Praise for *Protect the Joy*

"Protect the Joy is an important resource in a time of crisis for youth sport. As I discovered with my own son, well-intended but misguided coaches and leagues can make a child hate a sport they once loved. I wish I had this resource when my son was struggling to find any joy in a sport he no longer competes in. As parents and guardians, we feel helpless on what to say or what to do. We want our children to participate in sport and get the most out of themselves that they can, but we don't always feel like we have the right to ask questions or allow our child to be on a different path than their peers. The youth sports industry has gotten so big and powerful, but for many, joy has been left behind. This book is a guide on how to get that joy back and allow children to have a holistic approach to sports that will truly enhance their lives and help them to grow from sports in positive ways."

Kara Goucher,
Two-time Olympian,
World Championships 10,000m silver medalist,
and bestselling author of *The Longest Race*

"Dr. Amanda Stanec and Richard Way have provided a much-needed course correction for sport. In *Protect the Joy*, they expertly guide us on how to let our kids thrive and to utilize sport as a vehicle for growth and development over the long haul. This should be required reading for anyone involved in sport, especially parents and coaches."

Steve Magness,
Bestselling author of *Do Hard Things* and
Peak Performance

"An inspiring and empowering read, *Protect the Joy* counters the increasingly prevalent 'win at all costs' youth sport culture, embraces a holistic approach to developmental sport success, and serves as a pragmatic source of truth for those who mentor young athletes. With its profound insights into character development, resilience, and the potential transformative power of sport, this book is a must-read for anyone passionate about nurturing the next generation of leaders on and off the field. In her role as an expert advisor for USADA's TrueSport program, we've long known that Dr. Stanec brings great wisdom and wit to the youth sport landscape. I wholeheartedly recommend this remarkable work for its invaluable contribution to the conversation around ethical and sustainable sport systems."

Travis T. Tygart,
CEO, United States Anti-Doping Agency

"Let's bring back the joy! Finally, a book that guides us through the true meaning of growth and development in sport. Dr. Amanda Stanec and Richard Way share their expertise in a witty and authentic way. *Protect the Joy* is a must-read for anyone in youth performance."

Dr. Beth McCharles,
Certified Mental Performance Consultant® (CMPC)

"If only we could transport parents into the future to witness the impact of their child's sports journey on the adults they will become, they would realize that what truly matters is the joy, life skills, and sense of security experienced by their child along the way. While time travel may elude us, *Protect the Joy* lays the pathway to ensure that every child lives the most fulfillment from their sports journey."

Richard Monette,
Managing director of Activeforlife.com,
and performance coach for Olympians and
professional athletes

"Joy is the foundation for everything good in sports. But in today's increasingly commercialized youth sports landscape, it's easy to think the purpose of play is something else. Amanda and Richard are your trusted guides in creating an experience for kids that will change lives—and our society—for the better."

Tom Farrey,
Author of *Game On: The All-American Race to Make Champions of Our Children,* and founder of Aspen Institute's Project Play

A Positive, Collaborative Approach to Youth Sport

Amanda Stanec, PhD

with Richard Way, MBA

an Imprint of Amplify Publishing Group

www.amplifypublishinggroup.com

For more information, please contact:
Amplify Publishing, an imprint of Amplify Publishing Group
620 Herndon Parkway, Suite 220
Herndon, VA 20170
info@amplifypublishing.com

Library of Congress Control Number: 2024905686

CPSIA Code: PRS0624A

ISBN-13: 978-1-63755-520-0

Printed in the United States
Book design by Amy Stanec

*To every courageous child
doing their best in sport while others watch on.*

*To every youth-sport director, coach,
and parent trying to get it right.*

This is for you.

–A.S.

*To Vanessa and my extraordinary family, who have
cheered me on every step of the way. Your unwavering
support and understanding have allowed me to pursue
my passion of quality sport for everyone.*

*To Amanda and sporty friends, whose positive energy
and actions inspire belief that together we can
protect the joy of sport!*

–R.W.

CONTENTS

I Batter Up
Understanding Youth Sport Development

Chapter 1: The Play-by-Play   1
How to Use This Book

Chapter 2: Game-Day Strategies   19
Navigate Success Models and Frameworks in Youth Sport

Chapter 3: Score   53
How to Find Joy in Youth Sport

II Setting Youth Up for Success

Chapter 4: Where Are the Multisport Players?   81
The Benefit of Trying and Sticking with Multiple Sports

Chapter 5: Good Game   107
Ensure Youth Athletes' Well-Being

Chapter 6: There's No "I" in Team   133
The Art of Competence, Confidence, and Belonging

Chapter 7: Call the Shots   157
The Importance of Communication on and off the Field

III How to Clear the Hurdles

Chapter 8: Go the Distance   191
Set 'Em up for Success

Chapter 9: Put Me in, Coach   211
Prioritize Development over Winning

Chapter 10: Get ahead of the Game   231
Make Informed Decisions for Young Athletes

Chapter 11: How You Play   251
It's about "Fun"

Notes   277

Additional Resources   287

Acknowledgments   289

PART I

Batter Up

Understanding Youth
Sport Development

CHAPTER I

The Play-by-Play

How to Use This Book

"For me, success is not about the wins and losses.
It's about helping these young fellas be the best
versions of themselves on and off the field."

–Ted Lasso

Perhaps it was the fact that we'd all been navigating life with COVID-19 for more than a year, and we were in desperate need of something we could actually agree on. Or maybe it was the fact that we're suckers for a great sports TV show. Either way, the television series *Ted Lasso* delivered big time in August 2020. Everyone seemed to be talking about the show that touched our hearts, and it's not surprising that so many of the shows' clips went viral. At this point of the pandemic, most parents needed the perfectly pitched blend of Coach Ted's warm and fuzzy inspiration and spot-on lessons through sport as much as we appreciated Roy Kent's f-bombs.

Ted Lasso is a fictional American football coach who is hired to coach a soccer team in England. Unbeknownst to Coach Lasso at the time, the owner of the soccer team, Rebecca Welton, hired him with the expectation of failure. Rebecca thought tanking her ex-husband Rupert's favorite soccer team would be a great way of getting back at him for his infidelities. This sounds like a wacky sports show, we know. But early in the show we got to know Coach Lasso and came to appreciate his caring heart and the compassion he shows his players. Ted Lasso centers his players as humans, and it's impossible to ignore the positive impact of his doing so.

He gets it, we thought. *He really gets it.*

We connect with much of what Ted preaches, because as parents and professionals, we've been questioning norms in youth sport for decades. Every time an adult version of sport is applied to the youth-sport experience, we cringe at the contradictions between the youth-sport research and widely published best practices and what's actually happening in youth sport in our communities.

- Why are kids benched during childhood and early adolescence when they are chosen for a team?
- Why are kids punished with exercise or for being late when physical activity and fitness are only going to positively contribute to their health and sport performance?
- Why do kids get yelled at for making a mistake in sport when professionals make mistakes every game?

When sport is delivered in ways that are misaligned with research and best practice, it robs kids of a joyful sport experience.

Ted Lasso reminds us that sport can, in fact, be beautiful. The coaching on display is athlete-centered and heart-centered and looks more like a script out of a Brené Brown book than a sports book. Alas, this is why we loved it so much. This is what the world needs. More love and humanness to balance the macho and tough-love approach that any athlete knows all too well.

Yep, the *Ted Lasso* hype was, and continues to be, well deserved, and his messages around curiosity, teamwork, and, yes, even goldfish, are ones that every parent, coach, and athlete would benefit from understanding.

Perhaps what's most remarkable to us about *Ted Lasso* is not that we learned new things from it; rather, it's how the show took the learnings from sport psychology and pedagogy and presented it in uplifting ways.

The series made us start asking questions like: *What if we could write a book in a way where it was understood that we're all doing our best as parents and coaches *and* that be combined with increasing ability in the pursuit of excellence at all levels? What if we challenged current practice with an approach of empathy and understanding while inspiring people to do better, because every kid deserves the best?*

These questions, and others, continued to percolate until we simply couldn't put this book off any longer.

Le voilà! Thanks for joining in the conversation!

What Led Us Here

Given Amanda's unique background, which is a combination of physical education, research on theories of sport psychology, and pedagogy (teaching and coaching), she's been fielding phone calls and email requests for youth-sport advice for well over a decade. After thriving as a tenure-track professor, Amanda pivoted to meet the needs of organizations who were asking her to help write curriculum and lead professional development for teachers and coaches. In this capacity, she founded Move + Live + Learn, which combines the best of physical education, sport, and health literature to take a comprehensive and positive approach to enhance physical activity experiences for youth through a social justice lens. Since the requests for guidance and insight began well before Amanda was a parent, she couldn't draw upon experience in that capacity early in her career. Instead, Amanda responded to requests by applying her firm grasp of the research, best practices, experience, and understanding of sport development frameworks in hopes to support the youth being discussed on the calls.

Simply put, parents sought Amanda's advice when things didn't feel good about their child's sport experience. They would often state that their gut told them something was off, and they just didn't know what to do.

When there are hiccups along an individual's education journey, parents don't think twice about calling a teacher or a principal. But the fear of being labeled an *overbearing sport parent*, along with the reality that policies exist in youth sport that actually discourage concerned parents to communicate with coaches and directors, may leave parents in quite the pickle. When things go wrong, it's not common practice for them to pick up the phone and talk to a coach or sport director. Rather, they do nothing and hope for the best, or they pick up the phone and call someone independent of the situation—someone like Amanda. It's not uncommon for parents to express their confusion by proclaiming they don't know what the hell to do about the dilemma they find themselves in.

Parents aren't the only ones who have been calling Amanda for guidance in the youth-sport space. Thoughtful sport directors call when they need help developing coaches in informative and inspiring ways or when they are curious about her thoughts regarding certain parental complaints. Developed coaches seek guidance in how to balance demanding and unrealistic parents who care more about what level team their child is placed on than about what team has a skill level that is most appropriate for the athlete. These same thoughtful coaches and/or sport directors equate youth-sport success with athlete development, enjoyment, and retention and not a strong win/loss record. They wonder how to get parents on board with defining success in this way rather than running off to find a coach who is most concerned about an upcoming tournament win.

Most youth coaches are extremely well intentioned, but it's important to understand that most aren't required to complete any formal education in coaching. Similarly, most parents are also well intentioned, but they aren't required to complete any formal education before they become parents or before their child participates in sport. Yet, while most are doing the best they can, society often pits coaches and parents against each other, and people come to Amanda complaining that coaches are out of touch and unrealistic and parents are nuts.

Yes and yes. No and no.

Some coaches are unprepared and do a terrible job in leading a youth-centered sport experience, and some parents are unrealistic about their child's skills and abilities. Yet, other coaches are caring and do a terrific job at developing youth's skill, game sense, and character, while other parents strike the perfect pitch in combining high expectations with a warm and supportive environment.

Although Amanda didn't advertise formalized guidance in youth sport as part of her day job, her grasp of the literature on the topic, her love of kids, and her unshakable belief that sport should be joyful prompts her to make time to talk to many concerned parents and sport directors whenever they reach out. The apparent need to get research and best-practice material in the minds and hearts of parents, coaches, and sport directors alike continued to grow since the phone calls began coming in. People seemed to really want help navigating the unique challenges to youth sport.

Ted Lasso affirmed the original inspiration behind this book as the idea of writing one began to percolate on Amanda's morning runs more than fifteen years ago. As the miles ticked away, she pondered:

- How come so many parents are so frustrated with their child's sports experience?
- What would it take to help coaches understand just how much power they have in their role?
- Why are parents trying to rewrite their own sport accolades through the achievement of their children?
- Why are parents afraid to communicate with coaches?
- Why do coaches generalize all parents as "crazy"?
- Why do youth coaches often share wisdom from college coaches when they aren't coaching college athletes?
- Why do so many people speak about adolescents in such a degrading manner?
- Why are people learning about youth sport from people who aren't educators or haven't formally studied sport models and

youth development through sport?

- Why is there such an emphasis on winning and achievement at very young ages, and not enough attention paid to sustainable development and coaching the whole child?

Alas, life got hectic. Amanda continued to study and think about these questions on her runs, but the idea of writing a book was placed on a proverbial bookshelf for more than ten years. Amanda kept herself busy raising three daughters, working in the youth sport and physical education spaces, volunteering at her kids' schools, and coaching some of their teams. While she couldn't imagine making the time to write a book, the hours required to respond to people who sought guidance in youth sport increased each week. As more parents, coaches, and sport directors reached out asking for guidance, writing a book to address the themes that emerged from these calls seemed to be the most caring and sustainable way to help serve the youth-sport scene. *Let's give the people what they seem to want*, she thought.

If you're wondering what the types of questions parents were asking Amanda, examples include:

- Why is my son getting benched at soccer when he's nine years old?
- Is it okay if I ask my daughter's coach why she's not going to play much at age eleven, or do you think she'll be punished?
- Do you think I should tell my thirteen-year-old son he has to go to basketball when he has seven games over the weekend and he's curled up on the couch asking not to go?
- Does it make sense that my child only plays twenty minutes a game while others play eighty minutes every game? They are twelve years old.
- The coach punishes the team with exercise if anyone is late; does that seem reasonable to you?

Before she committed to writing a book on youth sport, she did a deliberate search for what she was imagining. Amanda assumed that such a book to answer the questions she was being asked existed. But after an extensive search, she realized the book didn't exist.

Most books on youth sport were written by men who coach or coached predominately at the college or professional level. While Amanda learns a lot by reading content created by these professionals, these books don't address many of the questions that parents were asking her, and problems arise when solutions presented by a college coach who works solely with eighteen- to twenty-two-year-olds are applied by a well-intended youth coach of six- to fourteen-year-olds. Sometimes the tone in these books pit parents and coaches against each other, and this vibe doesn't connect with Amanda's curious mind, teacher's heart, or her collaborative spirit.

Another theme that emerged after reading myriad youth-sport books is that they tend to romanticize more traditional versions of sport where the adult version of toughness is prioritized as lessons that youth ought to learn. There also seemed to be little room for nuance, which is especially problematic when youth coaches take these lessons—sometimes shared by college and professional coaches—and apply an unfiltered version to adolescents. Amanda wondered why youth coaches often quoted college coaches to "defend" decisions that stole joy from kids in sport, such as benching players or punishing them with exercise rather than really listening to the critiques brought forth to them.

As a parent and a youth coach, Amanda struggles with the seeming desire in these books to skip kids' adolescent years and treat youth more like adults as soon as they transition from childhood to adolescence. In raising her own kids, she noticed the bizarrely few years that existed between when parents talked about potty training to when they would bring up the potential for their child to receive college athletic scholarships.

But Amanda has found awesome, wonderful books that have pushed her thinking on related topics such as adolescent development and psychology. She's quick to offer her favorite book titles as recommendations to the parents, coaches, and directors who call and email her each week. (See the Additional Resources section on page 289.) Anyone who raises or works with youth will benefit greatly from an understanding of the rapidly and vast changing stage of adolescence. Based on their positive reviews of the non-sport books Amanda recommends to them—which are evidence-based books that weave in fictional and non-fictional stories to help bring the research to life—Amanda was more convinced than ever that a book like the one she dreamed up while running would be appreciated. With a PhD from the University of Virginia, more than two decades in this professional space leading inspiring projects on behalf of national and international sport federations, and with confidence gained from the positive feedback reported by those who sought her advice, Amanda took the book concept sitting on her bookshelf and moved it onto her desktop.

It was time to write her book.

While Amanda's college soccer career ended more than twenty-five years ago, she still loves being a teammate. With a deep love of the collaborative process, something she credits to her years playing team sports, she knew she wanted to write this book with someone who had a lot of experience working in youth sport, who coached youth sport extensively, and who experienced youth sport as a parent. Who she should write this book with was a no-brainer. She immediately reached out to her friend and global changemaker Richard Way. Richard loved the idea, as he is also passionate about the potential power of youth sport to make a positive difference in the lives of youth and adults alike.

Richard also has a great perspective on the purpose of sport and what's most important when raising kids. He and his partner are the proud parents of three young adults. When Richard's first daughter was born, the nurses indicated to him and his partner that there was a slight rushing sound in her heart. They were told to take their baby back to the hospital so she could be examined further before she turned one year old. So, when their little girl turned ten months old, they returned to the hospital for the examination. As the doctors approached them, it was impossible not to notice the worried look on their faces. They told Richard and his partner that their precious daughter would need open-heart surgery within the next two weeks.

This first surgery was the beginning of a journey that included four open-heart surgeries, a stroke, and too many angiograms to count. This experience left them with a clear sense that there is only one thing important in life when raising kids: their health and well-being. While Richard leads a dedicated and successful career in sport, he never loses sight that the purpose of sport is to *enhance* lives. While living with significant health challenges, Richard's daughter was still able to experience great joy in sport. Amazingly, in her teens, she even represented her province of British Columbia in the national field hockey championship tournament!

Richard's daughter's participation in sport often found him on pins and needles because he worried about her. Her participation was also important, as he was well aware of the psycho-social benefits that sport provides. Without a doubt, sport increased her quality of life, but there was always a piece of him worrying about her heart. Guiding his daughter, with his partner, through her sport journey galvanized messaging that wins and losses in sport are a distant second to healthy participation, which includes joy in participating. He also experienced firsthand the power that caring coaches carry in creating an environment where every child can thrive.

Of course, Richard, as a parent of three children—as any parent would know—would get into trouble if he only spoke of the journey of one of his children, as all three are sporty kids. Each is on their own unique physical literacy journey, although they share the common experience of participating in multiple sports while growing up. Both his other children went on to play soccer at the university level and have the opportunity to play in European leagues, even though one was an early developer and the other a late developer. Of the two, one translated lessons from sport into the start of a successful business career, while the other's path is playing professionally.

Richard's passion for coaching development and changing stale systems to a more logical, stage-before-age approach to skill development may position him as someone who cares most about international podium performances. But Richard and Amanda share their deep conviction that if the focus on youth sport is joyful, collaborative, and evidence-based, there will be many more athletes achieving their personal potential with the by-product being podium performances on the international stage. And there will be many others still who go on to build enriching, fulfilled personal lives supported by connection, movement, and a healthy approach to challenges as well as impressive professional lives built outside of sport. The key point is the journey toward personal potential and well-being, which includes development of physical, technical, tactical, mental, and life skills. All those skills benefit each person in a plethora of ways, thanks to the valuable life lessons that are gained in the absence of unnecessary and unhealthy levels of stress, anxiety, and heartache during their youth-sport experience.

So, Richard, with his years of working with hundreds of different national sport organizations (NSOs), experience coaching and administering from the local to national level, along with raising three sporty kids, could not refuse Amanda's book-writing invitation, relishing the chance to help partners navigate the complex decision-making to protect the joy of sport participation while creating the environment for their child to be the best they can be.

While we reflected on our favorite authors in the coaching, parenting, and self-help domains, we discovered some commonalities. We both appreciated a no-bullshit, down-to-earth writing style as well as when authors were willing to be vulnerable to illustrate their own growth. We believe that sharing some of our own missteps demonstrates the humility required to keep readers from feeling shame. This is all about learning and doing better once we know better. The title of this book references the importance of protecting the joy in sport for our kids, and we set out to write a joyful book on this topic. There is no room for embarrassment or shame, as we've been brought together in the spirit of understanding and growth.

Do not mistake our stance on a joyful youth-sport experience for one that is devoid of rigor, or perseverance, or resilience. If you know us, you know that's not our modus operandi. But, before youth can benefit from a rigorous environment or before they will want to persist, many conditions must first be established. If you're wondering what conditions, keep reading.

How This Book Is Structured

This book is divided into three sections. First, we introduce our hopes and dreams of the book and then provide some background foundational knowledge that helps frame what's to come in the following chapters. In this first section titled "Batter Up: Understanding Youth Sport Development," we define the Long-Term Athlete Development (LTAD) pathway, which is a stage-before-age approach to developing quality sport experiences throughout the lifespan. We also highlight some key characteristics of adolescence and present the social-emotional learning core competencies, which are a set of cognitive and behavioral skills, such as building and maintaining healthy relationships, goal setting, and emotional regulation, that help individuals navigate life in fulfilling ways.

The second section, "Setting Youth Up for Success," highlights what we know from research on the potential benefits of quality sport experience. It also takes us on a deep dive into the hot topics such as finding the right sport(s) for your kid, addressing the realities of multisport participation, and understanding how and when to have courageous conversations. This section explores the unique and specific challenges for student–athletes and how these challenges influence their overall well-being, presents fascinating research on confidence and communication, and helps adults understand how to support youth in acquiring both confidence and communication skills.

The third and final section, "How to Clear the Hurdles," explores issues adults commonly seem to get wrong. We explain why development should always take priority over winning at the youth-sport level and why doing what we know is best for kids during a delicate stage of development is better than what is being done at adult levels of sport. Finally, the book culminates with sharing an evidence-based framework of FUN for youth sport. Indeed, fun is not a four-letter word.

At the end of each chapter, we share reflection questions in the hopes that you take time to answer them. Sport directors can use these questions to facilitate discussions at coaching development sessions. We sometimes offer summaries in the form of do's and don'ts, suggested readings, and action steps that parents, coaches, or sport directors can apply to transfer the learning from the book in ways that benefit kids. We hope engaging with the content in this way helps to initiate thoughtful discussion and an openness to change when current practice is deemed less than optimal.

Our Hope for This Book

Our intention for writing this book hasn't wavered since we began writing it. Our hope is that you find it to be an inspiring and relevant overview of the youth-sport landscape and that it helps you to be prepared to get your child or athlete's youth-sport journey right. To us, "getting it right" means that all decisions made related to youth sport are done with perspective, a knowledge of the research, and kids and their hearts at the center of all decisions. We unapologetically believe that the youth-sport journey should overall be an extremely joyful one filled with positive experiences that teach kids how to form and maintain positive relationships, overcome challenges, be resilient, as well as set and achieve goals.

But let's also be very clear here: We are not selling an idea that the youth-sport journey should consist only of unicorns and rainbows. We all know valuable lessons and life skills are often acquired through moments of discomfort, as that is how we grow. But resilience isn't gained from harmful and embarrassing tactics, just as mental toughness is not defined as compliant kids who never question what a parent or coach is asking of them. Words such as *resilience* and *mental toughness* are often misunderstood by well-intentioned parents and coaches. We believe that a better understanding of these terms and others will eventually lead to more individuals exhibiting higher levels of both, so we examine them deeper in the book.

Quality sport may help place a select few on a pathway to elite sport, but elite sport shouldn't be the *goal* of sport. Rather, the lessons that are to be gained on a quality sport journey are reason enough for kids to play sport. Notice our choice to use the word *quality* in front of *sport*. That's intentional. You see, the youth-sport landscape looks very different than it did only a couple decades ago, and not all of it is high quality. Adults changed the former model, and now it's up to us—up to all of us, collectively—to try and recommit our focus on providing youth-sport experiences that meet their promise of positively impacting kids' lives.

It's not uncommon for us to hear parents talk about the potential of athletic scholarships when their kids are as young as seven years old. They are unaware of just how few athletic scholarships are available or the fact that sport performance at age seven doesn't predict where performance will be at age seventeen. Parents have confided in us that they think they should keep their child on a particular team despite the fact that their child doesn't connect with the coach because "they know how to get their child a scholarship."

A Toronto-based parent recently shared with us her sadness that lessons from sport that she acquired, such as, "If you work hard, you can make the team you have your eye on," are no longer realistic for her kids. Her children play in a hockey league that recently received national attention due to parents "buying coaches" and "choosing lineups," which was simply proof of what she suspected was happening throughout the league. In other words, even if her child is on a lower team and works their way up to make a higher-level team, they may never receive the opportunity due to the practice of bribing coaches. Extreme examples such as this aren't something we hear about every day, but hearing it once is enough to sound the alarm. It's time parents and coaches put in the work to fix what they've broken.

Adults must keep focus on a quality sport journey that provides victories along the way, rather than a destination or outcome. Victories come in the form of things such as new friendships, overcoming challenges as individuals and as a collective, increasing self-confidence and empowerment, and learning new things and being brave enough to apply them in game situations with people watching. It is absolutely critical to understand a quality youth-sport journey is a safe one, devoid of maltreatment or abuse of any kind.

For this to happen, the traditional definition of success in sport ought to be broader than just winning. We're not asking people to refrain from celebrating a big win or qualifying for a regional tournament. We just want to elevate the fact that success in the form of learning life skills that can be a foundation to successful careers in many professions should not be underrated. Of course, the game on the weekend ought to be celebrated and can be joyful, and it also can be a way to measure success. But, as you will come to learn or be affirmed, championship wins sometimes aren't joyful. Sometimes they aren't won the right way.

Unfortunately, we have also fallen witness to the havoc that bad sport can cause—and if you haven't yet, you likely will too. For example, we've heard parents cursing at coaches and officials, read about doping scandals, observed parents fighting on the sidelines, and felt icky watching nine- and ten-year-olds be benched. *Yuck.*

We are both realistic and idealistic. We know there are a lot of current problems with the youth-sport system, but we also feel that we will be able to fix these fractures more effectively and efficiently with solutions, empathy, and understanding. We don't want to drive people out of sport, even if the sport environment they are providing currently falls short of reaching joyful sport status. We do not believe that bad sport-related decisions are intentional or that coaches making misguided decisions are bad people. In fact, we suspect that most bad sports decisions are made by well-intentioned people who simply are not adequately versed in coaching education, pedagogy, and sport psychology, and that's a big reason why we wanted to write this book.

While you read this book, we invite you to pause and reflect on your own coaching and/or parenting in sport to identify your current strengths and areas for growth. We hope that you'll take comfort in knowing that while we reflected over the years, our egos took some healthy punches to the face. No shame allowed! None of us are perfect parents or coaches, but striving for continuous improvement and awareness will allow us to improve the next generations' experiences in sport and beyond.

We hope that parents, coaches, and sport directors learn the background knowledge necessary to understand these pivotal truths:

- The youth's perspective should be front and center in every youth-sport decision they make.
- The importance of having a firm grasp of key adolescent concepts and sport development models to make informed sport-related decisions for youth.
- That ranking kids' performance within a team at fourteen years and younger is not in the best interest of any kids.
- How confidence is developed among individuals and the collective team and its relationship to motivation.
- Why prioritizing development and improvement over winning at the youth level will help every athlete be more likely to reach their full potential.
- What success in sport looks like.

When Amanda first spoke about writing this book, a man told her this book needs to be written for moms because moms are more likely the ones completing sport registration forms and entering sport schedules into family calendars, and they are more likely than dads to be on the receiving end of kids' thoughts and feelings on a daily basis. Since Amanda's closer to age fifty than forty, she is used to hearing comments such as these.

However, she'll continue to call bullshit at such suggestions. Not only do these comments suggest female parents are the only ones to coordinate and facilitate these experiences, but it also assumes there aren't many youth with same-sex parents sharing these responsibilities, regardless of gender, and many others still who are from single-parent households where one parent does it all. In general, the youth-sport space is very male dominated, and it is important that coaches and parents understand conversations regarding an enriching youth-sport experience need to involve *all* parents. As a father, Richard certainly attests to that, as dads don't get a free pass to poor decision-making based on gender. Everyone making decisions on behalf of youth sport needs to have a certain understanding of the related research.

Dads' willingness to step up and volunteer and coach in the communities should not be overlooked or underappreciated. Given the number of dads coaching, it's at least equally as important that they read this book, especially considering the fact that most of the youth-sport books are written by men. It's time for conventional sport approaches to be challenged based on what we know about learning and teaching—a female-dominated space. When diversity of thoughts and ideas are presented, the best solutions emerge.

It is our hope that everyone reading this book, including ourselves, continues to reflect, learn, and grow accordingly. In doing so, we can project the joy of youth sport while kids acquire life skills throughout the youth-sport journey.

Questions to Ask Yourself

- What current behaviors do you model with your child or athlete that you feel are helpful in protecting their joy in sport?
- What current behaviors do you model with your child or athlete that you feel could be more positive and helpful in protecting their joy in sport?
- What current challenges do you have with your child's sport experience? What are possible solutions to these challenges?

- Do the coaches who coach your child act in a manner in which you want your child to act when they grow up?
- If you were a kid, would you be comfortable with your sideline behavior or would you be embarrassed?
- What current challenges do you have coaching the youth you currently serve? What are possible solutions to these challenges?
- As a club director, how can you create and cultivate a culture of humility and empathy?

Action Steps for Consideration

Youth-Sport Club Director

- Survey parents at your club and ask for specific feedback on the topics within this book. What the director requests her coaches to do doesn't always happen. It's important she receives feedback and parents have anonymity.
- Take notes of topics in this book that you think warrant more reflection and discussion with your coaches, and use them to facilitate a discussion with them.
- Prioritize the study of adolescent development and choose a favorite book to guide a discussion with coaches on its key findings and how these findings might inform their coaching practice.

Youth-Sport Coach

- Survey athletes on their experiences. Anonymity is encouraged. Ideally the community and culture would be one that it wouldn't be necessary. Be sure to ask what they appreciate about their youth-sport experience and what they would change if they were in charge.

- Ask the kids you coach who their favorite teacher is and why that individual is their favorite teacher. Take note of what they tell you about the teacher and take notice of any emerging trends that can enhance your coaching practice. These insights will show you how athletes feel most supported by the leaders around them.

Youth-Sport Parent
- If you picked up this book because your child seems to have lost their joy of sport competition, identify what could have happened along the way. Identify ways that you could help bring joy back to their experience.

CHAPTER 2

Game-Day Strategies

Navigate Success Models and
Frameworks in Youth Sport

"If you don't know where you're going,
you'll end up someplace else."

–Yogi Berra

n early 2023, at a recent youth-sport event hosted by a national sport
federation in the United States, Amanda's daughter and her teammates
found themselves in a less-than-desirable position heading into their
fifth and final game of a tournament. The girls entered the final game
with a record of 3–1, which was good enough to be tied for first in their
pool with another team. The team they were tied with was a team they
beat earlier in the tournament. Given results leading up to the fifth game,
it was likely that these two teams would win their final games, and in
doing so both would end the tournament with a 4–1 record.

For this particular tournament, the rules established to determine the
winner in the event of a tie state:

- Goal differential will be used to break the tie and declare the
  winner.
- If the tie remains after goal differential, goals scored will be
  used to break the tie and declare the winner.
- If the tie remains after goals scored, the winner of the head-to-
  head between the two teams is declared the winner.

Entering the final game, Amanda's daughter's team had twelve fewer goal differential points compared to the team with the same record. Therefore, to win their pool several things needed to happen:

1. They needed to win their game.
2. They needed to score enough goals to overtake the twelve-point goal differential.
3. They needed to hope the other team didn't score many goals if they won their game so they would win by goal differential of goals scored.

If they won their pool, they would be crowned tournament pool champions. The other team allegedly entered their final game assuming they just had to win their game, because what were the chances the team tied in record would score thirteen goals in their game?

During the final pool game, Amanda's daughter's team began scoring rapidly. Before long, the kids began to believe that they could actually score the thirteen goals needed to win their pool. While they felt proud for doing what was needed to win given the rules placed upon them, athletes, coaches, and parents alike felt uneasy about running up the score against another team at the 14U level. Three parents discussed how the other team must have felt as balls continued to pile into their goal with a relentlessness that seemed obnoxious, overwhelming, and even cruel. Amanda wasn't at the game, but as she received text updates from the group chat, she felt queasy due to her understanding of the research related to sport motivation and enjoyment (which we will touch on later in this book).

What was being described to her certainly wasn't aligning with what research-informed youth-sport competition should look like. She even wondered if members of the losing team would feel like quitting the sport after this experience, considering they were twelve- and thirteen-year-olds, which is an age range that experiences a high sport dropout rate among girls. Despite efforts in some sports to have policies that discourage the running up of scores, it's still surprising that the ability to do so exists at all, and it's incredibly disappointing that the rules at this tournament actually encouraged it.

The adults weren't the only ones concerned about the game. Some players on the winning side felt extremely torn. These girls were elated to win the tournament, but they felt empathy toward their opponents, as they could imagine what it would have felt like to be on the losing end of a game like that. Several teammates commented that some of the opponents were crying, some were rolling their eyes and sounded very frustrated with their teammates, and some just looked down during the final minutes and quit trying their best. Amanda's daughter's coach was professional and communicated with the other coach and official as to why they were trying so hard to score a lot of goals; she felt very conflicted as well and did not appreciate the rules that were in place. This club prides itself on character and something felt off by winning in this manner. However, the rules of competition drove the decisions, even though they went against everyone's values.

....

While we focus deeply on development throughout this book, we aren't naive; the purpose of developing individuals and teams is to help them be more successful. While success doesn't always mean to win in sport, sometimes it does. Regardless, prioritizing development should *always* guide decisions at the younger ages. Rules created to declare a winner should not replace the focus on athlete development and enjoyment, as was the case when kids found themselves having to score thirteen goals in one game. These kids did what was needed to win, given the rules created, but they didn't feel great doing it, and their parents and coaches didn't enjoy watching it. Given that winning is a part of sport and rules weren't broken, a reasonable person can say they did the right thing and should celebrate. The question is: *Why were these the rules?*

Over the past several decades, there has been a surge in credible research, theories, and frameworks that—when considered together—provide the variety of brushes and colors needed to paint a joyful youth-sport picture with a development focus that will support youth athletes as they grow and mature into healthy, thriving adults. We're left to wonder why such a beautiful youth-sport painting isn't the norm. Despite the plentiful and readily available body of knowledge, one would think that rules that promote "running up the score" and other joy-sucking experiences from youth sport would no longer exist in youth practices and competitions, but unfortunately, they do.

Any instance of community sport experience not reflecting evidence-based best practices is one too many. Too much is at stake given the important psychological stages of development our kids pass through during their youth-sport years. And when development is not honored over performance and winning, the long-lasting impacts on youth psyche and identity can be shocking. In this chapter, we present you with some of this important foundational work along with some pertinent research that we are convinced can help us improve the current landscape of youth sport— together. This information is necessary to inform imperative changes to current sport systems, coaching development, and detrimental behaviors by coaches and parental alike. Equally impressive work, such as the mental toughness framework and Fun Maps, are introduced later in the book to help coaches and parents identify the plethora of life skills youth can obtain from sport and also how to establish the best environment for them to be able to learn, practice, and hone these valuable skills.

For a variety of reasons, it's necessary that parents, coaches, officials, and sport directors understand what Long-Term Athlete Development (LTAD) (global) or Athlete Development Model (USA) is and how they can serve as excellent guides to creating joyful youth-sport experiences. Additionally, we can't write a book for adults to best support kids during the pre-adolescence and the adolescent phases of development without identifying and thinking deeply about key concepts of adolescent development. Finally, understanding what social emotional learning (SEL) is and why school districts throughout North America are formalizing its role in schools—even before the COVID-19 pandemic caused death and disruption throughout the world—will help frame what's to come in the following chapters.

It is our hope that you will find the messages in this book as foundational knowledge that will be extremely useful as you journey with your child(ren) through the rapids and whirlpools that youth sport can be. We hope you can refer back to the chapters as a reference when issues arise so that you can best protect the joy of playing sport. We understand that everyone's journey through sport looks different, and the varied topics covered in this book will resonate with you at different points of your journey.

So, let's get this started.

Excellence Takes Time!

A journey is often defined as a trip that one takes to a particular place, and it usually takes a long period of time. We love using the term *youth-sport journey* in our coaching development work, as we see how helpful this visual could be for coaches as they educate parents about how the experience mirrors a marathon more than a sprint. Some parents and coaches focus too much on the short-term realities of youth sport rather than the long-term goals. For sport directors and coaches to optimally plan for this journey—one we believe can be full of quality development and joyful experiences—it is helpful to start with the Long-Term Athlete Development (LTAD) model.

What Is the Long-Term Athlete Development (LTAD) Model?

The Long-Term Athlete Development (LTAD) model was created so athletes would do the right things, in the right way, at the right time, led by a person with the right training to coach a person at their current stage of development.[1] LTAD is based on research, science, and experience that concluded that individuals will get active, stay active, and even reach high levels of sport if they have a pathway that ensures the fundamentals of movement (e.g., run, hop, jump, leap, etc.) are developed before the fundamentals of specific sports, and that technical skills (e.g., speed dribbling in field hockey, dribbling with feet in soccer, shooting a wrist shot in ice hockey) needed to be developed before more complex tactics (e.g., offensive press in field hockey, zone defense in basketball).

The LTAD model was created at the beginning of the twenty-first century in response to the notion that the traditional sport approach included shortcomings that often resulted in negative physical and psychological consequences. A group of experts who created LTAD believed that if they articulated a better framework for sport development, many of the shortcomings and consequences of the traditional system could be improved upon through the LTAD pathway.

Problems with Traditional Sport Models
Traditional approaches to sport development determined what should be taught to individuals based primarily on their chronological age, which may not seem that problematic at first consideration. However, the problem with this was that individuals come to sport with different genetics and experiences, and often times grouping or planning for a specific age doesn't result in the most appropriate environment for many of the participants. Sport differs from the classroom learning environment in that the learning occurs publicly, which increases the learner's vulnerability, and while students come to school with varied understanding of the material presented, teachers are trained on how to differentiate instruction to meet the various needs within one classroom during a lesson.

Sport-relative age can vary greatly based on factors such as the number of years a child has participated in the sport, what calendar month a child was born in relative to the age range of the group, or the age a child starts a growth spurt.[2,3,4] Amanda's two oldest daughters, Scottie and Kassie, are twenty months apart and were born in 2010 and 2011. Every other year, they are teammates in two of the sports they participate in, and Kassie (who is younger) is challenged to keep up with Scottie and others who are bigger and more experienced than she is. *Developmental age* differs from relative age, but it produces similar discrepancies. Developmental age refers to the physical, mental, and emotional maturation of youth that can vary greatly in their developmental age.[5] As a result of both relative and developmental age factors, sport ability can range greatly among youth who are the same chronological age. It then becomes difficult to deliver the best training, competition and recovery, coaching, and experience to youth when we acknowledge they come to sport at different levels, have different motivations and aspirations, and grow and develop at vastly different rates, meaning their developmental experiences need to be individually tailored.

In addition to being organized by age groups, traditional sport models had a fixation on short-term goals, such as winning an upcoming game, versus ongoing development through competition. Such a traditional approach is illustrated by a soccer coach who refuses to play a player on the left side at age twelve because they are weaker and more vulnerable on that side of the pitch. Thus, rather than giving the player opportunity to play and develop on both sides, they stunt the player by playing them only on their strong or dominant side. The LTAD framework recognized that in most cases, traditional sport development predominantly benefits adult males because it was, in fact, designed for them. Problems arise in traditional models because they were not created for the kids who frequent them.

Benefits of a Sport Framework
Organized by Stages of Development

The creators of the LTAD pathway set out to build a way to better develop fundamental skills to increase the potential of all players. They developed a long-term framework to consist of seven stages of athlete or participant development, which are preceded by two pre-stages. Richard, along with a group of experts, has collaborated for the past two decades with sport-specific experts to develop frameworks for more than sixty sports across more than half the nations in the world. Those sport-specific experts would collaborate to design LTAD pathways to best suit the development in their sport. If you're a parent reading this book, be sure to google the sport your child is in and add "LTAD" or "ADM" to find a development framework for your child's sport. The LTAD experts first worked in Ireland, creating Irish Pathways in Sport, then Sport England, Wales, Northern Ireland, which led Sport Canada to support Sport for Life working with the almost sixty sports they fund.

Richard reflects on how exciting it was to collaborate and create a new system of sport development. The results have been mind-blowing, as organizations who invest energy into change have a dramatic impact on performance and participation. Just look at Tennis Canada, who adopted the LTAD pathway in 2008 and now Canadians enjoy cheering on and celebrating the generation of LTAD babies challenging for and winning major championships. Athletes such as Bianca Andreescu, U.S. Women's Open champion; Leylah Fernandez, U.S. Women's Open finalist; and Felix Auger-Aliassime and Denis Shapovalov, both whom have reached top ten world rankings. Amazingly Tennis Canada's LTAD generation has led Canada to men's World Champion Davis Cup winners in 2022 and women's World Champion Billie Jean King Cup winners in 2023! Basketball Canada now has the second-most NBA players of any nation after adopting the LTAD pathway in the early 2000s. Judo Canada's adoption of the LTAD pathway has resulted in multiple international medalists, while Snowboard Canada took home six medals from the recent Olympics. These are only a few of many who have changed their system of development to improve the quality of the experience, understanding that excellence takes time, and an athlete only participates if they *enjoy* the experience.

Now that we've introduced you to the LTAD pathway and shared its impact in countries that have adopted it, let's examine one example of how LTAD has helped evolve resource creation and coaching development.

Almost a decade ago, Amanda was hired by an international sport federation, United World Wrestling (UWW), to write a stage-before-age sport program to introduce kids to the sport of wrestling through the LTAD framework. Luckily, Scott and Luanne Fockler—master physical education teachers and youth wrestling coaches in Canada—were willing to lead the skill development aspect of the project that Amanda managed. The wrestling deliverable consisted of five stages of fifteen lessons/practice plans in each stage. If it was the kids' first day of the program, regardless of if they were age five or fourteen, they would often begin in the first stage of the program, but they could begin at a later stage if their movement proficiency determined that would be a more appropriate environment for them. Then, within the programming, kids are partnered with kids of similar age and size. But what they learn is more aligned to their experience in the sport. Likewise, at a more advanced stage of the LTAD wrestling curriculum, a ten-year-old may be properly placed in that group because they have wrestled for five years.

This differs a bit from a classroom knowledge approach. Typically, classroom curriculum is written and benchmark assessments are determined for each grade level and in each subject area. For example, we may want all sixth-grade math students to be able to demonstrate specific competencies before they are ready to move on to seventh-grade math. Thus, everyone in the class is of similar age and all are being asked to demonstrate competencies in the same mathematical concepts. What they learned previously was controlled by the school district, the math curriculum leader, and their previous teachers. Each year, teachers have targets and work their magic to help all students—or as close to all as possible—achieve the high standard that has been set for them.

However, in movement, there isn't the same amount of ability to determine what is learned, practiced, or gained previously in sport, especially as kids experiment with different sports, move with their families, or take breaks from sport; coaches and program directors don't always know the exact development stage an athlete is in when they begin on a team.

Individuals have widely varied backgrounds and experiences, as many schools don't have physical education, and oftentimes when they do have physical education, classes don't meet very often and class times are short. Moreover, physical educators are tasked to teach many things, not just sport competencies. Quality physical education programs certainly teach fundamental movement skills, skill combinations, and tactics during game play, but they ought to be equally as focused on educational gymnastics, dance, and outdoor lifetime pursuits as they are games. Plus, some individuals may have had access to community or club programs to develop their ability or have had sporty parents to play with outside of the classroom when many other students may not have those opportunities.

Thus, developing sport skills by taking the same approach as teaching math doesn't work in terms of helping everyone to develop a particular level of competence necessary to feel confident in one's ability in the physical domain. In setting up programs based on the LTAD framework, you avoid having groupings where some are bored because they aren't challenged, and some are frustrated and unmotivated because they aren't able to experience success. The emphasis of LTAD is development through the stages based on experience, competency, and so forth with the idea that it will manifest into confidence and motivation.

LTAD does more than guide us regarding what skills to teach and when or how kids should train. At least just as powerful is the way an understanding of the framework leads to wise decisions during competition, because it keeps the focus on development over winning. At all times. The result?

- Small-sided sports for younger children with a gradual increase starting with less players on a smaller field with appropriate equipment and smaller goals
- Practices that have more games and less drills
- Practice and games that are fun! More fun than the games they play on their computer or phone!
- Appropriate rules for competition

Ah, yes! Rules for competition. This brings us back to the tournament Amanda's daughter competed in. The rule stated that in the event of a tie, the winner will be determined by goal differential. In other words, the difference between goals scored and goals allowed. If the tournament committee created the rules with LTAD as the framework, the focus would have been on *development*. Thus, they would never have had the tie breaker as goal differential.

The second way to break the tie was goals scored. The tournament committee would also never set this to be the tie breaker if adhering strongly to an LTAD approach. Why? It promotes running up the score over development. Think about this for a second: They would have capped the goals at eight, or whatever we decide isn't demoralizing. Then, coaches can switch focus and challenge their team to try new things, play in different positions, and even insert their own rules such as "every player has to touch the ball without it being intercepted or without losing possession before we are allowed to shoot" or "only defenders are permitted to shoot." Inserting such constraints in the game can be subtle and give the team who is winning a chance to develop in their sport by stretching themselves or maybe even giving those kids on the bench more playing time! As you learn in Chapter 5: Good Game—Ensure Youth Athletes' Well-Being (page 107), stretching oneself and learning from everything are key pieces of mental toughness. There is very little mental toughness on display by the team scoring thirteen goals on another team. We'd argue the emotional control on display by the opponents was the real marker of mental toughness in that game.

All decisions related to practices and competition (including tournaments) should stay in alignment with the LTAD pathway of sport development, which means in this situation they should break a tie in pool play based on the objectives of that stage of development. There are many ways to break a tie that don't drive inappropriate actions by the coach and kids. You break the tie based on who won in a head-to-head game, but if there was a tie in that game, there are other ways to determine who wins. We now see many tournaments break ties based on least yellow or red cards, or least penalties, least fouls. *Imagine rules that promote fair play.* Or if time permits, it could be penalty shots or foul shots or some other easily measurable skill in the sport. *Imagine rules that promote skill development.* If it was a three-way tie, flip a coin. We would rather see thirteen-year-olds lose on a coin toss than rules promoting bad behaviors like running the score, leaving kids glued to the bench, and demoralizing other adolescents. At an age where youth sport decline in girls is particularly alarming, this is an easy fix with several potential benefits.

Physical Literacy's Role in the Creation of LTAD

The Long-Term Athlete Development (LTAD) was created when a working group of national-level coaches and sport scientists noted that many athletes progressing to junior and senior national teams were missing fundamental movement skills. For example, national program basketball coaches had players coming into their national team development camps who could not do a crossover step well in *both* directions, while national-level ski racers could not do a somersault or other basic movement skills proficiently, which limited their potential in their sport because basic fundamental movements are essential in both performance and injury prevention. When the working group concluded that many kids participating in sport didn't have a range of fundamental movement, and this missing piece of development appeared to negatively affect their confidence and motivation to participate as well as limited their ability to achieve their potential, they decided to try to do something about it.

Physical literacy is the motivation, confidence, physical competence, knowledge, and understanding to value and take responsibility for engagement in physical activities.[6] It's a mouthful, but it's a beautiful mouthful if that's even a thing.

Physical literacy

is the...

physical
competence

motivation
knowledge
valuing

confidence

...to be

🍁 Sport for Life   **active for life**

Figure 1: Physical Literacy[7]

We'd like you to pause reading for a moment and analyze the diagram depicting physical literacy and think about the kids on the losing team in the tournament described earlier in this chapter. Do you think they felt competent? Confident? Motivated to continue playing the sport? It's doubtful that at that moment they felt any of those things. Of course, that's just one game at one tournament, and hopefully the other positive sports experiences far outweigh the negative feelings they experienced that one day. But it is important to think deeply about those on the receiving end of rules we create.

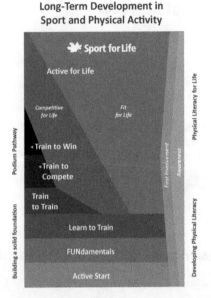

Figure 2: Long-Term Development in Sport and Physical Activity[8]

The Seven Stages of the Long-Term Athlete Development (LTAD) Framework

Pre-stages

The **Awareness** and **First Involvement** pre-stages engage individuals in sport and physical activity. They are critical. There are well over one hundred sports available to learn and play in North America. The reason for that is everybody has different characteristics. As an example, there are individual sports for introverts and team sports for the more social extroverts. Of course, that is a broad generalization. However, the point is parents should be aware of many sports so they can find the sport that their child can be passionate about. Then when their child has the first few experiences in the sport, their experience needs to be positive so they will come back and participate. They need to have proper-fitting equipment and smiling instructors ensuring they feel welcome.

Stages 1 and 2
In the **Active Start** and **FUNdamentals** stages, kids should try as many sports as possible to see what they like and have a passion to continue. In doing that, you lay the foundation for excellence or to be active for life.

Stages 3 and 4
Learn to Train and **Train to Train** are the stages that make or break an athlete. Often due to early specialization, the overall athleticism required to thrive at these stages was not developed in the earlier stage and is not being developed in this stage, leaving gaps in one's ability. Learn to Train is key in this multisport experience, which then leads into reducing the number of sports in the Train to Train stage. For example, a kid in the Learn to Train stage who grew very tall and plays basketball may experience success in basketball due to their height; however, it's important that they do other things to aid in their footwork and coordination, as both will be needed for them to continue to experience success when they enter the Train to Train stage. In both stages, high-quality coaches are critical to create the right training, competition, and recovery. However, since the child is participating in multiple sports, the parents need to guide their journey to defend against burnout and injuries.

Stages 5 and 6
The **Train to Compete** and **Train to Win** stages provide a high-performance training environment for those who want to specialize in one sport and compete at the highest level, maximizing the physical, mental, and emotional development of each athlete.

Stage 7
Active for Life stage is about staying physically active through lifelong participation in competitive or recreational sport or physical activity. It also refers to being active in volunteering, coaching, or officiating.

....

If you're a director looking to revamp how your sport club is organized or a parent looking for a sport framework that has a clear pathway for development, the LTAD model is for you. It is perhaps likely that your club has pieces of the framework in place, and we encourage you to think of how to adopt it more fully. Successes mentioned throughout this section highlight why we recommend this framework, but we're fully aware that organizing for sport development programs through a stage approach isn't going to result in an automatic joyful youth-sport experience. However, a LTAD approach will absolutely enhance the quality of the sport experience more than not having implemented a developmentally appropriate pathway if both sport experiences have equal coaching quality.

Adolescent Development: Youth Don't Deserve a Bad Rap

We know that both coaches and teachers have a huge impact in children's lives, so it is quite surprising to us how little formal training and education on adolescent psychology is required before coaches are permitted to work with children. Teachers study this topic extensively through their teacher education preparation for good reason, and they're often required by their states to complete continuing education courses each year, yet coaches need seemingly very little to none in order to coach. Before you get annoyed with us, please know we're fully aware that *some* coaches have extensive training in this area.

Adolescents often and unfairly get a bad rap. Adults speak of teenagers as though they are monsters among us, and if Amanda had a dollar for every time someone rudely commented on the living hell her three daughters would bestow on her family while they moseyed through their teen years, she'd be retired and living in Hawaii. We loathe this rhetoric because we find adolescents to be funny, caring, honest, empathetic, and inclusive—at least most of the time, and certainly as much as the adults in our lives. And while we may be very (to put it mildly) removed from our own adolescent experience, if we're honest we can admit that it wasn't always a cakewalk.

Adults stand to learn a lot by listening to passionate teens. Generally speaking, they care about the world around them, including vast social justice issues. We think it's pretty incredible how they navigate—and often excel in—life while experiencing plentiful changes in their bodies at rapid rates. Most adolescents find ways to be good students, thrive in their extracurricular activities, and hold part-time jobs. They have long days and accomplish so much in them.

The fact that adolescents sometimes exhibit traits of being somewhat scatterbrained, self-centered, and very focused on their social relationships is also worth mentioning. During this time of rapid change and growth, individuals will experience an increase in both maturity and in risk-taking, an increase in prioritizing their social lives, as well as vast structural and functional brain development.[9]

In this section, we point out some key concepts of adolescence as well as make a call to action based on the information presented. This book will introduce you to many new concepts and approaches, while reinforcing or challenging your existing knowledge. Even with the many pages you will read, we, admittedly, barely scratch the surface of adolescent psychology in this book. This is by design. It is not because we don't believe adolescent psychology doesn't deserve to hold center stage in a book about youth sport. On the contrary, throughout this book we introduce you to some of our favorite scholars and authors on the topic of adolescent development by disseminating their findings while adding a youth-sport lens to their work.

Physical Activity's Role in Adolescent Development

Did you know that adolescents should have at least sixty minutes of moderate to vigorous physical activity daily for healthy growth and maturation? We're not talking about high levels of fitness training here; we're simply sharing recommendations for how active kids should be for optimal growth. But kids are falling short of meeting these physical activity recommendations, and this should concern us all.

Most of us reading this book have children or raised children at a time that differs greatly from the time we were growing up. For starters, the only gaming system that was at Amanda's house when she was an adolescent was a Commodore 64 that she used to play an Olympic Winter Games video game via a floppy disk that was stored in a soft white case that resembled parchment paper. She recalls playing *Frogger* on her brother's Atari before her family got a computer and had only one channel—two when the rabbit ears were placed in an exact way—until they purchased a satellite dish for the primary purpose of watching NHL games. Like many parents in their mid-forties, when she was a child Amanda's time wasn't being pulled by a device or social media, which left ample free time to head outdoors in search of neighbors who shared her boredom so that they could play. Pickup games of soccer, baseball, and ground hockey manifested from such neighborhood gatherings, and conflicts during these games were resolved without the help of hovering adults, score clocks, or officials. When picked last for a neighborhood game or, worse yet, when told she wasn't welcome to play that day, Amanda was left to sit with her disappointment momentarily before finding something else to do. This usually resulted in riding her bike or juggling a soccer ball, both of which helped her to feel happy just a few moments later.

Let's examine Amanda's current neighborhood, which is located in the suburbs of West County, St. Louis, Missouri. Her home was built in 1971 and is approximately a half a mile away from a busy road devoid of sidewalks. After teaching her kids to ride bikes on tennis courts located within her subdivision, Amanda received a politely worded email as a "friendly reminder" that tennis courts are, in fact, for tennis only. While we understand that bikes can damage a tennis surface and want to point out that the email makes sense upon reflection, it is interesting to note that there is nowhere for young kids to ride their bikes independently and safely.

Lee Furnace Jr., a wrestling coach in St. Louis, Missouri, shared with us how basketball nets were removed from neighborhoods in St. Louis City because the police viewed Black kids who were gathering to play as a threat of violence to the community. A lot of people love to say kids' physical activity rates are at an all-time low because kids are lazy. We think it's because too many adults are lazy—they aren't dissecting the cause of decreased physical activity rates. Nor are they identifying the hurdles that exist for them to be active so that they can fix these fractures.

We can try to bring back neighborhood and community play by ensuring sidewalks accompany new neighborhoods, which allow for active modes of transportation such as scooters, skateboards, and bicycles so that kids can independently and safely gather to organize and participate in pickup games of their choice. Communities can also put in appropriate drainage systems and lights on local fields that result in them being accessed for more months throughout the year. These are changes that won't occur overnight, and they will never occur without advocacy and effort by your community members such as yourself. While it won't be easy, research suggests our kids will be happier and that they are more likely to engage with sport for a longer duration than if we continue in the current fashion of decreasing physical activity opportunities.

Physical activity has not become normalized in many ways outside of youth-sport participation. In fact, once in the spring of 2017 Amanda was outside with her five-month-old baby and five-year-old while her seven-year-old went for a mile run (out and back) in preparation for the upcoming mile run in physical education class. Amanda was soon shocked to see a police car pull up to her front yard where she was playing with her two youngest daughters. Officer Josh stated that he just found it odd to see a child out running on their own, and he wanted to be sure that the little girl returned home safely. Josh was very cool and stayed for a while so that Amanda's girls could explore the cruiser, turn on the lights on top of the police car, and learn what all the equipment in the car was for. The neighbors were certainly curious as to why the police car was in front of the

Stanec family's home for over an hour beginning at 7:30 a.m. on a beautiful, clear-sky Sunday morning. Perhaps this moment is the best way to illustrate just how much we've normalized kids not moving their bodies outside of sport.

It's not that kids are lazy and don't want to interact with their friends; rather, adults have often built neighborhoods in spaces where it's simply not safe to let young kids play outdoors, and this has normalized that the only activity that occurs is structured and supervised closely by adults.

As a result, parents like Amanda register their kids for formalized activities, which leads to a mass exodus of kids from the neighborhood on weeknights and weekends alike to attend structured sport activities. While there are many benefits of such organized sport activities, there are also limitations when organized sport replaces any opportunity for unstructured play. When kids participate predominately in activities facilitated and closely monitored by adults, opportunities to gain authentic social skills are stripped away. Today, social skills aren't learned primarily through peer-to-peer interaction during unstructured play, as they were years ago when Amanda grew up in rural Nova Scotia playing with her neighbors. Conflict resolution is one particular skill that was refined on the dirt road adjacent to her home where the after-school road hockey games got very intense!

We agree that the kids attending structured sport each night is a far better option than no physical activity or social connection at all. Kids need to disconnect from Wi-Fi and connect with each other for endless reasons. And, while they may not be solving problems without adult intervention, they clearly are gaining social skills through organized sport participation. Unfortunately, physical activity rates decrease during adolescence—a time when its benefits are as important as early childhood. In fact, an alarming number of youth-sport participants, 30 percent, dropout annually, and as many as 70 percent quit sport by the onset of adolescence.[10] Given the many unique and specific benefits we believe sport can provide for youth, it is extremely concerning to see the data on dropout rates.

Specific benefits adolescents may gain from youth sport include the following:

1

Physical activity supports optimal brain development.
Physical activity plays an important role in optimal brain development during adolescence, a time when significant changes in the brain regions supporting cognition, learning, and emotion occur.[11] The prefrontal cortex region is a part of the brain that covers the front part of the frontal lobe of the cerebral cortex. It is an important brain area for executive control (the ability to carry out goal-directed behavior using mental processes and cognitive behavior).[12] The prefrontal cortex is responsible for planning, prioritizing, and decision-making. Humans have a larger prefrontal cortex, which distinguishes them from other mammals and allows them to take intentional steps toward higher-level goals, speak a language(s), process complex social information, and to be introspective.[13] Prefrontal cortex-based "top-down control or regulation" networks continue to develop during adolescence and researchers suggest that a more physically active lifestyle during adolescence may be linked with a more efficient use of the prefrontal cortex when performing goal-directed tasks. Goal-directed tasks include controlling one's emotions, behaviors, thoughts, and emotions (inhibitory control) or learning about the relationship between two different stimuli (learning associations).[14]

We know that adolescents are less likely to engage in after-school unstructured play and physical activity than they did during their younger years. We're also well aware that many school districts have cut physical education instructional time in recent decades, and that most middle schools cut recess from the daily academic schedule. Understanding the benefits that physical activity has on brain development, including emotional regulation, it's necessary to highlight here that organized sport may be the one only time of the day that many adolescents are physically active. This is especially concerning when we remind ourselves that almost half of adolescents in North America don't engage in sport at all, and thus many are missing out on the benefits to brain development brought through physical activity. A positive sport experience is essential to keep kids in the game, and therefore to receive ongoing benefits due to participation.

2

Physical activity has the potential to enhance sleep behaviors.

Dr. Gail Moolsintong, a pediatrician who happens to be one of Amanda's best friends, explains three big contributing factors that interfere with teenagers getting enough sleep. First is the normal, natural shift in the body's diurnal rhythms. Nearly all teenagers' natural sleep and wake times shift a few hours later during the adolescent years. Unfortunately, most high schools across the United States actually start classes earlier than they do during the elementary school years. The second factor is (no surprise) screens. Everyone wants to blame the blue light, and that's a factor. But more importantly, every single app or activity on these devices is designed to be stimulating and engaging. The best bet is to just get the screens out of the bedroom at bedtime. The third factor is schedules; so many teenagers are over scheduled. Between school and homework and part-time jobs and athletics, there isn't much time left in the day for downtime, including sleep.

Dr. Moolsintong further explains that sleep is crucial for optimal functioning of all parts of your brain, including concentration, logical planning, and emotional regulation. Chronic sleep deprivation, the kind that goes on over days and weeks, can be insidious. Often you feel like you are functioning okay. But in reality, your brain is suffering. This can even look like or worsen mental health problems like ADHD or clinical anxiety disorder.

It's important to understand that ongoing and regular physical activity can help youth to get to sleep earlier and to sleep more soundly. You're likely aware of the many benefits of consistent and quality sleep, such as elevated mood, mental clarity, and a healthier/more resilient immune system. Unfortunately, even though adolescents need as much sleep during their adolescent years as they did during childhood, sleep behaviors typically decrease dramatically during the adolescent years.

Physical activity can help individuals sleep better and to sleep more soundly. Unfortunately, researchers concluded that adolescents who play sports have actually been found to get less than the recommended hours of sleep as a result of factors such as stress, overtraining, travel, and academic demands.[15] When adolescents have too little sleep, they may fall asleep at inconvenient times at best (like taking a nap in class) or life-threatening times at worst (such as while driving themselves to or from school). Too little sleep can decrease motivation in tasks deemed not exciting and can lead to a dependence on caffeinated drinks.[16] In worst case scenarios, too little sleep can lead to negative thoughts and suicidal ideation.[17]

Therefore, it is really important that those involved in sport scheduling do all they can to provide environments where kids' sleep isn't negatively impacted. For example, don't hold sports practices too late in the evening so that adolescents have time to wind down and get a good night's sleep. While we realize this isn't always an option, we are concerned with those who aren't sleeping, as it can hinder brain development during this critical stage of development. As well, coaches should not provide a win-at-all-cost mentality at training and competition, and parents should not put unnecessary stress or unrealistic expectations on their kids' performance, as both can lead to unnecessarily high levels of stress and anxiety and, indirectly, hinder sleep behaviors.

3
Sport can provide healthy risk-taking opportunities for adolescents.

The prefrontal cortex was introduced and defined earlier in this chapter, and it is one of the parts of the brain that takes the longest to fully mature.

During the same time that the area that controls emotional regulation and decision-making capabilities is taking its time to develop, adolescents enter a stage of life triggered by a remodeling of the brain's dopaminergic system, which increases their desire to seek reward, especially in the presence of peers.[18] The combination of a not-yet-developed prefrontal cortex and an increased desire to have peers' approval can result in unhealthy risk-taking behaviors in adolescents when the perceived social benefits outweigh potential harm in the moment.

In an important piece in *The Atlantic*, Dr. Daniel Seigel explains how changes in our brain's dopamine reward system are responsible for risky behaviors and not the hormonal imbalances that often get a bad rap by parents of adolescents.[19] Dr. Seigel explains how this imbalance leads to greater impulsivity, more susceptibility for addiction, and increased hyper-rationality whereby adolescents place more emphasis or value on potential benefits of a risky behavior and less value on the known and realistic risk. In other words: the adolescent brain craves risk. Interestingly, the adolescent brain can get its "risk fix" from sport engagement, as it can satisfy the desire for reward. Basically, the adolescent brain doesn't discriminate between harmful risk, such as jumping off a roof into a swimming pool, or good risk, such as competing in a sporting event.

While sport can provide healthy risk-taking for youth, it seems necessary to highlight it can sometimes harm one's brain and lead to long-term negative side effects. For example, researchers from Boston University conclude that children who play American-style tackle football before the age of twelve have more behavioral and cognitive problems later in life than those who started playing after the age of twelve. The athletes who participated in this study were also at threefold risk of clinically elevated depression scores. As a result of this research and other studies that found similar cause for concern, adjustments have been made in some communities while they are recommended in others. For example, some youth football programs are now operated as flag football leagues rather than tackle so that contact is eliminated during the early adolescent years when the brain is experiencing rapid changes and growth.

4

Sport provides adolescents
with necessary social connections.

At this point of the chapter, it's no secret that adolescents place a higher priority on peer relationships and peer approval than in earlier stages of development. Any of you with teenagers have experienced a time when they begin to spend more time in their room and less time with you, and they seek increased opportunities to interact with their peers. Brain development during adolescence accounts for individuals to prioritize peer relationships and social experiences at greater levels, and this is a normal part of development.[20] This is why, when my friends and I share stories about when our own kids annoy us because they want to be with their friends more than us, we end up laughing and reminding each other that this is actually a good sign, as they appear to be hitting the normal stages of development at the appropriate time—eye rolls and all.

The COVID-19 pandemic illustrated just how vital in-person social peer interaction is for kids. Because this generation is so intensely attached to communicating through technology, these pivotal social interactions need much more support from adults and coaches to ensure kids are reaping the social and emotional benefits of these connections. Many parents shared during the height of the pandemic that their children were struggling due to isolation at varying levels. A middle-school principal commented to Amanda that when schools reopened, she was observing immature social behaviors among sixth graders that she never observed throughout her previous thirty years as an educator. When we wrote this book in early 2023, the world had opened back up to resemble life pre-COVID-19 in school and sport. But, if you observe your own children or the kids you coach, it is likely that many of them have a smartphone in their hand (not all, but many). Adolescents can connect in some ways through technology, but technology falls short in many ways of helping kids to build and maintain healthy relationships.

At a time when a lot of interaction among youth is virtual and even carefully curated through social media, sport provides an avenue for adolescents to gather and develop peer relationships in person. The important social connections made at sport aid in brain development and lead to many helpful interpersonal gains that will serve adolescents well throughout their lives. These experiences are perhaps more necessary than ever before to help younger adolescents catch up in social skills that may have been hindered during the necessary-but-difficult lock-down phases of the pandemic.

Understanding the specific benefits adolescents may gain from sport participation is necessary to not only be inspired to keep them engaged in sport throughout this critical stage of development, but to understand specific ways parents, coaches, and sport directors alike can establish purposeful settings so this worthy plight becomes a reality. Throughout this book you will learn about coaching strategies and parenting approaches that can help ensure kids will want to stay in the game. You will also be encouraged that sometimes it's necessary to step in and speak out—as coaches and parents—to evoke necessary and positive change in a sport system that does not place youth well-being at the center of all youth sport–related decisions. For example, if your child is not in an environment where they are able to develop and maintain positive social connections with peers or the coach, it may make the most sense to try another environment, understanding how critical social connections are during adolescence.

When examining specific benefits that sports can provide participants during adolescence, examples such as executive function or the ability to plan and meet goals and display self-control were provided due to the specific and rapid changes that occur in the adolescent brain. It is true that controlling one's emotions, setting goals, and forming healthy relationships are important skills for all youth who participate in sport. A wonderful framework that can be used to help parents, coaches, and sport directors understand how to design sport programs and parent in ways that support positive behavioral and cognitive competencies (skills) is the social emotional learning (SEL) framework.

Social Emotional Learning:
SEL Deserves the Hype, So Ignore the Haters

If you've worked with a school leader in the past decade, it's likely that you've heard the term *social emotional learning* often referred to as SEL.[21] However, we want to acknowledge that there are some vocal American politicians attempting to brand SEL as a negative and something that should not be the focus of schools. We'd like to help you understand what SEL actually is so you can draw your own conclusion. From our experience, SEL is a key piece of the ideal relationship between parents, education, and sport. Social emotional learning is a process through which individuals acquire and apply behavioral and cognitive competencies. If you're wondering why there is such a focus on SEL in schools now when there wasn't before, refer to some of the societal norms and community planning issues covered earlier in this chapter (e.g., neighborhoods not conducive to outdoor free play, smartphones providing opportunity for adolescents to socialize virtually rather than in person). When Amanda and her siblings played outdoors with their neighbors, they gave and received feedback regarding what was reasonable and appropriate behaviors. By removing unstructured physical activity norms for youth while at the same time decreasing recess time in school, we've stolen youth's ability to acquire SEL skills informally. Now, intentional SEL curricula are being implemented in schools to help facilitate students' acquisition of SEL competencies because teachers and education leaders recognize that students aren't able to learn optimally when their SEL skills are underdeveloped.

We appreciate that the SEL literature highlights homes and communities and the roles in which they play in individuals' SEL skill acquisition. Schools are often tasked to be everything for everyone, but it's not their sole responsibility to develop SEL skills in youth. Sport falls under communities and community partnerships. Here, we define each of the five SEL competences and share how each can show up in our youth-sport spaces. It is likely that you, like us, believe in the power of sport. So, let's be intentional in seeing sport reach its potential.

There are five core competencies of social emotional learning. In order for youth to gain these valuable skills, it is recommended that these skills are learned and practiced at home, school, and in all types of extracurricular activities. Let's explore each of the core competencies and examine how these skills can be gained specifically through youth sport.[22]

The Five Core Competencies of Social Emotional Learning (SEL)	
	1. Self-Awareness *The abilities to understand one's own emotions, thoughts, and values and how they influence behavior across contexts.*[23]
	Ways to help develop self-awareness in your children or in youth you coach: • Teach and celebrate fair play/sportsmanship. • Ask athletes to identify emotions when winning/losing/struggling to learn a new skill. • Ask athletes to identify current strengths in sport. • Ask athletes to identify current opportunities for growth. • Explain what it means to give one's best effort for the purpose of improvement/growth.
	2. Self-Management *The abilities to manage one's emotions, thoughts, and behaviors effectively in different situations and to achieve goals and aspirations.*
	Ways to help develop self-management in your children or in youth you coach: • Teach and celebrate when athletes manage their emotions during big and small moments in sport. • Teach ways to calm typical nerves before competition or before learning a new task, such as taking three deep breaths. • Help athletes understand how self-discipline can increase their skills and help them feel more motivated. • Teach goal-setting related to their skill development and effort and be sure to follow up with athletes on their goals periodically throughout the season.

Continued…

The Five Core Competencies of Social Emotional Learning (SEL)

3. Social Awareness

The abilities to understand the perspectives of and empathize with others, including those from diverse backgrounds, cultures, and contexts.

Ways to help develop social awareness in your children or in youth you coach:

- Provide athletes time to ask others for their perspectives, ideas, and thoughts.

- Invite athletes to verbalize to the group peers' shining moments from training and competition.

- Provide space for athletes to share how they feel after a disappointing loss or when someone is injured or appears to be sad or struggling.

- Teach athletes that it's okay if they notice the heartache of a losing team and feel for them, while at the same time they are elated and pleased to have won.

- Thank your athletes when they appear to do their best and teach them to thank whomever drove them to sport and to thank each other for the opportunity to help them get better.

- Teach and celebrate when an athlete helps an opponent up during a stoppage of play or when they share uplifting words with an opponent in the handshake line.

- Teach your athletes that they ought to compete with the utmost respect when competing against people from all backgrounds, cultures, and contexts.

Continued...

The Five Core Competencies of Social Emotional Learning (SEL)

4. Relationship Skills
The abilities to establish and maintain healthy and supportive relationships and to effectively navigate settings with diverse individuals and groups.

Ways to help develop relationship skills in your children or in youth you coach:

• Make time to foster positive relationships with the athletes and guide activities that help them develop positive relationships with each other.

• Educate on pertinent cultural competency, as needed.

• Use positive and effective communication when speaking with all youth (chapter 7, page 157, is dedicated to the topic of communication).

• Overtly teach teamwork and how to solve problems within a team in ways that ensure everyone is heard and feels seen.

• Teach and model conflict resolution positively and effectively.

• Speak up for the rights of others, even when it's uncomfortable to do so.

5. Responsible Decision-Making
The abilities to make caring and constructive choices about personal behavior and social interactions across diverse situations.

Ways to help develop responsible decision-making skills in your children or in youth you coach:

• Celebrate curiosity and open-mindedness.

• Talk to youth about the importance of thinking about each potential consequence for their actions.

• Teach youth that decision-making can be clouded when emotions are heightened and remind them that emotions are often heightened in sport.

• Encourage youth to take initiative to solve problems as they arise throughout the season, and to do so by thinking critically and collaboratively.

Just as it's not the sole responsibility for the school to help youth acquire SEL skills, it's not the coach's sole responsibility either. However, if current sport practices take a 180-degree turn from what's presented in this section, coaches and sport directors may want to reflect and consider switching things up. If you're reading this from the parent lens and feel uneasy about how little of your child's sport experience seems to develop SEL skills, you may want to think about whether or not your values align with the current club your child belongs to. (For a deeper conversation on ensuring youth receive appropriate development opportunities in sport, see Chapter 3: Score—How to Find Joy in Youth Sport on page 53.)

Throughout this chapter, you read about the history and purpose of the Long-Term Athlete Development (LTAD) model, explored myriad benefits sport can provide youth during the rapid surge of changes they experience during adolescence, and learned how social emotional learning (SEL) skills can be intentionally acquired and applied in a sport setting. If you were charged with setting the rules for the tournament discussed at the beginning of this chapter, while considering LTAD, key characteristics of adolescence, and SEL skill development, would you prioritize goal differential or goals scored? We have no doubt that those in charge of the tournament care deeply about the athletes' experience. It is likely that they adhere to the LTAD/ADM in their work, as it is praised in their sport's level 1 coaching certification. That said, we didn't name the sport, as we're not in the business of shaming people for making a mistake.

While we certainly don't dwell on this one mistake in an otherwise incredible annual tournament, we believe that it is a great example of how, sometimes, really good people fall short in doing what is truly in the best interest of all kids. Sport coaches, parents, and directors will inevitably make mistakes because they are human, and empathy and grace belong in such instances. Amanda wrote to tournament organizers when her daughter returned, thanked them for the incredible event, and humbly suggested they reconsider the tie-breaking ruling. Because, if we know better, it's up to us to care enough to do something about it. While she didn't receive a response, that won't deter her from doing so again in the future, because kids are worth it.

It is most likely that the rules for the tournament were established a long time ago and haven't been reconsidered since then as, let's be real, it's unlikely that a team tasked to score thirteen goals is able to do it very often. Personally, we love reading books that push our thinking and current thoughts on a particular topic, as that's how we grow. We don't take it personally when our favorite authors call out our shit as though they are speaking directly to us. You likely will disagree with some of what we are suggesting in this chapter and going forward, and that's okay too. Trust us, we've initially disagreed with ideas we now advocate for! Our thinking is constantly evolving as we continue to learn and as more work is published. So, please proceed with this foundational knowledge in your back pocket and an open mind in the spirit of creating sport experiences that are so epic, no one wants to quit.

Questions to Ask Yourself

- As a coach or parent, do you read rules for tie-breaking before a tournament? Would you reach out if you felt a rule misaligned with the Long-Term Athlete Development (LTAD) model?
- What are three things you would suggest a coach do to encourage their athletes want to come back for the following season?
- Consider the ways to develop social emotional learning (SEL) skills in athletes. What are you currently doing? What might you be able to build upon? How might you do this?
- If you're a parent or a coach, do you model SEL skills on the car ride home from practice or games? During competition? How might you better model SEL?
- Were you surprised to learn that up to 70 percent of youth quit sport by the time they reach adolescence? Why do you think this happens?

Do's and Don'ts

Do's

- Observe athletes' skill levels and establish their stage of development before age sport model.
- Understand the concepts of developmental age and relative age so that you're not unintentionally hindering the experience of athletes by assuming they are all at the same place in their sport journey and physical development.
- Provide Long-Term Athlete Development (LTAD) education to coaches, parents, and youth. If you're a parent, consider learning more about this model and encouraging your child's sport organization to do the same.
- Adjust current training according to the stages of the LTAD pathway. If you're a parent, observe the training your child is receiving and take steps to fold in the appropriate training for their level or encourage your child's sport organization to do so.
- Work to create supportive sport environments among peers so that youth will be more likely to continue sport engagement throughout adolescence.
- Understand the vast and rapid changes occurring in an adolescent brain to better coach them and parent them throughout this stage of development.
- Become familiar with the core competencies of SEL.
- If you're a director or coach, consider choosing different SEL skills to home in on as you notice where your athletes may be falling short (e.g., relationship-building among teammates).

Don'ts

- Establish sport models based on chronological age.
- Allow an unhealthy social dynamic to permeate on a team, because social connections are critically important to adolescents and a bad social environment can lead kids to quit sport.
- Assume kids have particular SEL skills at any particular age, as they are skills that have to be learned and practiced to be acquired.

CHAPTER 3

Score

How to Find Joy in Youth Sport

"Sport has the power to change the world. It has the
power to inspire. It has the power to unite people
in a way that little else does. It speaks to youth in a
language they understand. Sport can create hope
where once there was only despair."

–Nelson Mandela

M eet Theo,[24] a soccer player in Ottawa, Ontario.

Theo's 12U Soccer Season

Theo is a twelve-year-old boy who tried out for the most competitive 12U
soccer team offered in his city. He was elated when he found out that he
made the team, because soccer is something he enjoys very much. As a late
developer,[25] Theo practiced on his own consistently since the end of last
season because he wanted his technical skills to be at a level necessary for
this team. The team was coached by a parent–coach who played college
soccer twenty years ago, but he has a professional life outside of sport.
The coach did not have any formal coaching credentials but was enthusiastic about his team's overall ability. As such, he planned organized and
thoughtful practices. At the beginning of the season, the coach communicated that every player would receive at least 50 percent of playing time
during each game. However, midway through the season, he emailed
parents and said their playing time philosophy would be tabled for the
rest of the season and that a minimum time was no longer guaranteed.

Throughout the season—without warning or communication from the coach—Theo was benched periodically. He found himself feeling less excited to go to soccer practice because he felt the players were treating him like he didn't belong on the team. When he did get playing time, Theo was convinced that teammates weren't passing to him because they didn't have faith that he could get the job done. His parents noticed that his love of the game seemed to be decreasing and asked him if he'd like to take a season off. He said he still loved soccer but didn't understand why the coach treated him in ways that made him think they didn't believe in him. This made his parents sad, as they wanted him in soccer to have fun with his friends, to learn time management and dedication, and to have something that gave him a sense of community, especially as he approached his teenage years. Theo's parents were realistic in that he was, in fact, playing with less speed and confidence than some teammates, but they also realized that growth and maturation occur at different rates during adolescence and that he likely would improve in these areas as he got older. Theo's parents don't expect everything in sport to be handed to their son, and they aren't afraid for Theo to experience disappointment throughout his sport journey. But they also felt very uneasy with this situation, which was crushing their son's joy in a sport that he loves so much.

Theo's 13U Soccer Season

Most of Theo's teammates switched clubs, and Theo remained on the same team for the next season with a new coach, as the original coach also departed. During the offseason leading up to the beginning of 13U season, Theo independently practiced key technical skills and also took one hundred shots on goal each day. Theo would play his favorite music while doing so, and sometimes he'd invite friends over to join him. Theo attended a few soccer clinics during the offseason because he loved meeting new friends and learning from coaches who really studied the game and provided guidance that gave him confidence on the field. His parents reported that he seemed relieved to be no longer playing with his 12U teammates and coach. Theo shared with his parents that his former coach and teammates added unnecessary stress to his sport experience the previous year. The new coaches—who were also parents—communicated that playing time would be equal or very close to equal at all times (no exceptions), because their primary goal was to develop every single player and the entire team. They communicated that since there were tryouts, everyone deserves to be on the team and to receive adequate playing time so that they could all improve their decision-making and ability to take their skills to games.

The new coaches did not waver from their playing-time commitment. Theo made sure that whenever a teammate tried a new skill in practice to cheer them on regardless of their success in that moment, because he knew that with enough practice the new skills will be effective soon enough. Theo didn't want anyone to feel nervous trying new things, like he felt the previous year, so he took his role as a leader on the team very seriously and used his position to build other teammates up. Theo's parents noticed Theo's joy from soccer seemed to return. No longer was their son playing out of fear, and he would light up when it was time to go to practice. Athletes and parents seemed much more friendly compared to last season and less anxious, and everyone seemed to fully support each other.

....

Throughout our combined decades of experience, we have observed all that is amazing about sport. We've been moved to tears watching athletes overcome adversity and achieve what naysayers said was not achievable. We've felt connected in our communities and countries when local and national teams make a run for a top spot on the podium. Amanda's research background includes sharing stories of female elite athletes who experienced upward social mobility gained through sport, while Richard has shared stories from the local perspective of an athlete, coach, leader, and dad regarding athlete development around the globe. As such, there is no doubt in our minds that sport can do a lot of good—when sport is in fact *joyful.* We suspect you agree, or you wouldn't have chosen to read a book on the topic of protecting youth's joy in sport. Joyful sport is achieved when coaches and parents take a holistic approach to athletic development that does not solely focus on performance and competition, and it is achieved when it's successful in instilling helpful life skills such as confidence, interpersonal intelligence, and discipline in athletes.

Joyful sport is made of research-informed programs, intentional and thoughtful people, and safe spaces for kids to thrive. The tenets of joyful sport include the following:

- Joyful sport models good education; it is collaborative and thoughtful and keeps the youth at the heart of all decisions.
- Joyful sport treats participants in developmentally and age-appropriate ways.
- Joyful sport is led by coaches who set high expectations related to all participants' development and offers a supportive environment for players to improve.
- Joyful sport is supported when adults effectively communicate with youth and invite youth to do the same.
- Joyful sport has meaningful competition formats that ensure all participants are challenged appropriately.
- Joyful sport focuses on development over wins and losses—always.
- Joyful sport enhances well-being through sleep hygiene, nutrition, and rest and recovery because the adults guiding the athletes understand that all are necessary for the youth to reach their potential.
- Joyful sport aims to end each season with youth loving the sport more than they did at the beginning.

Joyful Sport Is Developmentally *and* Age Appropriate

When youth experience sport in developmentally and age-appropriate settings, it can provide a plethora of positive outcomes,[26] including, but not limited to:

- Enhanced social health
- Improved physical health and wellness
- Elevated sleep hygiene
- Strengthened resilience
- Refined time-management skills
- Increased confidence
- Developed goal-setting behaviors
- Sharpened stress management skills

Conversely, when youth find themselves in an adult version of sport (highly competitive, exclusive), sport can actually hinder their overall well-being. In these instances, sport becomes the stressor rather than an escape from other life stressors, and this should be as unsettling to you as it is to us. Although adult sport settings can provide older players with the necessary environment to reach peak-level performance, when youth are exposed to it, it leads to a bad version of sport.

What Is a Bad Version of Sport?

Bad sport occurs when youth are experiencing a sport environment that prioritizes the product (outcome; win/loss) over the process (development). Adult version of sport in youth settings can rob sport of its ability to do good, and in turn, it keeps youth from gaining the extremely valuable benefits that sport has to offer. Theo's first soccer season consisted of elements found in the adult version of sport, which is very common throughout the youth-sport scene in North America.

When sport is developmentally and age appropriate, it is better positioned to enhance the lives of all involved. A beautiful example of joyful, developmentally, and age-appropriate sport can be found at your local ice rink. If you've never visited a 6U ice hockey practice, you should. Trust us. Each practice begins with some large group skating games, and then children are divided into groups based on skill level and experience. These groupings are important, because research concludes that youth are more likely to continue with sport when they have higher levels of enjoyment and motivation. Enjoyment and motivation are unlikely without some perceived or actual success. If a beginner child is grouped with players much more skilled and experienced than they are, they will be less likely to experience success and the environment won't be enjoyable or motivating.

Each station at a 6U hockey practice has minimal (if any) lines, so each child receives a lot of opportunity to practice. The stations consist of inclusive and fun small-sided games, such as soccer or monkey in the middle. That's right, kids are playing soccer on skates at ice hockey practice. It's truly a beautiful thing. Spectators are treated to toothless grins that can be seen across the ice and through kids' helmet cages. If seeing these smiles doesn't warm your heart, nothing will. There are no scores posted; there are no championship trophies. Score clocks and championships are for the adult version of sport, and they can steal the joy of play from kids when placed on them too soon. When we observe 6U practices, we notice the joy.

Unsurprising, a joyful 6U hockey practice like the one we describe parallels a morning routine for a kindergarten class led by a master teacher. When Amanda's daughter Ginny, a kindergartner in Emily Riechert's classroom in the Parkway School District in St. Louis, Missouri, arrives to class each morning, she along with her classmates are invited to visit various learning centers. In sport, learning centers are known as "stations," but the concept is the same. Ms. Riechert's classroom centers include various math games, art options, such as painting or drawing, and engaging letter or sight-word activities, to name a few. Each center provides the child an opportunity to practice developmentally appropriate and intentional skill sets carefully planned so they are both motivating and fun.

When coaches and teachers structure learning environments with the intention of using enjoyment and genuine interest as a springboard for growth, the potential for youth is immeasurable. Coach Zane Truman, a coach with the 6U St. Louis Lady Cyclones hockey club may choose monkey in the middle at a practice because he feels players would benefit from practicing passing, pressuring the puck, and communicating in a fun and age-appropriate manner. Ms. Reichert may choose a particularly fun sight-word activity because it will help her students begin to read at a developmentally appropriate level.

Now, let's think about what a 6U hockey experience might look like if Coach Zane placed an adult version of hockey on them. Perhaps instead of everyone practicing at a station, there would be a full-ice scrimmage with most players on the bench. A score clock would be on display, and some kids would likely get played a lot more than others. A tiny human would be placed in a large net and expected to stop the puck as it comes toward them.

If Ms. Reichert set up her kindergarten classroom like a high school class, where students enter the classroom, read the instructions on the board, and are expected to begin an instant activity with little verbal guidance, her students would struggle and become frustrated very quickly. They wouldn't understand the expectations or direction, because most of them can't even read; this approach would not be developmentally appropriate. Since students wouldn't have the chance to move around from center to center or engage in silly and fun learning tasks, it also wouldn't be age appropriate or engaging for them.

All of us wearing coaching and parenting hats should keep the youth in sport when we speak and travel in youth-sport spaces. Students learn at different rates, and it may take some kids longer to read than others, but they all get there thanks to well-trained, intentional, and creative teachers. In sport, players will develop at different rates, and where they are at age seven does not predict where they'll be at age seventeen. As such, we need to provide all participants with warm environments, with high expectations, and with support to meet these expectations.

While the example used is for 6U, if you look up ADMkids.com (the site for USA Hockey's American Developmental Model), you will see these principles are appropriate for older age groups. Our children will grow up soon enough. As they say, "The days are long, but the years are short." Let's help our children enjoy their youth and keep the fun in sport; ironically, they will have a better chance of participating in college or professional sports if they enjoy sport and develop appropriately.

Coaching Development: Youth Shouldn't Be the Only Ones Expected to Improve

coach
kouCH/: **noun**

A covered carriage that takes a person
of importance from point A to point B.

The origin of the word *coach* lights us up, because it places the human at the center, and we know that every youth who shows up to sport practice and competition is worthy of our attention, teaching, and support. We also appreciate the visual of a coach guiding an athlete from point A to point B, because sport development is exactly that, and helping kids progress throughout the development pathway ought to be a primary objective of any coach.

We likely all agree that a positive, knowledgeable coach who places children and youth at the center and focuses on their development is absolutely essential to a sport experience. If that sounds easy to do, it's not. Coaching well is very difficult, and this is why we have a lot of patience for coaches who are doing their best, even when they fall short. In other words, we don't expect coaches to be perfect—hell, we're coaches and we're far from perfect. But we do expect coaches who step up to serve to take their role seriously, regardless of if they are a paid coach or if they are a volunteer.

Without community members stepping up to coach local youth, there would be no youth sport. While we should always be grateful to coaches for sharing their time, we believe it's a minimal—albeit high—expectation that they make time to learn about best practices as well as how to apply them to the setting that they are charged with leading.

For starters, good coaches are students of the sport. This includes appropriate coaching certification by a national sport organization (NSO). Most level 1 coaching certifications are available for a minimal fee and online. If you sign up to volunteer, it is a reasonable expectation that you become certified at least with a level 1 coaching class. These classes have valuable information that will set coaches up for success.

If sport is only joyful with good coaches, it is imperative that we ask ourselves the question: *What do good coaches do?* What follows are examples of what to strive for when coaching youth, and what to look for when deciding if the environment for your child is the right fit.

Good Coaches Are Reflective, Just like Good Teachers

They regularly ask themselves what they're doing well and what they could improve on. They allow themselves to learn from other coaches and educators. They may even ask athletes who their favorite teachers are and then make an effort to observe them and talk to them to find out what it is that they do that makes their class so enjoyable. It is important for them to observe themselves and others to ensure their own growth and development.

After practice and competition, they ask questions such as:

- Did they look confused when I explained that skill or drill?
  If so, did I explain it well? Would a visual help? Would sending a link to a complex drill in advance help them?

- Did they appear bored? Was the drill fun and upbeat? Did I bring high energy tonight?
- Did we lose because we didn't try, or do we simply have things to learn?
- Did they seem uninvested? Did I explain the "why" to this drill?
- Did I plan too many "structured" drills, or did I create small games where kids could learn technical skills along with decision-making skills?
- Were they laughing and smiling during activities and in between them? Did they seem to have fun while staying on task? If not, were the activities not challenging or too difficult?
- After this practice, will all the kids be excited about coming to the next practice?

Good coaches will then use the information gained during reflection to either refine their explanations, change their behavior, or, in some cases, they will be affirmed that their efforts seemed appreciated by the kids.

Good Coaches Establish Warm, Safe Environments

Most of us have seen the social media videos that go viral as students perform their special handshakes with their teachers upon entering the classroom. What's so powerful about these videos is that it highlights the teacher's effort to prioritize every student. Sport participants should feel seen at every practice and every game, just like every student feels seen while performing their unique handshake upon entering a classroom. This doesn't mean they are given unearned opportunities. It means that coaches should greet the team members, and teammates should have learned that welcoming each other is an expectation. In establishing strong relationships between coaches and players, youth will feel safe to be creative and try new things free of reprimand.

Good Coaches Use Positive Skill-Specific Feedback

Positive skill-specific feedback specifies what the athlete is doing well. Skill-specific feedback is a better option than positive *general* feedback statements, such as "good job" or "nice try." An example of skill-specific feedback is, "I'd love to see you follow through a bit more toward your target." Elementary physical education researchers concluded that teachers tend to give general positive feedback to girls and specific positive feedback to boys.[27] The teachers were only trying to encourage the girls, likely because they are aware of the alarming rates that girls decrease their physical activity as they get older. However, an unintended consequence of this is that the girls weren't getting the feedback that could help them develop their skills as proficient as the boys. The boys increased their skill competence more than girls at an age whereby growth and maturation would not account for different measures between girls and boys. In other words, at an age where boys and girls should have no difference in skill ability, teachers' general feedback behaviors appeared to hinder girls' abilities to develop their skills to the same level as boys who received specific feedback.

Researchers interested in better understanding "change-oriented" feedback, more commonly known as "negative" or "corrective" feedback suggest that athletes are open to receiving it when it is delivered in an empathic tone, is equipped with tips or solutions for the athlete's mistake or challenge, and includes clear and attainable objectives.[28]

Good Coaches Understand How to Establish a Motivating, Athlete-Centered Environment

In simple terms, achievement goal theory is a theoretical framework often applied to help researchers understand motivation. Researchers first used the theory to examine motivation in education, specifically in the classroom setting.[29] Other researchers then applied the goal orientation theory to examine motivation in physical education and later in sport. The achievement goal theory suggests that competence plays a major role in achievement, and that individuals can move toward ego or task goals while working toward achievement-related tasks. "Ego goals" are goals where success is defined as winning or being superior to others, while "task goals" are goals where success is defined as improving or mastering a task.

Sport practices can be set in ways that promote either ego or task goals, or as often and most typical, practices can promote *both* ego and task goals. The practice environment established by the coach used to promote either task or ego goals is called the *motivational climate*. If a motivational climate is established with intent to promote task goals, it's called *a task-involved motivational climate* whereas if it's established with intent to promote ego goals, it's called an *ego-involved motivational climate*. To be clear, the type of motivational climate youth find themselves in will absolutely influence which type of goals they will move toward. For example, a high ego-involved motivational climate will encourage youth to set ego-oriented goals, while a high task-involved motivational climate will encourage them to set more task-oriented goals.

We advocate that coaches prioritize a task-involved motivational climate over an ego-involved motivational climate to enhance athletes' experience, because the research concludes youth are more motivated and enjoy their sport experience more when they are setting task-oriented goals within a task-involved motivational climate. We also encourage parents to understand task-goal orientation to help teach their kids how to set task goals.

Here's why.

Task-oriented goals are within the athletes' control, while ego-oriented goals are not. For example, if a person or team has their eye on the state or provincial championship, there are many variables that aren't within their control, such as officiating, injuries, ability of the other team, facilities (or, lack thereof), etc. However, if the environment is established that constantly asks for participants' best, and their best is celebrated, the person or team will continue to progress in their development and, in fact, be better situated to win the championship.

The research supports our encouragement for coaches to establish a task-involved motivational climate and for parents to help their kids set task goals versus ego goals, including one study Amanda was the primary investigator on.

Amanda's interest in the intersection of sport psychology and best teaching and coaching practices began more than twenty-five years ago when she enrolled in her master's degree. The culminating requirement for her degree was to complete a thesis study. Amanda's study set out to determine if adolescent girls are able to recognize a particular motivational climate established for them by a teacher or a coach. Fifty sixth-grade girls participated in this study over a seven-week period. For the first three weeks of the study, half of the students attended daily physical education class in an established task-involved climate with one teacher, while the other half attended daily physical education class in an established ego-involved climate with another teacher. Students completed a survey about their experiences on the final day of PE during the first three-week block. Then, students went on spring break for a week. Upon return of spring break, the students remained with the same teacher, but the teacher now planned for and taught daily PE using the opposite motivational climate for the second three-week block. Upon completion of the second three-week block, students once again completed the same survey, which would help Amanda determine if students recognized the characteristics established.

Findings of this study conclude that students were able to identify the characteristics of their class accurately as task- or ego-motivational climate. Specifically, they recognized that in the three-week task-involved motivational climate block that the teacher (1) defined success as students doing their best or learning something new; (2) wanted them to celebrate effort; and (3) would not reward those who were more skilled during class. Conversely, upon completion of the ego-involved motivational climate, students noted that the teacher (1) defined success as being the best or winning; (2) rewarded the winners; and (3) had consequences such as "losers pick up the equipment" for losing teams in small-sided games.

This is an important finding because the research also concluded that the students enjoyed their physical education experience during the three-week task-involved climate far more than they enjoyed their experience in the ego-involved climate. The teacher participants in the study noted that when students participated in the task-involved motivational climate, they offered to help more, they encouraged their peers, and they arrived early to class. However, when these same students participated in an ego-involved motivational climate, they more frequently rolled their eyes, arrived late to class, and did not enjoy the lesson. While the teachers were the same and the students were the same, students' behavior and perceived motivation was not. Additionally, the teachers reported feeling more discouraged with their students in the ego-involved climate versus the task-involved climate. If you're wondering what a task-involved motivational climate looks like and how to establish one, we have you covered. When creating a task-involved or mastery motivational climate, there are six dimensions that need to be planned for. These six dimensions are known as Epstein's TARGET framework[30] and include:

1. **Task:** design of activities
2. **Authority:** location of decision-making
3. **Recognition:** use of rewards
4. **Grouping:** selection of working groups
5. **Evaluation:** assessment criteria
6. **Time:** pace of instruction

Years later, a group of researchers from the United States and Australia validated Amanda's master's thesis findings with a longitudinal study involving 283 student–athletes who ranged in age from fourteen to eighteen. The student–athletes were placed in one of two groups: a control group who participated in their regular sport practices and an experimental group who participated in their sport practice that was designed using Epstein's TARGET framework. Both groups participated in their sport experience for twelve weeks. Participants were asked to complete question-naires before the study began (pre), as soon as the twelve-week program completed (post 1), and again six months after the program ended (post 2). The coaches who were assigned to be in the experimental group agreed to learn about the TARGET strategies and understand how to apply them while coaching.

Researchers concluded that the coaching climate can be manipulated by the coaches using Epstein's TARGET. In other words, coaches can plan practices that steer athletes toward task-oriented goals rather than toward ego-oriented goals. Just like in Amanda's master's thesis study, athletes were able to identify when a task-involved motivational climate was established. Moreover, athletes experienced an increase in cooperative learning, autonomy, social relationships and perceived competence, self-determination,[31] persistence, and effort, and significantly decreased their levels of boredom. The researchers stated that the most remarkable finding of this study was that some of the benefits were maintained six months after the program ended.

If you're thinking we're nuts and about to ruin every competitive kid's competitive drive, let us quickly put you at ease. Competitive kids are competitive, regardless of what the goal is. Therefore, they will work as hard as they can in improving and being the best they can be. Just because these athletes won't get to watch their peers carry the balls or water bottles if they lose a scrimmage, it doesn't mean that their competitive spirit will crash and burn. We promise.

Given the positive effects of using the TARGET Framework to establish a task-involved motivational climate for your athletes, we are hopeful you're interested in establishing such a climate if you are a coach. At the end of this chapter, we've provided an action step—*Plan for a task-involved motivational climate* (page 76)—to help you nurture the best climate possible for developing athletes. If you're a parent, we're hopeful that understanding the important benefits your child can gain by steering them toward task-oriented goals motivates you to do so.

Key findings from the research on motivational climate include:

• Coaches and physical education teachers can plan practices and lessons in a task-involved motivational climate.
• Youth can identify a task- or ego-involved climate.
• Youth will experience greater levels of autonomy, social connection, self-determination, persistence and effort, and perceived competence in a task-involved motivational climate.
• Youth will experience lower levels of boredom in a task-involved motivational climate.
• Youth are more motivated to help others and to arrive early when they experience sport or PE in a task-involved motivational climate.
• Coaches and teachers will enjoy coaching and teaching more when they plan for and deliver practice and class using a task-involved motivational climate approach.

Parents: With Great Power Comes Great Responsibility

While it is important that youth directors and coaches do not put youth in the adult version of sport—and that coaches should be reflective students of both the sport as well as sound pedagogy[32]—they aren't the only adults who play a key role in determining if a youth-sport experience will be a good one.

Parents and caregivers are essential to a good sport experience and have the power to aid in their child's youth-sport experience, especially in those moments where the child may need their guidance the most. Sport can provide many wonderful life skills such as resilience and persistence due to the struggles that may arise in sport. Parents will hear examples of such struggles after a difficult game, practice, or tricky interaction with a teammate or a coach. Parents ought to remain curious in these moments and avoid meeting an emotional child with panic. For example, when an emotional child communicates a struggle they are experiencing, parents can take a deep breath and calmly ask questions and try to get the full story. Their calm demeanor can help calm the child. The expression that "there are two sides to every story and then the truth" comes to mind as we write this section. Sport is public and can be relentless and unfair. Marry that with an adolescent brain, and it can be a recipe for an outburst or two. Adolescents have an excuse; their brains are undergoing a total rewiring during these years and emotional bursts are expected. As parents, we don't have that excuse. It is our job to be the mature adult in the room, which admittedly isn't always easy because our children are typically the center of our world.

It is important for parents to differentiate between a difficult situation and an abusive situation. This is an issue that is continuously left out of snarky tweets from people who love to criticize parents. It would not be wise to eliminate every hurdle your child might face in sport, yet parents should hold sport to a standard whereby it is more often than not the highlight of a kid's day. If a parent has been observing things that make them feel icky, they should trust their instincts. Those feelings mean it's time to step in and—at the very least—have a courageous conversation (see chapter 7, page 169). Parents who support joyful sport don't avoid confrontation because it might upset someone; they approach it from a place of empathy and with the intention for everyone to feel better after communication transpires.

Parents who support joyful sport let their kids know that sport is something they do, but it does not define them.
They also offer to role-play difficult conversations with their kids before they encourage them to have these said conversations with adult coaches or other players. Parents who support joyful sport avoid looking at an experience in sport through a toilet paper roll and step back to see the full picture in an attempt to gain perspective. They help their kids understand all they

have to be grateful for, while sometimes acknowledging that the kid has a right to feel pissed off. These parents also remind their children that while a sport(s) may be part of their identity, it should only be one part of them because they are fully human.

Parents who support joyful sport don't treat their children like mini-professionals.

They don't try to rewrite their sports dreams through their children, and they don't foster a sense of entitlement in their kids. These parents educate themselves on adolescent psychology and childhood development so that the expectations they place on their children are age and developmentally appropriate.[33]

Parents who support joyful sport don't berate any child related to sport.

They never lose sight that sport is a game, and games are played for fun. They avoid any temptation to compare their child to others. When parents tell their kids to pick up the same habits as another youth, they can cause resentment. Such parents can make their kids feel they are in competition with their teammates, rather than developing *with* their teammates for the good of the team's success.

Parents who support joyful sport remember that fun is the key ingredient in a recipe of staying in the game.

In November 2022, during half-time of a Big 10 field hockey final between University of Michigan and Northwestern University, Amanda nodded and smiled while Coach Marcia Pankratz was interviewed on the TV. When asked what her goals were for the rest of the game, Coach Pankratz said—among other things—for the girls to have fun. She continued, "They came to Michigan to be student–athletes and to have an awesome experience. Fun has to be a part of that." *Hell, yeah!* It is not unlikely that this approach and focus helped the Wolverines capture the title that day in a 2–0 victory over the D-I NCAA defending national champions. Parents who teach their children that competing is fun, doing their best is fun, and doing better than they ever did before is fun will help them to understand that laughs and smiles belong in competition and can, in fact, positively influence performance.

Joyful Sport Has a Welcoming Environment

We fully believe that sport can't reach its potential if it's not responsive to issues related to diversity, equity, and inclusion. To begin this section, we must acknowledge our own whiteness, biases, and privilege. Amanda is a first-generation Canadian on her mother's side and became an immigrant to the United States. She holds citizenship in Canada and the United States. Richard is a first-generation Canadian and lives on the west coast of Canada. Even though we have completed immigration papers and participated in citizenship tests and interviews, we've received a great deal of privilege due to our Eurocentric roots. For example, we've never faced the same biases or stereotypes of immigrants who did not speak English as a first language, who are not Christian, or who are people of color. We understand that recognizing our privilege and how it has helped position us in our careers is an important fact to highlight. It doesn't mean that we didn't work hard; rather, it highlights that our start line was further ahead of our peers and colleagues from underrepresented groups.

Cultural humility is a process of self-reflection and discovery for the purpose of building honest and trustworthy relationships.[34] We first read about cultural humility in the context of healthcare settings where the importance of physicians, nurses, and clinical researchers having ongoing self-examination of their own beliefs while seeking to understand others is well documented. Cultural humility requires someone to have a personal lifelong commitment to reflection in the context of beliefs and identities for the purpose of evaluation and critique. Coaches who demonstrate cultural humility may ask themselves questions such as:

- Which parts of my identity are privileged and/or marginalized?
- How does my own identity shift based on context and settings?
- How might my own biases hinder or limit my athletes' experience?

We rightfully feel ill equipped to write about race and equity for many reasons, but we are committed to continuous reflection and education on the topic.[35] It's imperative that we encourage all adults working with youth to understand systemic racism in sport so that we can serve as active participants in removing barriers for youth who are underserved. This requires coaches and club directors to see color, to understand different religions and cultural customs, and to create a space where kids can be their true selves when they go to their sport practice and competition. It is equally as important for parents to talk openly about any privilege their family might have as well as have zero tolerance for racism and bigotry. Additionally, parents ought to teach their children to be upstanders for those with less privilege and those who are marginalized.

On a recent run with a friend, Amanda was told of an incident where her running buddy's neighbor was called the n-word by a teammate on his high school hockey team. When another teammate informed the coach about the incident, he was labeled a "pussy" by the slur-slinging teammate and a few other teammates. The kid who used the racial slur said what adults needed to hear to think he had learned his lesson, but behind the scenes he proceeded to taunt the boy who reported the slur. Amanda's legs felt heavy as she heard this story and her stomach felt nauseous. These types of incidents do not belong in sport. Coaches must make it known and athletic directors should provide training on how coaches can talk about these issues at the beginning of season and set clear expectations with severe consequences to ensure situations like this are eradicated from sport.

If sport has the power to do a lot of good, we ought to be committed to widening the net of who gets to participate in sport. Trends over the past several decades have increased a lot of sport-related travel and often make it cost prohibitive for many families. Youth as young as eleven and twelve years old are traveling out of state to compete several times each season. We're not suggesting youth competing with others at the same level is a bad thing, or that taking your kid out of the region to compete makes you a bad person. We are concerned about the travel hours required when these trips are frequent, as it hinders kids' ability to spend time riding bikes, climbing trees, and just being kids—all the while costing families a lot of money.

When we choose to cut sports at the school level—K-12 or collegiate levels—we should consider diversity, equity, and inclusion in those discussions. When we move to cut a sport like wrestling and replace it with a sport such as golf, we are replacing a low-cost sport that welcomes kids in every size and replacing it with another sport that is extremely exclusive and costly at the youth level. We are not knocking specific sports or ones that require significant time or financial investments—we truly believe that *all* sports have the power to do good. But sports that require little equipment and low registration fees must be highlighted when talking about inclusive sports.

Amanda's friend Senegalese Olympic freestyle wrestler Isabelle Sambou shared with her how her experiences in wrestling resulted in upward social mobility. Isabelle literally supplies electricity to her village due to her accomplishments in wrestling. Isabelle was the flag bearer for Senegal in the 2016 Rio Olympic Games, and her story leads us to wonder how many other kids like Isabelle are denied a chance to compete due to the cost of certain sports and due to the sport system created in developed countries.

When we organize youth sports in communities, we should work hard to offer adapted sports, and it should not just be the parents of children with disabilities making this plea. Youth with disabilities have far fewer opportunities to participate in sport because parasport[36] is not as common. Moreover, costs of para or adapted sport are much greater due to the nature of the modified equipment. Also, families typically have to travel further to find an option. Special Olympics is one sport offering for children with certain disabilities, however in Missouri alone there are currently 100,000 individuals who can't access Special Olympics due to living in rural parts of the state too far from practices or competition hubs.

When coaching any youth, it is a good idea to survey them prior to the season to get to know them. Ask about their family's background, culture, and traditions and invite them to expand upon these topics. It is helpful to know if they have religious holidays that will cause them to be absent, and coaches should honor that and not make them feel guilty or badly for missing. Ongoing surveys can be a very helpful way to better understand the youth participating in sport. Coaches can gain a lot of insight and learn important information that they can then build on when conversing with the youth.

Keyboard warriors and twitter sport celebrity types love to put out sound bites and memes about parents saving kids from any disappointment in sport, and in some cases, they may have a point. There are people out there constantly complaining about parents and how they are helicopters and bulldozers, and perhaps some are. But we don't buy the idea that "coaches are stupid" and "parents are crazy." We believe there are exceptional coaches and some misguided and misinformed ones. We believe that there are overbearing and unreasonable parents, and that there are caring parents who just want to raise good citizens who contribute positively to society.

Research concludes that the number one reason kids play sport is to have fun, while the number one reason they quit sport is because it's no longer fun.[37] Do not mistake our use of the word "fun" as some unicorn rainbow with butterflies surrounding it. Fun is doing one's best, doing better than one ever did before, and competing as hard as one can. Joyful sport is fun, and all adults play an important role in ensuring that the environment is fun.

How to Spot Joyful Sport

- Athletes are excited to go to practice and competition.
- Athletes try new skills because they know creativity and effort are celebrated.
- Success is defined as doing one's best, improving, or mastering a skill or tactical play never mastered before.
- Laughter and smiles frequent training sessions and competition.

The Good That Joyful Sport Can Do

- Enhances well-being
- Better sleep
- A stress relief/outlet
- Leads to positive relationships
- Increases success in short and long term. Success can be defined as working toward one's potential and applying skills that will support that journey.

How to Spot Bad Sport

- Athletes don't want to go to practice or to competition.
- Athletes perform far below their potential due to a culture of fear.
- Athletes don't know where they stand with the coach.
- Success is defined narrowly as winning or being the best.
- Poor body language and defeated posture is recognizable during training and competition.

The Harm That Bad Sport Can Do

- Leads youth to have negative associations between themselves and physical activity.
- Damages relationships among youth but also children and parent relationships.
- Leads to youth quitting sport permanently.

Questions to Ask Yourself

- Does the sport I provide for my athletes treat them as youth? Or does it assume they are mini adults? If I am providing an adult version of sport, what can I do to modify my current practice?
- Based on my child's relationships with teammates and the coach and their feelings when it's time to go to practice or a game, do I think they're loving their sport environment? If not, what seems to be off?
- Do I punish my athletes if they lose? Do I reward them if they win? Or do I praise effort and development?
- How do I establish a safe and caring community for my athletes? What could I do better?
- Do I speak to my child about privilege and appreciation for their sport opportunities?
- Do I talk to my children about being upstanders for teammates, even when it's difficult for them to take a stand?

Action Step for Consideration

- Plan for a task-involved motivational climate using Epstein's TARGET approach in order to promote task goals among athletes.

Epstein's TARGET Framework and Motivational Climate in Sport	
T	**Task: Design of Activities**

Design activities in ways that kids are focused on their own development and improvement and not on social comparison.

Example: Have soccer players practice juggling for one minute and ask them to count how many times they can juggle in a minute. If the ball drops before the minute ends, they can begin again immediately, and they don't have to start over to count. Ask kids to keep track of their score. Allow them to reflect on what they did well and what they can improve on. Have them repeat with the goal of improving their score.

A	**Authority: Location of Decision-Making**

Learn about the Teaching Games for Understanding model of instruction and plan activities whereby you ask athletes questions so they can come up with a creative solution rather than telling them what to do.

Example: In a five vs. five small-sided game, pause the activity when you notice no one is wide and open to receive a ball. Ask players what they can do tactically and offensively to help their team. Prompt them for answers. Repeat the solutions that can be very helpful.

R	**Recognition: Use of Rewards**

• When you notice things deserving of praise, be sure to give it in a one-on-one setting.
• Do not reward with things such as, "You don't have to help pick up equipment."

Example: Recognizing effort in a one-on-one setting helps kids feel seen. Every team member should help set up and take down equipment, as no one should be above those tasks. Reward and recognition should be on effort, development and improvement, and reaching a new goal.

Continued…

Epstein's TARGET Framework and Motivational Climate in Sport

G	**Grouping: Selection of Working Groups**

- Establish groupings for kids to help build team chemistry.
- Encourage cooperative learning and the idea of athletes helping each other share their knowledge.

Example: Provide small groups for activities and pick the groupings. Be sure to switch groupings often. Establish a plan with the athletes on how team members will treat all group members during such drills.

E	**Evaluation: Assessment Criteria**

Assess athletes on their individual goals and stage-specific standards and ask them to assess their own effort in accomplishing tasks.

Example: Provide progress reports mid-season and report cards at the end of season summarizing findings. Make sure these reports stay between the coach and the athlete who is encouraged to share with their parents. Do not post assessment criteria publicly for others to see.

T	**Time: Pace of Instruction**

- Modify time allocated to accomplish a task or to learn a new skill as needed to help the task seem attainable and therefore help increase motivation.
- Provide time for athletes to think thoughtfully before responding to a question. It's okay to have ten seconds of silence!

Example: Deviate from your practice plan if your athletes are needing more time than you thought to work on a new skill. This may mean not doing everything you initially planned to do, and that's okay. Sometimes less is more!

PART II

Setting Youth
Up for Success

CHAPTER 4

Where Are the Multisport Players?

The Benefit of Trying and Sticking with Multiple Sports

"I played everything. I played lacrosse, baseball, hockey, soccer, track and field. I was a big believer that you played hockey in the winter, and when the season was over, you hung up your skates and you played something else."

–Wayne Gretzky

Athlete I: Early Specialization

Jordan, a kindergartener, has been showing a natural talent for gymnastics since she was able to walk. Given her apparent love of flips and jumping on furniture, her parents enrolled her in parent and tot gymnastics classes. Jordan was a star upon arrival. While other children clung to their caregivers during the lessons, Jordan was mimicking the older gymnasts in nearby groups. Now, at age five, Jordan attends gymnastics for approximately sixteen hours a week and practices with girls twice her age. When asked if she'd like to join the no-cut and low-cost kindergarten youth soccer and field hockey teams organized by parents in the grade, Jordan's parents respond that while she'd love to, there is no time due to gymnastics, so Jordan is unable to participate. They also share that the owner of the gym Jordan attends reminds them that if she takes a season off gymnastics, it will be especially challenging to come back to the level she is currently at because there are really no off seasons in gymnastics training. Jordan appears to be a happy child, but her parents have noticed that her age-appropriate behavior sometimes annoys the older kids because they are more mature, given they are twice her age. However, Jordan's advanced physical abilities and love of learning new gymnastics skills have convinced the gym owner that it is best for Jordan to train with the older girls. Jordan is the oldest child in her family, and her mom is a former competitive gymnast who competed at the collegiate level, so spending this much time in the gym training for gymnastics doesn't seem out of the ordinary for her mom. She and Jordan's dad subscribe fully to the thought that gymnasts who strive for the podium need to put in a lot of work during the early years.

Athlete II: Early Multisport, Sport Sampling or Sport Diversification
Latrice, an active kindergartner, is the daughter of parents who believe that—regardless of talent—early exposure to multiple sports is essential to helping their child have a well-rounded childhood. They've done their research and concluded that those who avoid early specialization in sport are more likely to find the sport that they enjoy, more likely to reach higher levels in their sport of choice, and are less susceptible to injury and burnout. Their family sport philosophy is that sports should change when seasons change. They've also decided that a sport commitment during this phase of childhood should never exceed three hours per week, but more ideally two hours per week. Latrice's parents have witnessed their older children's friends burn out from early sport specialization. Latrice's skills in her multiple sports are much more advanced than her peers, as she's an early developer with a natural ability for skill acquisition. Coaches repeatedly ask her to continue for a second consecutive season upon completion of specific sports, but Latrice's parents politely decline and share that she will continue switching sports with the seasons throughout her elementary school years.

....

The history and variety of sport goes back millennia, and historians count more than eight thousand indigenous sports developed throughout world history. Today, more than two hundred of these are recognized with either national or international federations supporting their development. There is a reason a wide variety of sports exists today—it is because sports have been created and evolved in response to various cultural needs and/or interests. A positive consequence is that kids who have their own broad range of interests have a plethora of sports to experience and choose from. There are individual sports for kids who like to do things on their own, team sports for those who like to work with others to accomplish tasks, target sports for kids who appreciate precision, combative sports for kids who enjoy physical contact, racquet sports for kids who like a strategic battle, artistic sports for those who wish to combine technique and elegance, and adventure sports for kids who love to take sport risks.

Many youth enjoy more than one type of sport, and it's difficult for some to determine which one or two are their favorites until they have tried them all on for size. This likely makes a lot of sense to you if you're a dedicated runner, as you understand it's impossible to find the perfect running shoe without running a couple miles in them. Trying a variety of sports is sometimes referred to as *sport sampling* and *sport diversification*.

Once someone finds a sport(s) that they enjoy participating in, the sport system often quickly suggests to families that the young athlete needs to commit primarily to that particular sport. The concept of participating in only one sport year-round at an intense level at the exclusion of other sports is known as *sport specialization*. Traditionally, sport specialization has primarily only been the norm in a few sports such as figure skating and gymnastics. While most youth do not compete in gymnastics and figure skating, the age that kids specialize in sports such as hockey, soccer, and basketball at the community level is trending earlier than past decades. We hear often in our communities about young athletes specializing by the time they are ten years old.

Sport specialization may make sense for some kids, such as an elite-level gymnast or figure skater. Keep in mind we use the term *elite*[38] literally. It may also make sense for individuals well into their adolescent years to specialize in a sport, but it's important to consider the legitimate concerns around sport specializing that are well documented in youth-sport research. Converse to sport specialization, someone who participates in *multisport* is an athlete who participates in two or more sports throughout the year.

In this chapter, we discuss how sport sampling plays a vital role in kids determining which sports bring them joy. We also examine the research on potential issues related to early sport specialization as well as the potential benefits of multisport participation.

One day, someone told Richard, "My kid just isn't an athlete. He tried soccer and hated it." The parent was speaking about their six-year-old son who, more often than not, appeared more interested in picking flowers than chasing a soccer ball. When they were asked questions such as, "Oh, have they tried archery or curling?" the parents replied, "Nah, I just have a robotics kid."

First things first: robotics is cool and anyone who participates in it should be applauded. Also, playing a sport and participating in activities like robotics aren't mutually exclusive, and it's a shame if anyone thinks that is the case. We share this example to alert parents that if your child tried a sport and disliked it, was disengaged, or stood out for being timid and miserable rather than aggressive, it does not mean that your child can't have amazing experiences in sport. The reality is that this particular child maybe would have loved an individual sport such as archery. When a child seems uninterested in the first sport or two that they've tried, it doesn't necessarily mean they will be uninterested in *all* sports.

We love it when parents recognize that their kids aren't enjoying a sport, because that's important feedback, and we shouldn't force them into an activity they dislike. However, if we want kids to learn perseverance through sport, we say that parents ought to persevere in helping find the best sport situations for their kids. In other words, help their children find which sports they will enjoy and later learn valuable life skills from.

Trying a variety of sports at a young age, as exemplified by Latrice in the chapter opening, is an important piece to the youth-sport journey, because we don't want to pigeonhole kids into a single sport just as we don't want to become wrongly convinced there are no sports that our child will enjoy. We are convinced that you're more likely to help your child connect with a sport they love and foster a lifelong love of sport and fitness if you prioritize broadening their sport experiences during their earlier years (sport sampling or sport diversification) and then continuing with this practice as opportunities continue to present themselves during the middle and high school years (multisport participation).

Before we get too into the minutia regarding sport sampling or diversification and multisport participation, we want to be on record as being realistic to the challenges of both.

Potential Challenges to Multisport Participation

Participating in sport is expensive.

Sport registration fees and sport equipment can be very expensive. We believe sport ought to be a right for kids, but the shift from community recreation to for-profit sport clubs makes this more difficult than in recent decades. If organizations don't provide equipment to borrow or if they require expensive equipment to participate, it excludes a lot of youth. In fact, the Aspen Institute's Project Play Initiative reports that the average family pays $692 per child, per sport, per year. We can all do the math to determine how costly multiple sports are for families, and obviously the cost rises quickly with additional children. Travel costs are reportedly among the highest expenses for families in youth sport, which is really frustrating because, let's face it, youth-sport travel should be the exception and not the norm. Some sports charge over $500 per season (four months) and offer three seasons a year. Thus, it may cost a family $1,500 for one child to play one club sport, and that's before any costs associated with travel, tournament fees, and/or additional camps and clinics.

**Sport sampling and multisport participation require
a great effort on the part of caregivers.**
Logistics involved in taking kids to multiple sports increase when there
are multiple children in the home and/or when youth live in single-parent
homes, and they can be extremely complicated. This is compounded with
the fact that sport practice and competition are now typically located
further from one's neighborhood due to the shift from community recreation to club model where "elite travel" teams are created at ages that are
way too young, eliminating the opportunity to a "long-term" approach.

**When not implemented correctly, sport sampling and
diversification, and multisport, participation can lead to
an overscheduled youth.**
While sport specialization is known as a single-sport participation year-
round, multisport participation is defined much more broadly, because it
can look very differently among different kids. For example, some families
might adhere to the philosophy of Latrice's family. During her sport-
sampling phase described in the introduction of this chapter, Latrice
switched sports with the seasons during early elementary school years.
At some point, multisport participation might look different for Latrice.
For example, when she's in fourth grade, she might play one sport several
seasons a year but play additional sports here and there for a shorter duration and/or attend summer camps in sports other than her primary sport.
Or, for feasibility, she may play two sports for several seasons—one at a
recreation level and one at a more competitive level.

If Latrice, like some kids we know, play several sports year-round at
a competitive level, it can be challenging on a growing body and also can
lead to unnecessary stress levels on an adolescent who is also responsible for
completing more schoolwork outside of the school day. How much extracurricular activity time a child can manage while remaining happy varies
greatly among individuals and perhaps siblings. Just because one sibling
thrives with a busy schedule doesn't mean another will.

In other words, trying new sports and/or playing multiple sports requires both privilege and effort on the part of parents who—let's be honest—are already slammed with careers, managing households, and trying to maintain balance in their own well-being. Thus, as you read this chapter, please know that we understand these challenges. Hell, we live these challenges as parents of kids who participate in multiple youth sports. The last thing we want to do is to shame you into thinking you are failing your kids if they aren't truly adhering to a multisport approach when you are doing the best you can with what you have.

There are hundreds of sports, and each offers something a little different physically, socially, and mentally. Trying different sports will increase the likelihood that a child finds one or several that bring them joy. When feasible, we encourage parents to expose their kids to various types of sport and sports from different categories such as individual, team, combat, artistic, target, and racket sports to name a few. This is what Latrice's parents chose to do. We also encourage sport directors and coaches to encourage their athletes to try sports other than the ones they offer and coach. This might seem counterintuitive to their business model, but an understanding approach to sport sampling and multisport participation can lead to positive bottom-line outcomes for sport organizations. For example, more multisport athletes will choose their club because it is known as a supportive, flexible space to learn and grow, and families will get an understanding that the club has their child's best interests and well-being in mind. When youth are encouraged by both parents and coaches to sample sports at various levels, they are more likely to continue their sport involvement for the long-term.

We already highlighted potential challenges of sport sampling and multisport participation, but the reason we promote both is that the benefits to be gained from both are well documented in the data-backed published literature in the youth-sport field. But, before we dive deeper into the specific benefits that can be gained by those who try a variety of sports and end up as teens who participate in multisport, we want to introduce you to three brothers who experienced a childhood filled with both. To preface this story, it's important to note that the purpose of sport is not to gain the same level of success as these boys did in their sport—although it's a bonus when it does. This story illustrates why parents should take a step back regarding when it's time to specialize (or not specialize) and let your kids make the decisions, as this can result in individuals' greatest success and happiness. These three brothers went on to excel in a single sport when they decided it was time to pursue this route. We share this to inspire you, but also to acknowledge that there may come a time when sport specialization is appropriate. We believe wholeheartedly that this time is likely later than many sports parents suspect, and youth athletes often know when that time comes for themselves.

Pat and Marissa Tocci are the proud parents of three sons, Patrick, Marco, and Nico. The Tocci family lives in Lititz, Pennsylvania, and Pat and Marissa, like many of us, juggled a lot of logistics getting the boys to various sports throughout their childhood and youth. If you are lucky enough to be personal friends with the Toccis, as Amanda is, you might assume that they spent these years at Little League wrestling tournaments and traveling to the famous Fargo wrestling championship, but that didn't happen until their boys were well into their teen years.

Pennsylvania is known as a youth wrestling mecca. When Amanda's husband, Jim, was an assistant coach at the University of Virginia, he traveled to Pennsylvania frequently with the goal of educating great student–athletes on why they should come and wrestle at UVA. When asked where he recruited the most, the answer was always Pennsylvania. Understanding that wrestling is as loved by Pennsylvanians as hockey is loved by Canadians is important, because it helps illustrate just how unique the path is that the Tocci brothers traveled. Despite the fact that their father, Pat, wrestled in the Ivy League for Brown University and spent over two decades working for the National Wrestling Coaches Association, none of the Toccis' children engaged with the sport of wrestling until ninth grade. That's right, they didn't jump into the sport until they were in high school. This is even more surprising when you see them. The three brothers look like quintessential wrestlers. Patrick, the oldest, is twenty-two and a D-II student–athlete at Millersville University majoring in business administration. Nico is nineteen and a freshman at the D-I Air Force Academy who is preparing to be a fighter pilot with a major in systems engineering. The youngest, Marco, is finishing up his senior year of high school and will wrestle at the D-I at University of North Carolina at Chapel Hill. He plans to study sports administration and sports law.

Patrick, Nico, and Marco all played lacrosse, basketball, football, and ran track and cross-country growing up. Wrestling wasn't something that they participated in until they were in high school.

Yep. Even though the boys didn't begin wrestling until high school, they are all wrestling in college or have plans in place to wrestle in college. It would be misleading to suggest that gifted athleticism doesn't play into their current reality, as most kids who pick up a sport in high school do not go on to earn a college athletic scholarship. However, in this instance, great genetics coupled with a relentless work ethic did just that. The boys are convinced that playing a variety of sports while growing helped lead to their wrestling success and the ensuing opportunities that accompanied this success. Their parents believe that their late entry to the sport may have helped them to avoid burnout or injury, and they described to us how skills transferred from other sports helped them develop in the sport of wrestling.

The message you take from this story is not supposed to be that if you begin a sport in high school, you might receive an athletic scholarship. It's that parents don't have to micromanage their kids in order for them to experience their greatest successes.

The Tocci brothers' story is a fun one, as it illustrates what can happen when parents get it right and permit the kids to drive the train. They exposed them to a variety of sports and allowed their boys to choose the path they enjoyed, which was a multisport path. Eventually, Pat and Marissa permitted them to specialize in wrestling during their junior year of high school, as they believed this was a time when the boys were old enough to set personal sport-related goals.

It was as though Pat and Marissa Tocci had the Building Blocks of the American Development Model (ADM),[39] created by USA Hockey, as their guiding principles. The USA Hockey Building Blocks of ADM read:

PLAY
Playing the game is where kids learn that the game is, in its simplest form, *fun*. And if you can mix in age-appropriate training and practice with skills and athleticism introduction, kids will have even more fun. And to keep it fun, there should be a low priority placed on winning and losing and a high priority placed on just introducing the game to a young kid.

LOVE
Once a kid learns to play the game and begins to develop skills and athleticism, hockey starts to take priority among other activities. Skills become more refined, their physical and mental makeup is stronger, and the friendships they developed early on continue to grow. The games become more important, and hockey in general becomes a bigger part of their life.

EXCEL
Now that they play and love the game, a higher premium is placed on excelling at it. Tougher competition and more of a focus on mastering skills play an increased role in their development. Hockey starts to take a larger priority over other activities. But, above all, the game is still fun and the friendships that were forged back in Mites are as strong as ever.

When we write about sport sampling or diversification and multisport, we emphasize the importance of the purpose being to help kids discover what they enjoy. Ideally, they find several sports they love and continue participating in several throughout their elementary school years. Participating in several sports is represented by the PLAY phase of the USA Hockey ADM Building Blocks. Around thirteen or fourteen years old, there is a lot of pressure on some kids to specialize in one sport, which is represented by the EXCEL phase. However, we strongly encourage folks not to skip over the LOVE phase. While they may not play at the highest level of multiple sports, continuing to experience sport in the LOVE phase will help project the joy and ensure that sport is not becoming too serious too soon for your child.

After reviewing the literature on benefits gained from multisport participation, we concluded that those who participate in multisport are more likely to: have an increased level of athletic development, have an ability to transfer skills to a variety of sport contexts, gain a mental refresh or reset, experience less burnout, and continue participating in sport for more years.

Benefits of Multisport Participation

Let's dive a bit deeper to learn more about the studies and stories that led us to draw these conclusions.

Sport sampling leads to increased athletic development.

Serbian researchers concluded that 77 youth approximately 7.5 years old scored significantly higher in motor coordination than 70 peers the same age who were enrolled in soccer only,[40] and they suggest that sport programs for young children ought to be multisport in design. In a meta-analysis[41] of 51 international sport studies that included a sample size of over 6,000 youth athletes, including 772 of the world's top performers, researchers answered the question: *What makes a champion?* in their article published of the same name in *Perspectives on Psychological Science* in 2022.[42] Specifically, they found that world-class athletes were more likely to engage in multi-sport practice, began their main sport later, practiced less in their main sport, and progressed more slowly than national-level athletes. While we share this finding, the researchers in us likely have more questions than assumptions. Questions such as: Were these athletes simply more gifted, because giftedness does play a role at the elite sport level? A lack of giftedness is why Amanda's soccer aspirations ended at the provincial level and not the national level! And questions such as: If parents could afford multi-sport, were they able to offer their kids more resources and opportunities than those who couldn't? We don't have the answers to these questions, all we have is the data. But we believe it's important to understand the findings while remaining curious.

Multisport participation promotes skill transfer.
In our experience, it is not uncommon to hear parents say that their child is participating in one sport because it will help them with another. While we hope that these parents understand the many social and emotional gains of playing multiple sports, we agree that skill transfer can be a positive effect of multisport participation. An article published in the *International Tennis Federation's Coaching & Sport Science Review* examined skill transfer between tennis and hockey. Specifically, the article highlights how hockey can provide excellent preparation for tennis in the physical (concepts of balance and control while tracking a puck or ball, agility, strength, timing and coordination, sending and receiving objects), affective (ability to acquire and apply skills leads to increased confidence in ability to do so in other environments), and cognitive (social-emotional skills such as goal-setting, relationships, navigating challenges) domains.[43]

This information is really helpful to parents who find themselves in the "my child can't take a season off because they'll get behind" mindset. There are many technical and tactical advantages from taking a season off one sport to pursue development in another. Parents shouldn't be surprised if coaches, sport directors, or other parents don't want to hear this because we find they seldom do. So, it's best that you simply do what you think is best for your child.

Participating in several sports allows for mental refresh and reset between seasons.

In researching for this book, Amanda surveyed and spoke to many coaches and sport directors. One conversation piqued her interest when the topic of multisport came up. Aim Field Hockey owner and director Lauren Cornthwaite shared the additional gains she's observed in athletes who participate in multisport throughout her twenty-five years of coaching field hockey at all levels. Lauren, who founded Aim over fifteen years ago, shared, "The piece a lot of coaches don't recognize enough is what athletes who play multisport bring to each sport. They gain so much from using different muscles, learning from different coaches, and understanding game IQ in different sports. Whereas, in athletes that only play one sport, there may be holes in certain aspects of their development because they are so singularly focused. Multisport athletes learn things that would be really difficult to acquire from just one sport."

During our interview with Lauren, she also reflected on how the mental toughness she gained during her high school track career served her during her playing days on the Dartmouth University field hockey team where she served as team captain. While talking with Amanda, she questioned whether many of her field hockey accomplishments would have been realized without the mental lessons she gained from her track experience at The Principia School in her hometown of St. Louis, Missouri.

Known for both her wisdom and human-first approach to coaching field hockey, Lauren, like any master educator, highlighted the fact that while not all youth can balance several sports throughout the duration of their high school experience, that decision should be up to them. Coaches or sport directors should never be the ones telling a youth what to do and should respect that each teen will have their own academic journey and athletic journey. Those decisions should be made within a family without external pressures from coaches who don't have the full story or understand exactly how that human responds to a certain workload and schedule.

Sport sampling leads to a decrease in sport-related burnout.

Some parents report to us that they hesitate to encourage or initiate breaks for their children from certain sports they enjoy to try other sports. With the topic of burnout in mind, we typically push back with what we hope are thoughtful questions that will help the parents in their decision-making. Consider the following questions while deciding which decision is right for your child and family:

- What makes you hesitate to take your child out of the sport for a season? Are you afraid that others will become more competent than them after they return? If so, why do you think that bothers you?
- Does your child ever cry before practice or competition? If so, why do you think that is?
- Does your child ever complain before going to practice and competition? If so, do they share why that is?

When we probe parents for details after they share with us the reasons why sport sampling won't work for them during the early years, they often state that they are scared their child will fall behind their peers who aren't taking a break from the sport. There is a genuine concern on behalf of parents that their kids won't remain on a top team if they take a break or that others will pass their kids in terms of development.

We're grateful for parents' vulnerability when they share that sometimes their kids are crying before it's time to go to practice. This is a clear indicator that their child isn't having fun in that sport or that the child is perhaps burning out and needs a break. Recognizing these cues your children are giving is key to ensuring sport is enhancing their well-being and not hindering it. To be clear, when we reference burnout, we are thinking of an overtired and overscheduled nine-year-old crying on the couch because he doesn't want to go to his sixth basketball game over the weekend. We're also thinking of a twelve-year-old hockey player who played on a spring team and attended summer training all summer who is sick of ice hockey and wants to play other sports but is afraid to tell her parents. Sometimes the messages from children are very subtle, especially when they don't want to let down their parents or the team. They come in the form of tiredness, a desire for sleep, or asking, "Do I have to go to practice tonight?" Those messages must be met with listening to determine if this is just laziness or if it is lack of commitment, which is a message that maybe they are not really enjoying the sport or they are experiencing "burnout" in a sport they love. Either way, a break is usually needed.

Burnout in youth sports is real.

Robin Vealey and Melissa Chase wrote a book titled *Best Practices for Youth Sport* in 2016, where they define burnout as a negative psychological and physical state in which young people feel tired, less interested in the sport they participate in, and less able to perform at their best.[44] Keith Kaufman wrote about student–athlete burnout for the NCAA Sport Science Institute and explains that sport burnout is caused by too much training with too little recovery.[45] It is important to remember that overtraining at *all ages* can lead to burnout and injuries; parents and coaches need to be watching for signs of burnout consistently to best support youth athletes.

One's level of motivation influences their risk of burnout. Promoting sport that is fun, joyful, and age appropriate will increase youth's intrinsic motivation (participating in an activity because of pure satisfaction instead of a consequence), while sport that is too serious, too competitive, and too frequent will decrease their intrinsic motivation. The saying "sometimes a change is as good as a break" comes to mind as we examine this topic. Intentionally taking a multisport approach can help families avoid overscheduling their kids in one particular sport and decrease the risk of burnout and injury associated with early sport specialization.

We're here to assure you that where kids are skill wise at age seven will not predict where they'll be at seventeen. Think back to the Tocci brothers' story from the beginning of this chapter. They pursued sports that filled them with joy, then decided as teenagers to pursue a different one and experienced great success. Did you know that only 15 percent of players who signed a professional contract at the age of sixteen in the Union of European Football Associations (UEFA) soccer academies play a game with the first team? If you follow the NHL, you may have heard of Drake Batherson. Batherson almost quit hockey in his teens, as he was told he was too small to reach his dreams of playing professional hockey and thought perhaps he should pursue golf. Alas, a growth spurt ensued and Batherson is now enjoying a successful professional hockey career with the Ottawa Senators. Still not convinced? Perhaps you'll find it interesting that there are more undrafted players in the NFL than first-round draft picks. If professional scouts can't always predict talent, we can't assume that any parent or youth coach can either.

The surest way to see where your child can be at age seventeen is to take steps for them to avoid early burnout.

Multisport participation fosters a long-term love for an active lifestyle.

Researchers of a five-year longitudinal study of 756 participants who were age ten or eleven at the study's inception concluded that those who were sport samplers during their childhood had higher levels of physical activity during adolescence than those who specialized early in sport or who did not participate in sport.[46] It is no secret that regular and ongoing physical activity aids physical, mental, and social health. Thus, sport sampling should be promoted throughout childhood, if possible, with this link to increased physical activity levels during the adolescent years.

Jean Côté is a well-published professor of positive youth development through sport and has published extensively on the topic of sport sampling and early sport specialization. Côté and colleagues report that there is no data existing currently that links sport sampling to youth dropping out of sport. Conversely, empirical evidence shows that when children specialize in sport early rather than continue to sport sample, there is an increase in sport dropout, regardless of ability.

Researchers suggest that youth are more likely to engage in sport when they take a multisport approach for a couple reasons. First, some youth who sport sample do so in what's called "deliberate play." *Deliberate play* is child-led, unstructured, and includes activities such as pickup basketball or street hockey. "Deliberate practice" is a more formal sport experience that is often led by adults in a highly structured environment. It is highly plausible that youth have more fun in deliberate play environments. Another reason children may be more likely to continue playing sports through adolescence is because they have avoided injuries related to overuse from a single sport. In his work, Côté notes that young athletes who engage in high volumes of deliberate practice have higher incidences of injuries, and this can lead to sport attrition.

Ideally, throughout a kid's childhood, they can engage in deliberate play. If adults don't create spaces that allow kids to gather safely outside, we can't expect them to engage in deliberate play. If deliberate play is not an option for kids due to where they live, ideally they will be able to sample sports through deliberate practice. That said, since we promised you we'd keep it real, we have to talk about the cost of deliberate practice. It's not cheap. In fact, let's be real, it's *ridiculously* expensive. Now, multiply the cost of deliberate practice by the number of children in a family, and it's even more cost prohibitive. This fact greatly reduces access and opportunity for many youth, especially considering economic hardship many have faced over the last several years. The logistics involved in deliberate practice are often time consuming and labor intensive. Amanda's husband jokes that they became part-time Uber drivers without the payment or the five-star rating by the time their three kids engaged in sport which is, of course, deliberate practice. We share all this so parents don't beat themselves up if their children aren't engaging in a variety of sport experiences throughout their elementary and adolescent years. Current challenges around deliberate practice that are stated here are not meant to depress us; they are presented to inspire us.

- If you're a youth coach and offer sport year-round, and you find the same athletes keep coming to you, are you willing to suggest they take a season off?
- If you're a parent, are you more concerned about your child "falling behind" in the short term than their long-term enjoyment of sport? If so, why do you think that is?
- Do you give your athletes or children a couple weeks off in between seasons?
- Do you promote deliberate play? If not, how can you?

These are important questions for us to ask ourselves once we understand the evidence-based benefits to be gained from sport sampling and multisport participation. If at this point, you're committed to helping your child find the sport(s) that bring them the most enjoyment, it's time to set aside your own biases.

Helping Your Child Find the Sport(s) They Enjoy

It's awesome if you're not sure which sports your child will choose to participate in because it shows that you aren't forcing kids into the sports you currently play, used to play, or the sports you enjoy watching. When Amanda was expecting each of her three children, a lot (seriously, a *lot*) of people would ask if she was going to have a wrestler, as her spouse wrestled at Cornell University. Amanda would laugh it off but internally shook her head at the question. Shouldn't youth join the sports that they love and not the one their parents succeeded in?

She's not knocking people for making small talk, and she's very proud of Jim's wrestling accolades, but it struck her as odd that so many would allude to their unborn child as a "future wrestler." Amanda and Jim just hoped that their little one would find something they loved as much as she loved playing soccer and he loved wrestling while growing up, but she'll admit she was naive about the amount of effort on her and Jim's part to make it happen! Interestingly, after coaching their kids in the sports they each played as well as others, their three kids have all shown passion for sports that their parents never participated in. So, either Amanda and Jim (her partner) were terrible coaches, or they did a great job of following their kids' lead.

Over the years, Richard has been asked repeatedly by new parents asking, "What sports should my kids play?" His answer is always the same and his approach a bit more systematic than most: "Begin with gymnastics (for fundamental movement skills), swimming (for safety and fundamental movement skills in aquatic environment), and a running sport (again for fundamental skills and often social engagement), then, when appropriate, try to add a sport with music to develop skills with rhythm. Doing these activities will lay the foundation of physical literacy and thus a base for all sports. While those sports in the most organized form can be costly, they can also take less conventional forms, like tumbling around the living room or backyard, swimming at the local beach, and soccer at the park with the neighborhood kids. We can approach these suggestions with both deliberate play and deliberate practice in mind. The variety adds spice to life and enjoyment for all for life.

Now that you're aware of the benefits of multisport and willing to set your own biases aside (because let's face it, we all like to think the sport we play is the best sport), following some established criteria can be helpful in determining when to try what sport. Since all sports are pretty much offered year-round for all ages, it can be overwhelming to try and organize sport sampling and diversification and multisport participation.

Sports should change when the seasons change.
Sport organizations will send registrations for the next season before the current season even ends. Those organizations led by folks focused on

anything other than kids may even try to coax parents and disseminate promotional materials encouraging them to hurry and register because "spots fill up quickly." When you switch sports when seasons change, the decision is made for you, and you can simply move on, even when administrators or coaches pressure you to remain with that organization. Otherwise, you may find yourself overthinking things or overscheduling your child.

A sport should be offered only one to two days a week during the early years to provide time for children to try other sports. When children are five through ten years old, sport shouldn't require them to be at that sport three to five days a week. When one sport is offered that frequently, it becomes difficult to add a different sport. Some soccer clubs are especially guilty for adding optional (but not actually all that "optional") practices for kids who are really young, and it's not uncommon for club soccer players who are age nine to be at soccer training four to five days a week.

Sample sports that come from different sport categories (team, individual, combat, artistic, etc.). Amanda's middle daughter, Kassie, was enjoying the ballet, jazz, and tap combination dance class she attended one night a week. While her older and younger sister chose to play ice hockey as their second sport that season, she chose dance. One night, Kassie went with Amanda to pick up her sister from ice hockey practice. They arrived a few minutes early and were watching the last ten minutes of practice. Kassie looked up at her mom as tears filled up in her big brown eyes. The vibe of the hockey practice she was watching gave Kassie a massive case of FOMO. She declared she wanted to try ice hockey. Kassie stated that while she enjoys dance, hockey just looked a lot more fun. A few phone calls later, she was added to a roster thanks to gracious volunteers who found a beginner-skilled team that she would thrive with.

Amanda thought Kassie loved her dance class, and Kassie did enjoy it. But seeing the team on the ice laughing while learning new things working together in the small-sided games really resonated with Kassie, and it was something she wanted to be a part of. She began ice hockey at ten years old, as did her older sister. This example highlights the importance of exposing kids to different sports and different ages. Kassie grew up going to public skates with her family, but never wanted to try ice hockey beyond a learn-to-play. Kassie has also wrestled, played soccer, dabbled in lacrosse, and developed a deep love for field hockey. And for six weeks each summer, she swims on the local recreation swim team with her sisters. By prioritizing a wide range of sport exposure, you allow your kids the opportunity to find what they enjoy most.

Now that you have some criteria in making a plan over several years for your child's sport-sampling phase, there are additional sport-sampling and multisport hacks that we wanted to share to help make this process go as smoothly and efficiently as possible.

Hack 1
Try the same sport at different clubs or a second time.

One point about taking a multisport approach that we don't hear about that often is trying the same sport at different clubs. This clearly isn't always possible, as some towns are too small for two clubs or some cities already have a well-established program where kids thrive so there is no need to add a second. But, when sport sampling at various clubs is an option, it should be at least considered.

Sport sampling at different clubs is different from club hopping (switching from one club to another) when things aren't perfect for your child. Club hopping is sometimes necessary to protect the joy, and there are times when club hopping affirms the old saying that the grass isn't always greener. Maybe the coach working with your child or the club that you've joined has a completely different sporting philosophy than you, and it's not what you are seeking for your child. In cases like this, you may need to try the same sport in a different environment. If the first experience wasn't fun for your child, we believe trying a sport that you think is a good fit for your child at another club is something to consider.

Clubs and families that frequent them each have their own vibe. If your child tries a sport where there is subpar coaching, it may be the environment and not the sport leaving a bad taste in their mouth. If the coaches do not seem well-prepared and are arriving at the same time you are arriving, you're going to wonder if it's the value the club promises on its website. Speaking of websites, when choosing a club, go to the website and read about the club's mission and then do a little digging to see if it's a mission-driven club. Check whether the coach has taken any training and has been certified. It's important to ask questions before you invest your time.

For example, if we see youth teams being called names such as *premier elite* and the athletes are below a truly high-performance level and the age of fifteen or sixteen (and we do—often), we're probably going to keep searching. Remember, we don't like when the word "elite" is used in youth sport unless it's literally talking about youth Olympians. In our humble opinion, if a ten-year-old developing athlete is participating on a team with the title *premier elite*, we're seriously questioning the club's motives. While it could certainly be the case that the club directors are educated and wonderful, there is also a red flag that they have some other motives such as feeding parent egos in order to keep registrations coming. Professionals who have kids' best interest and development at their core won't feel the need to convince you that their teams are good or that your child is proficient; they will simply create a culture where development and fun are the focus. You will feel this when you arrive at the club with your child, and it will be a feeling that remains as time goes on.

We've also known of many instances where a kid revisits a sport a year or two later after initial exposure and they experience a 180-degree shift in enjoyment. This could have happened as a result of maturity increasing, a better coach/athlete relationship, or the fact they met better friends the second time around. Regardless, if you think your child had a negative sport experience due to things that were in place by chance, don't be discouraged to try again.

Hack 2
Understand issues around the timing of specialization.

At some point, there may come a time when it makes sense for your child to specialize in a sport. This would be the EXCEL phase of the USA Hockey ADM Building Block model (page 90). Ideally, youth are in high school and still have other physical activity outlets at a social or recreation level to offset a more serious culture of competition. While adults enjoy placing an adult version of sport on youth, youth aren't wired to thrive in such a model, as having fun with their friends and feeling valued and seen are major sources of inspiration to play sports. So, even if your child is excelling and even though they show promise, be sure that the specialization is something that makes them happy and check in with them often to ensure that it's meeting their expectations in terms of enjoyment.

Richard's kids have all graduated from university and clearly benefited from trying various sports throughout their childhood. Specifically, his three kids played soccer, hockey, softball, lacrosse, rugby, badminton, gymnastics, swimming, diving, wrestling, field hockey, ice hockey, and track and field, along with various forms of dancing. Two of his kids garnered scholarships and played competitively in college while the third represented her province. Richard and his spouse observed how playing many different sports led to their kids gravitating toward the sports that they enjoyed. Some sports are very physical with a lot of contact, some are solitary, others are social where sharing is important. In trying so many sports, the kids could find what their personality matched, which brought them enjoyment. Their sport of choice matched them, and it resulted in them enjoying participating and enjoying training and competition, and it was key to making the level of commitment needed to enjoy performance. When it was time that they wanted to specialize, it made sense for them to do so.

Parents, it's okay to put your child's long-term development—social, mental, and physical—ahead of what a coach or sport director preaching early sport specialization is telling you is best. It is certainly okay to hear them out and ask them why they deem specialization to be best for your child. But it's also wise to understand the research and make decisions with your child at the heart of them.

When people ask Amanda why she invests so much time (and money) into her children's sports, she jokes that it's hopefully less costly than bail. She believes that busy (but not too busy) kids who frequent a variety of social settings through sport gain valuable lessons about working with others, time management, persevering toward a goal, and more.

Questions to Ask Yourself

- Are your kids participating in a sport because they like the sport or because you like the sport?
- Are you scared for your child to lose their spot if they take a season off?
- Does your child enjoy individual sports or team sports more?
- Does your child like target sports or judged sports?
- Does your child like physical contact sports or non-contact?
- As a coach, do you encourage your athletes to try other sports?
- Are you able to join forces with another club and offer a two-sport learn-to-play experience?
- Could you reserve facilities to provide youth a space for deliberate play in the sport you coach or another sport?
- Are you involved at the local level to help increase community sport offerings or spaces?

Do's and Don'ts

Do's

- Try different sports from different types of sport categories (team, individual, combat, artistic, etc.).
- Consider your child's personality in deciding what sports they should sample.
- If possible, try the same sport a year or two after the initial experience if the initial experience wasn't enjoyable. Kids' interests change as they mature.
- Try the same sport at different clubs, if possible, to find a club that has a philosophy that matches your family's sport philosophy.
- Choose clubs that don't just preach character but have a record of good character and a commitment to instilling character education into their programming.

Don'ts

- Only try sports from one sport category.
- Register your kids only in sports that you enjoy playing the most or that you enjoy watching.
- Think your child can't be successful in a sport just because they aren't interested at young ages or because they are very beginner skilled compared to peers their age. All kids grow and develop at different rates.
- Get caught up on what you think is a good club based on what was a good club twenty years ago. Get to know the philosophy and do some digging to ensure what they say they are selling is actually what's being provided.
- Get pulled into a club that uses the words such as "premier" or "elite" for youth ages.

Key Takeaways

- Kids grow and develop at different rates, and their interests change as they do so. Sport sampling is worth it to help a child find a sport where they feel they can develop and belong.
- Multisport is an investment in time, logistics, and cost but can benefit youth physically, mentally, and socially so it ought to be explored.
- The USA Hockey ADM Building Blocks of PLAY, LOVE, EXCEL are a great guide that can help parents make decisions with their children and for sport directors and coaches to use to guide decision-making and programming.

CHAPTER 5

Good Game

Ensure Youth Athletes' Well-Being

"For the longest time, I thought asking for help was a sign of weakness because that's kind of what society teaches us. That's especially true from an athlete's perspective. If we ask for help, then we're not this big macho athlete that people can look up to. Well, you know what? If someone wants to call me weak for asking for help, that's their problem. Because I'm saving my own life."

–Michael Phelps, most decorated Olympian of all time

K atie Meyer was a sister, daughter, friend, student, and teammate. She was a national champion and a captain during her time with the Stanford women's soccer team. Meyer died by suicide in March 2022 and is the inspiration behind the nonprofit Katie's Save, which aims to prevent other deaths by suicide on college campuses.

Katie isn't the first or only student–athlete to die by suicide. In fact, five NCAA student–athletes died this way from March through April 2022. Many of you may also be aware of Kate Fagan's book *What Made Maddie Run*, which dove deep into the life of Madison (Maddie) Holleran. Maddie ran for the University of Pennsylvania and also died by suicide in 2015. Fagan's book does an excellent job of spelling out the unique pressures student–athletes face and how these pressures can take a toll on their mental wellness. We explore such pressures in more depth throughout this chapter to prepare parents and coaches to guide student–athletes through these challenges with a healthy mindset.

Another nonprofit doing incredible work and inspired by a similar heartbreaking story is Morgan's Message. Morgan's Message exists to "amplify stories, resources, and expertise to strengthen student–athlete mental health, build a community by and for athletes through peer-to-peer conversations, and provide a platform for advocacy."[47] Morgan's Message was created to honor Morgan Rodgers who played lacrosse at Duke University and who died by suicide in 2019 after a dream-shattering knee injury manifested into mental health challenges. Morgan's Message gives voice to those who are navigating life as both students and athletes through a podcast and a blog series, *The Mental Matchup*.

One article, written by Cailin Bracken who is a student and lacrosse player at Vanderbilt University, was titled "A Letter to College Sports." Cailin's article went viral upon its publication, and in it she describes being student–athlete at the collegiate level like this:

"Playing a sport in college, honestly, feels like playing fruit ninja with a butter knife. There are watermelons and cantaloupes being flung at you from all different directions while you're trying to defend yourself using one of those flimsy cafeteria knives that can't even seem to spread room-temperature butter. And beyond the chaos and overwhelm of it all, you've got coaches and parents and trainers and professors who expect you to come away from the experience unscathed, fruit salad in hand. And, yes, I understand that all of these people with expectations of me also have lives of their own. I get that they don't spend every waking moment of their life thinking about the plays I make in practice, or the time I'm getting on the field, or the appointment I was late for, or the essay I handed in. But sometimes the worst part of all of this is that it feels like the people in your life—namely, the adults—aren't thinking about you at all. They're thinking about the result that you create: the wins or the losses. They forget that when you take away the accolades and the schedule juggling and the success, there's just a kid there. A kid who simply wants to feel safe—who wants their approval, their support and who wants to feel like they can come crashing down and have a cushion to break their fall."[48]

The landscape that today's student–athlete navigates resembles nothing of those who played a decade or more ago. In fact, it is likely that the internet barely existed (if at all) when you played youth or university sport, and social media wasn't even a twinkle in Harvard and Stanford dropouts' eyes. There was no transfer portal. There were no social media blasts thanking schools for official visits, offers, or announcing where athletes have committed to playing and learning. And there was no NIL (Name, Image, Likeliness) embedded into the college athletics experience.[49]

Years ago, applying for post-secondary education options was far less competitive, and recruiting didn't begin early on in one's high school years. To write a book about youth sport and not acknowledge the different experience youth athletes have compared to those in past decades would be an epic fail on our part.

It is likely at some point of your childhood someone of an older generation told you how lucky you were compared to generations prior. Typically, this luck was attributed, at least partly, to advances in technology. As much as it may pain some readers to admit, today's parents can't truthfully look our kids in the eye and tell them with certainty that they have it easier than we did. For many of us, that simply isn't true. The elevated competitiveness associated with achievement in sport for today's youth is very real, and current challenges aren't always ones kids gain empowerment from; unfortunately, they are ones that they simply survive or endure and usually wish didn't happen. Sometimes realities around sport participation for youth and older athletes are so unbalanced from a healthy youth-sport experience that they manifest into mental health disorders and illnesses. How sad that many parents who put their kids in sport so they can have fun and learn valuable life lessons have to realize that sometimes sport can be a major contributor to participants' hindered mental wellness.

Dr. Lisa Damour, a bestselling author and clinical psychologist communicates in her books *Untangled, Under Pressure,* and *The Emotional Lives of Teenagers* that stress and anxiety aren't always bad and shouldn't always be on the receiving end of a bad rap. In fact, she explains that oftentimes when individuals feel stress and anxiety, it is their body's way of informing them to do things to alleviate those feelings in productive ways. For example, when one feels stressed over an upcoming test, a wise decision would be to prepare for the test. Or, if someone finds themself feeling anxious in a social situation, it can be a warning sign that this situation is potentially dangerous. That said, sometimes stress and anxiety can hinder one's well-being, and if we are really honest, we can acknowledge that sport has the power to do both. Sometimes sport can create healthy feelings of stress and anxiety, which may help someone prepare for a big game. As a result, a player is focused and ready to compete. Other times, stress and anxiety levels can be so high that they hinder one's performance. Such high levels of stress and anxiety can be triggered by external factors, such as an overbearing parent, an authoritarian coach, or an exclusive and fear-based team culture. They can also be triggered by internal pressures to live up to a reputation or identity that sport and society have placed on them.

When feelings of stress and anxiety are so high and persist long term without the use of healthy coping mechanisms, it can hinder their mental health. But Dr. Damour is very clear that parents should understand a bad day does not mean a youth has poor mental health. In fact, if an adolescent received bad news or had a disappointing social experience that left them feeling sad, it is likely that good mental health is on display because feeling disappointed about a frustrating experience is the appropriate feeling. However, if one feels sad *all* the time and for little to no reason, this could be a characteristic of poor mental health. In other words, sound mental health can be summarized as when individuals' feelings seem reasonable based on a particular experience, not simply if bad feelings exist and certainly not when bad feelings exist for good reason. It is important to distinguish that good mental health does not mean the lack of challenging or complex feelings; an indicator of good mental health is an individual's ability to allow all emotions to be experienced and then released appropriately after their message is received. Sport is an incredible arena for parents and coaches to mentor youth through this incredibly important foundational life skill.

Let's look at some of the changes from the youth-sport landscape.

Many neighborhood recreation non-cut teams have been replaced with teams that require one to make the team before being granted permission to play. This can happen as young as age six. These teams typically train at locations farther away from kids' homes than in decades past, thereby increasing time and associated costs to participate while decreasing the number of youth who even have access to participate. As today's youth age in sport, pressures transition from simply making youth teams to navigating social media pressures as well as a much more competitive college admission environment. Pressures that stem from social media and other technologies have created unchartered territory for parents who are raising youth and coaches who are coaching them.

While it is impossible to truly understand what these young people are going through, throwing our hands up in defeat is not our style. We both have deep knowledge in the youth-sport space, but we are not psychologists or mental health experts. We hope you find the material in this chapter, and the whole book, helpful in supporting your student–athletes' well-being, but if you're finding a child is struggling with their mental health, please contact mental health professionals to support their healing.

We chose to frame this discussion around student–athlete mental well-being and to use the term "athlete mental wellness." *Health* is defined by the *Oxford Dictionary* as the state of being free from illness or injury. The World Health Organization (WHO) defines well-being as how one feels about their state of being and how they perceive their place in the world. Additionally, WHO clarifies that mental health *is not merely the absence of disease or infirmity*, as it is a state of well-being in which an individual realizes their own abilities, can cope with normal stresses of life, can work productively, and is able to contribute to their community.[50]

• Mental health is more than the absence of mental disorders.

- Mental health is an integral part of health; indeed, there is no health without mental health.
- Mental health is determined by a range of socioeconomic, biological, and environmental factors.

In North America, there has been a concentrated effort to reduce stigma around the topic of mental health. While many will proclaim these efforts have been successful, a lot of organizations are choosing the term "mental wellness" over the term "mental health" at the time of this book's publication. We suspect this is to help further reduce any stigma associated with the term "mental health," but we acknowledge that these terms' usage can create some confusion, considering many understand them to be the same thing. Therefore, for the purpose of this book, we use the term "student–athlete mental wellness." We appreciate the interconnectedness and the fact that wellness is indeed multidimensional. Dimensions of wellness often include, but are not limited to: spiritual, emotional, social, environmental, physical, and mental health.[51]

Student–athlete mental wellness exists on a continuum from languishing to flourishing.[52] On one end is thriving and on the other end are mental health disorders that disrupt a student–athlete's ability to function and perform in any or all aspects of their lives.

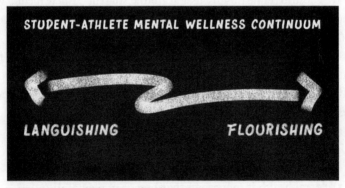

Figure 3: Student–Athlete Mental Wellness Continuum

TrueSport USA, a nonprofit organization powered by the United States Anti-doping Agency, recently published a Recommendations Report titled: "Humanizing Sport: Best Practices Guide to Support Student-Athlete Mental Wellness and Resilience for Anyone with an Athlete in their Life." In it, the authors (who include Amanda) highlight the importance of building mental wellness supports. Specifically, they state, "Building mental wellness supports student athletes' ability to move across the spectrum from languishing to flourishing while building resilience with each challenge, stressor, or adverse situation that is overcome. Athletes develop resilience through consistent and predictable support by the trusted adults in their sporting environments; adults who commit to developing mutual trust and respect in relationships with athletes, and prioritize athlete health, wellness, and safety above all else."[53]

All youth who play sport K–12 and in college are student–athletes. This term, "student–athlete," reminds us that these individuals balance the schedules and workload for both academics and sport. The term falls a bit short in centering the individual as a human first and foremost, which is something that we are cognizant to do. Regardless, we use the term "student–athlete" throughout the chapter and will specify if we are referring to the group of individuals who play sport prior to high school graduation or those who play in college.

As we explore issues related to student–athlete mental wellness at all levels, and in turn, their overall well-being, we want to be really clear that the focus of sport should be to enhance youth's quality of life. In other words, we aspire that sport increases perceptions of how youth feel about their place in the world. This is our north star. As such, we believe:

- Sport has the potential to enhance participants' overall well-being, but this is only likely when coaches, parents, and athletic directors are intentional to ensure this happens.
- Youth-sport participants deserve sport experiences that are developmentally and age appropriate.

- Effort can help increase opportunity and access so that *all* youth can benefit from rich sport experiences.
- Sport has the potential to do far more than just decrease risk factors attributed to sedentary lifestyles.
- Psychosocial issues in sport as well as adolescent psychology should be priorities from day one in a youth-sport experience rather than an add on.

We know sport has the power to do all this good, yet we wrestle with the complex reality of sport's current culture. At a student–athlete mental wellness conference hosted by True Sport USA in the fall of 2022, Dr. Kevin Chapman, a licensed clinical psychologist and the founder and director of the Kentucky Center for Anxiety and Related Disorders, pointed out that in order to fully understand student–athlete well-being, one must understand the cultural context in which sport occurs.[54]

In chapter 3, we introduced to you goal orientation theory and how success can be defined in two ways: (1) winning, being the best, and having the most accolades, or (2) it can be defined as doing your best, learning something new, or doing better than you ever have done before. (See page 63 for the full explanation.) Dr. Chapman's talk reminded the audience that the United States is an individualistic culture (me) instead of a collective culture (we). As such, youth and their families in individualistic cultures are more inclined to define success as an ego-involved orientation (winning) rather than a task-involved one (doing your best). In fact, the United States ranks first of all nations on individualism.

Perhaps you, like us, are wondering: *How can we support youth well-being in sport in a society that places great value on the success of the individual over development of all participants?* Obviously, that's the million-dollar question in this chapter. We're realistic while optimistic, so as we explore student–athlete mental wellness we recognize that the sports culture (we) often conflicts with societal norms (me) and, as a result, conflicts emerge.

Supporting student–athlete well-being is one of the best ways to ensure kids benefit from the joy in sport and life. Let's take a closer look at the specific and unique realities that student–athletes face.

Student-Athletes Face Unique and Specific Pressures

It always surprises us when parents are so keen on their child being a student–athlete post high school. While some may really be interested in the incredibly difficult and equally coveted scholarship opportunity sport brings to a select few, few seem unaware of the realities many current college student–athletes are facing. The rate of mental wellness problems among youth and college-age athletes are staggering. An NCAA student–athlete well-being survey completed by over 9,800 student–athletes concluded that mental health concerns increased post COVID-19. Student–athletes reported 1.5 to 2 times higher rates of mental exhaustion, anxiety, and depression than pre-pandemic.[55] Some studies have found that student–athletes report higher instances of mental wellness issues than their peers who do not play sport.[56] Less than half of the women and men who completed the NCAA survey reported that they strongly agree or agree that they would feel comfortable in seeking support from a mental health provider on campus. We suspect a big reason for this is that most athletes at that level attribute their success to their "mental toughness" and "ability to continue even when uncomfortable."

But the numbers are *staggering.* The specific and unique experiences that student–athletes face due to the combined realities they experience as both students and athletes are manifesting in mental wellness challenges for many of them.

Examples include:

- Missing class time due to travel
- Performance pressures to either make the next team or be recruited at the college level or to maintain scholarship or spot on a team at the college level
- Issues with injuries and expectations to return to play
- Social media pressures and expectations
- Body duality of the female athlete[57]
- Navigating the imbalance between what body type a sport might require at a high level versus what society deems appropriate
- Less down time and a schedule that is very structured
- Transitioning to life without sport, which may happen after high school or after college as very few go on to compete in sport post university

College student–athletes have different pressures than their peers. Sure, they share some of the same issues, such as moving away from home and an increase of difficulty between high school and college courses. But to compete at the next level is extremely difficult, and it is likely that many freshmen on college teams find themselves fighting for playing time for the first time in their lives. Issues such as little to no playing time for the first time at age eighteen can absolutely be enough to trigger mental health problems, especially when parents or coaches aren't aware that these new circumstances can cause these issues.

Schedule Challenges

A friend of Amanda's shared a story about one of her twin daughters who was playing D-I at a school in the western United States. When her daughter explained to her theology professor that she would miss class because she was traveling out of state for a game, the professor quipped, "No. You'll be here. Sport isn't more important than God." The student, then eighteen years old, was left bewildered. Clearly the professor understood that, of course, she felt both were important, as academics are extremely important to this young woman, as is her faith. This is one example of the unique experiences college student–athletes may have. This student ended up transferring to a D-III program where she is currently loving life (and her professors), as the original match wasn't the best fit. She was lucky in many ways. She has a supportive and loving family who communicate to her that her value is not tied up in a division or in sport at all. They wanted her to be in a school where she could do her best and that would be enough.

When this mom shared the story about her daughter, Amanda, a former professor, thought about how easy it is to work with student–athletes in a way that supports their performance in both the classroom and in competition, and how it doesn't have to cause unnecessary stress in the young person's life. From 2003 to 2006, Amanda taught then–University of Virginia soccer star Sarah Huffman (aka Huffy). At that time, Huffy was not only a physical education major, she was a key player for the ACC champion University of Virginia and the United States U21 National Team. When Huffy had to travel abroad for national team commitments, Amanda would receive papers from her electronically.

They communicated clearly in advance, and additional office hours were added at unconventional times to accommodate time zones. It was easy to help Huffy feel supported, and it was awe-inspiring to watch Huffy balance it all. But it had to be difficult to navigate the class time that she missed, even though she never complained about it. If Amanda could go back in time, the only change she would make is that she would send an extra email to ask Huffy if she needed any additional support and to let her know that if she did, Amanda would certainly be available to help.

Clearly not everyone gets to compete at the highest collegiate level or for their country. But busy schedules are a reality for a lot of youth who play sports. The additional pressure of maintaining high academic standards and trying to be noticed by college coaches makes it even more daunting for many kids. It's no wonder that multiple studies conclude that high-level athletes experience higher rates of emotional disorders in the general population.[58,59]

Physical and Emotional Impact of Injury

Injury is another factor that can negatively influence various dimensions of wellness, such as physical, social, and emotional. Therefore, it can be a serious stressor in the lives of student–athletes. When youth are injured, they may feel lost without their routine and their social network in addition to going from being very physically active to having little to no activity while they recover. When they are removed from their team due to injury, they can experience loneliness and extreme disappointment that few are able to truly understand, such as Morgan Rodgers's story we touched on earlier. It may seem to others like these experiences are small in relation to the big picture of life, but that is not the case. It is important to understand student–athletes navigate these experiences with deep emotions they often need help processing. These feelings are real, and it is essential that youth who are injured are frequently checked in on and understand they are still key members of the team community.

Social Media

The pressure to perform at younger ages is magnified for today's youth due to social media use and societal norms associated with social media. When those of us in our forties and fifties were thinking about what college we would continue our playing at, there was no way to announce who made us offers or what these offers entailed. Our mistakes weren't archived for life through social media, and we thought the word "brand" only meant a particular type of product.

Of course, social media can be good. Some student–athletes use it as a recruiting tool, which can be positive, and it also can be used to spread inspiring messaging. But parents and coaches can acknowledge that it increases pressure on young people, and sometimes that pressure manifests into feelings of inadequacy.

A friend of Amanda's reached out in the days preceding the June 15 date in which college coaches in some sports are permitted to reach out to student–athletes of interest who just completed, or are about to complete, their sophomore year of high school. Her child was feeling especially anxious about the date because quite a few college programs she was following in her sport were doing countdowns of sorts leading up to June 15, and whenever these feelings subsided, they would be heightened again when she would look at her Instagram feed. For student–athletes hoping to hear from a particular school or others hoping to hear from any school at all, this can be a time filled with unhelpful levels of stress, anxiety, and fear. The mom wondered if coaches thought about these in kids in this way. After the text exchange, Amanda looked at the Instagram posts and took an educated guess that once one high-profile program chose to post about getting ready to make their calls in search of future players for their team, others simply followed without giving it much thought. *What if,* Amanda wondered, *instead of showing off their campus and trying to sell their program to eager student–athletes who already are chomping at the bit to join these top programs, the coaches took time to put their followers at ease and remind them that sport is one part of them and that their worth should never be measured by their ability to make a particular team or be admitted into a particular college?*

Sleep

Sleep hygiene is a critically important contributor to overall well-being. Youth who play sports often dedicate a lot of time to sport, and hopefully they have other hobbies as well. Combined with schoolwork, this can result in some long days and decreased sleep, and youth athletes have been found to get less sleep than their peers who do not play sport.[60] Less-than-recommended levels of quality sleep will hinder a youth's performance in both sport and academics as well as recovery from vigorous training.

Parenting podcasts that address kids' phone use often assert that when parents give their children their first phone, they ought to enforce a no-device-in-the-bedroom policy. Technology in the bedroom is a huge detriment to the duration of quality sleep an individual gets, so this is one way to help encourage optimal sleep for a busy kid.

Disordered Body Image

Some sports are more likely to hinder mental, emotional, and physical wellness through higher instances of disordered body image. Student–athletes in endurance sports, diving, gymnastics, figure skating, and some weight-cutting sports may feel internal and external appearance demands due to gender norms, performance expectations, and expectations for lean-ness. A tricky part of body image issues in sport is that sometimes improved performance may occur in the short term and the eating disorder can go unnoticed. Physical wellness can be later stunted due to injuries and repro-ductive health related issues caused by an eating disorder.

Burnout

This section would not be complete without mentioning burnout. We address burnout more thoroughly in chapter 4 (page 81), but it's important to highlight it and how it can negatively impact one's mental wellness. The topic of burnout is of course concerning to youth at all ages and levels, given the trends that some sports morph into a year-long commitment when only several decades ago youth were more likely to switch sports with the season. The physical and emotional exhaustion that can result from sport burnout can leave athletes disconnected from the sport they once loved. In fact, burnout may cause an athlete to quit a sport entirely. If burnout leads to exiting a sport, physical inactivity may result if the previous sport wasn't replaced with a new one. Physical activity is important for typical growth and maturation, social health, and emotional health; thus, burnout can play a detrimental role in one's overall mental wellness.

Student–athletes don't need to be in college to face unique and specific pressures that can hinder their overall well-being. Since these dimensions of wellness are interconnected, it is most likely that when one dimension is hindered (e.g., physical wellness) more are to follow (e.g., mental wellness, emotional wellness, social wellness). As such, when a student–athlete has a concern in one area such as an injury (physical wellness), parents and coaches should check in with them periodically on other areas such as how they are feeling (emotional wellness) about their recovery and/or their current connections with teammates during this time (social wellness), for example.

Student–Athletes Are Humans First

As we've shared so far in this chapter, being an athlete at the youth and college levels can be really challenging. While the challenges hopefully come with rewards in the form of positive memories that will last a lifetime and friends who adore you for who you are, it is still difficult. So much of young people's lives can be wrapped up in their sport practices and dreams, that their sense of who they really are can get lost in the shuffle.

It is essential that student–athletes are treated as humans first and student–athletes second. They ought to see themselves as fully human and not just a student–athlete. It is equally as essential that parents, coaches, family members, and community members understand that they play a significant role in helping youth athletes see themselves in this way.

If you're wondering what that sounds like, we have you covered. If you are speaking to a younger person and you're making conversation with them, consider replacing sport-specific questions with questions such as, "What's going well for you these days?" or "Did you see any good movies or read any good books lately that you're willing to tell me about?" or "What's something you've done recently that you're proud of?" While it is likely that adults are just making light conversation when they ask a youth how many goals they've scored or when they will move up a level in gymnastics or if they perfected a new dive, it can manifest into a misunderstanding by the young person that their value and identity relies on their sport performance. By showing youth you're curious about aspects of their lives outside of sport, you're supporting their understanding that their value as a person is not attached to their athletic performance and those close to them care about their entire life experience, not just the one they're having on the field. When you ask well-rounded questions, you might learn really interesting things about the young person, and you're not contributing to perceived societal norms that they are an athlete before a human being.

In researching for this book, the idea to converse with youth athletes about things other than sport was shared to us by several current NCAA D-I student–athletes. They want people to know that they are well-rounded people with career aspirations outside of sport, friendships, and relationships completely independent of their athletic circles, and they enjoy hobbies such as knitting, writing, and hiking. They are so much more than the sport they play and the sport accolades they may or may not collect.

Parents may choose to check in with their kids periodically regarding athletics to make sure their joy remains as the competitiveness increases. Amanda asks her kids these questions before and after every season:

- "Did you have fun this season?"
- "Do you want to play again or take some time off?"
- "Are you ready to stop playing this sport, and would you like to try another?"

She'll end the line of questioning by telling her daughters that she doesn't care whether they play a particular sport, and it's their choice to play the sports that they enjoy the most—no matter how long they've been involved. The goal of doing this is to ensure that her kids know their goals in sport have to be their own, not their parents'. As well, she wants them to know they are loved unconditionally, and they don't have to perform in the sport domain just because their parents enjoy sport and enjoy watching them develop through sport.

The Mental Toughness Framework

We often hear the term "mental toughness" used incorrectly by well-intended parents and coaches. First, let's talk about what mental toughness is *not*.

- Mental toughness is not tolerating abusive behavior of coaches.
- Mental toughness is not playing through injury in ways that can increase the injury.
- Mental toughness is not staying on a toxic team where you are excluded and picked on.
- Mental toughness is not being on the receiving end of an overly competitive parent who places too much value on their child's sporting experience.
- Mental toughness is not keeping extreme feelings of despair bottled up inside to deal with in isolation.

The mental toughness framework presented here comes from the field of sport psychology.[61] We suggest parents and coaches familiarize themselves with this framework as they help guide young people in achievement settings, such as in school and sport.

Figure 4: The Mental Toughness Framework

Dr. Steven Danish, one of Amanda's favorite mentors whom she met early on in her graduate studies, told her that "sport has the power to teach magical life lessons, but the learning of these lessons doesn't happen magically." The message was clear. Coaches and parents must be intentional about: 1) ensuring life lessons in sport are overtly taught; and 2) ensuring the life lessons taught are good lessons, "magical" if you will. The key to ensuring that lessons learned from sport are positive and productive comes down to guiding athletes through processing, understanding, and accepting the experiences that come their way. To do this well, we look to the mental toughness framework.

There is no place for authoritarian leaders who do not understand the definition of mental toughness. The mental toughness framework consists of a collection of skills that youth can acquire. However, just as you learned it takes thoughtful planning to deliver a motivational climate that fosters task goals in chapter 3 (page 53), it also takes thoughtful planning and reflection to help youth acquire the skills necessary to result in mental toughness.

There are four pillars of the model—Control, Commitment, Confidence, and Challenge, and they are commonly referred to in sport psychology literature as the "four Cs." Each of the four Cs has several components. Once parents and coaches are familiar with this model, they can use it to help youth gain the skills necessary to combine into mental toughness.

Let's explore how parents and coaches can help bring this magic to life among the youth we serve and love!

The Mental Toughness Framework in Action
Control
• Model emotional regulation. • Teach coping strategies, such as taking ten deep breaths when upset, and model the strategies. • Teach relaxation techniques; build in time for recovery and relaxation.
Commitment
• Teach goal-setting and then be certain to revisit the goal-setting process to check in with goals and current strategies. • Offer to be an accountability buddy or share your goals and how you stay accountable in them. • Set goals alongside your child or your players and report back to them on your progress. • Remind youth that goals should be set up to bring joy to their lives.
Confidence
• Teach the principles of self-talk and explain self-talk helps with motivation. • Help youth understand what it takes to build true confidence (see chapter 6, page 133, for more information on this). • Provide opportunity for youth to practice so that they can increase competence and, in turn, increase their confidence in their abilities.

Continued...

The Mental Toughness Framework in Action
Challenge
• Help youth understand that even if they fall short of their goals, they can learn from the experience.   • Teach youth that there is joy to be found in the pursuit of a challenge.   • Ask youth to reflect throughout their journey in facing a challenge to help them identify feelings of empowerment and increased belief in self.

Teaching Student-Athletes to Be Strong, Positive Teammates

Quality youth sport and college sport experiences are ones where mental and social wellness are enhanced through participation, not stunted. For this to happen, we all have a role to play in developing strong, positive teammates. This may sound easy, but it's far from it. Sport is on display. Unlike a math test that a young person may take when no classmates are aware of their grade, peers and parents alike will observe the same young person developing skills and tactics through sport. Audible sighs and negative body language by peers, parents, and coaches have all been observed at youth competition with children as young as age six.

As mentioned briefly earlier in this chapter, the United States is an individualistic society—yet we celebrate team sports. Sometimes the ego of the individual player can hinder the result of the team, and sometimes coaches and parents play an effective role, albeit a negative one, in making this happen.

Those of us with kids who play sports can be grateful to those who step up to volunteer to coach youth teams, and we can expect them to take this role seriously in terms of developing their own skills in ways that allow them to coach in ways that are best for kids. *Best for kids* bears repeating. Unfortunately, sometimes the coach is taking the sport too seriously in terms of winning, and what's best for kids isn't central to the equation. Some coaches will pretend they don't know what's best for kids and revert to tactics that may (or may not) result in a short-term success defined as a win. But the potential damage of those choices cannot be overstated.

Coaches aren't the only ones who sometimes forget what's best for kids. Parents who cheer quietly against other people's kids when they fail, because they view that child as competition to their own child rather than a teammate, contribute to a toxic sport environment. Amanda's friend recently shared that she removed her son from his fifth-grade travel base-ball team. The coach set up a culture of fear, and she admitted that when the boy competing for her son's position didn't have a good game, she found herself feeling good about the situation because this meant her son would get to play the following game. Amanda's friend, a former teacher turned stay-at-home mom who gives back to her community in many ways, had the good sense to reflect on how inappropriate her feelings were and removed her son from this situation and moved him to a team where the focus was more on development and where kids at the young age of ten weren't pitted against each other. It should be noted her son, who once loved baseball, also dreaded going to practices and games because he was always getting yelled at by a coach who played head games with him until he switched teams.

No sport situation should pit ten- or eleven-year-olds against each other, and Amanda's friend knew that. She admitted they should have left this team sooner and learned to be on alert for early warning signs she missed going forward. So, before parents set out to teach your child how to be a good teammate, they need to look in the mirror and be honest about if they need to improve in this area as well.

We suggest that parents and coaches overtly teach youth about what it means to be a strong, positive teammate. This includes being welcoming and inclusive, competing at their best effort, communicating in a way that is direct yet uplifting, sharing compliments with teammates when they are genuine and come to mind, calling out a teammate who is behaving in a way that works against the team's core values, and understands that the goals of the teams supersede the desires of an individual. What we are not asking parents and coaches of young people to do is to normalize the adult sport model, which comes with practices such as benching players, set starters, etc. Those norms work against what is best for every kid on the team.

Ask kids if they are being good teammates and how they are doing so and ask them for examples of who showed up as a good teammate today and why they decided to name the individual they did. Ask them if they demonstrated respect for the sport by competing hard and also by competing fairly while treating opponents with respect. By asking these types of questions to youth, you help them to center the importance of serving their teammates and also shining a light on their teammates. It's impossible for every member of the team to be the star technical player, but it is possible for every member of a team to be a star teammate. Adolescence is a tricky stage of life, and this won't happen without an intentional approach.

No one is perfect, and there are always people who are better than you in a particular sport, unless you are Michael Phelps or Serena Williams. Thus, the focus of sport participation should always be on gathering lessons that will serve you well throughout life as a productive, giving, and happy citizen. When sport is the contributor to mental-wellness problems, it is important parents and coaches are honest about that. Sometimes it is necessary to remove a child from a team when it is detrimental to their mental wellness, and in many different situations a child will benefit long term from a healthy level of struggle in their sport experience. The key is that no coach or parent lets their own ego or their goals for a child trump the child's experience or goals in their sport.

We're hopeful that this chapter will help the overzealous parent to reflect on what's most important about sport. It's important that parents understand that only youth should determine if they want to play sports post high school. We ought to pause here and point out that the previous sentence is laced in privilege. Sport scholarships help many first-generation college students receive a college education, and that reality can't be overlooked as it can often complicate the realities and place increased pressure on these students.

In situations where sport is not the ticket to higher education, adults need to recognize college sport is absolutely not for everyone who may have the talent to succeed physically at that level. Give youth permission to hop off the pathway to high performance sport if their experience is detrimental to their well-being. Nothing is more important than our kids' well-being. Nothing.

Questions to Ask Yourself

- Does my child seem happy going to sport?
- Does my child seem happy when I pick them up from sport?
- Does my child have positive relationships with most teammates?
- Does my child laugh when with their teammates?
- Does my child feel a sense of belonging at sport?
- Is sport keeping my child from sleeping?
- Is sport triggering eating behaviors that hinder my child's well-being?
- Does my child appear to put unhealthy levels of stress or pressure on themself when it comes to sport?
- Does my child's coach put age-inappropriate levels of stress or pressure on my child?
- Do I notice a difference in my athletes' demeanor?
- Why is this athlete all of a sudden not showing up for practice? How should I respond to that?
- Do I ask my athletes about their lives outside of sport in ways that are appropriate?
- How can I create a culture where my athletes know I care about them as humans first?

Do's and Don'ts

Do's

- Ask student-athletes questions that aren't related to their school or sport. For example, "Have you read any good books lately?" "Do you have any movie recommendations?" "What have you been up to on break?"
- Equip youth with skills that build their mental wellness.
- Center the youth as a human first and athlete second.
- See and value every youth at every practice and competition.
- Ask student-athletes if they are okay or if the combined pressures of school and sport are finding them feeling overwhelmed. Let them know that it is okay to feel overwhelmed, and it is not a sign of weakness or incompetence. If they are feeling overwhelmed, offer to listen and to help.
- Reach out of professional help as needed.
- Help your child setup screen time limits and bedtime routines to promote sleep hygiene.
- Help your child explore other clubs/coaches/environments if the current situation is negatively impacting their well-being, but recognize that good sport should contain times where youth have to persevere.
- Teach and model adequate fueling and hydration behaviors.

Don'ts

- Use this chapter as a replacement for medical expertise.
- Feel embarrassed if you need professional help to determine if your child is experiencing normal levels of stress and anxiety or levels of stress and anxiety that can be detrimental to their mental health.
- Confuse disappointment from sport as an unhealthy sport environment.

- Say things that make your child feel their body is in some way inadequate.
- Make food and body image a focus of conversation.

Key Takeaway

- Youth face more pressure today than ever before. It's difficult for any parent today to grasp what they are going through. There are resources available to help ensure your child has support necessary to navigate adolescence.

CHAPTER 6

There's No "I" in Team

*The Art of Competence,
Confidence, and Belonging*

"The thing about confidence I don't think people understand
is it's a day-to-day issue. It takes constant nurturing. It's not
something you go in and turn on the light switch and say,
'I'm confident,' and it stays on until the light bulb burns out."

–Mia Hamm

A round the time we began writing this book, Amanda and her family were traveling by air from her native Nova Scotia to Toronto en route to their current home in St. Louis. They couldn't believe their luck when they were accidentally assigned seats in first class. What exhausted parent wouldn't want free headphones and new release movie options after two weeks of late nights and non-stop adventure visiting Canada's Ocean Playground? Amanda's luck continued when she noticed that *King Richard* (2021) was one of the movie options. So, she gave her kids an enthusiastic thumbs up as they all gleefully placed the free headphones on their ears and selected their movie of choice.

King Richard is a movie about Serena and Venus Williams's journey to legendary status. It zoomed in on how their father, Richard Williams, coached and managed them in unorthodox ways early in their careers. The entire movie captured Amanda's attention for a variety of reasons. Several years prior, she led a research study that examined the sport of wrestling as a vehicle for upward social mobility for women in developed and developing nations. *King Richard* highlighted parallels between the

Williamses' humble childhood in Compton, California, and the childhoods described to her by the Olympic and world-class wrestlers who also came from underserved communities. Amanda was also hopeful that the recognition of privilege—or in this case, the lack thereof—would help lead to more empathy among sport decision-makers and even inspire others to focus on decreasing cost-related barriers to youth-sport participation. But the scene that stuck with her the most is the one that depicts a 1995 interview with then fourteen-year-old Venus Williams conducted by John McKenzie of ABC News. McKenzie asked Venus if she thinks she can beat her upcoming opponent, to which she responded, "I know I can beat her." He continued, "You know you can beat her?" to which she flashed her adorable smile. "You're very confident?" he continued as her smile widened. She assured him, "I'm very confident." "You say it so easily" he pushed, "Why?" At this time, young Venus assuredly stated, "Because I believe it." It was then that Richard Williams interrupted the interview and told McKenzie to stop. He went on to say, "You're dealing with a little black kid. Let her be a kid. She answered with a lot of confidence. Leave that alone."

This scene was based on a real-life event, and we encourage you to watch the actual interview. It sheds light on how important confidence is in a child's youth-sport experience. Richard Williams understood, among many things, that while true confidence requires skills gained through dedicated and purposeful practice, it can be hindered or even stripped away instantaneously when adults question or undermine a child's natural pull toward confidence. There is no reason to assume that McKenzie was trying to hinder Venus's confidence, but his line of questioning had the power to do just that, whether he realized it or not.

....

Confidence is the belief that one has the abilities, qualities, and judgment to achieve success.[62] Real confidence plays a significant role in the youth-sport experience, as these beliefs can manifest into motivation to try new things, to work diligently at improving in certain areas, and to overcome challenges. Although the definition of *self-confidence* pertains to how an individual feels about themself, feelings, understanding, and beliefs about their abilities are influenced by other people's perception and attitude toward them, such as coaches, parents, and teammates to name a few. The beliefs that play into confidence are sometimes unconscious and can be influenced by others' actions and comments. Such beliefs absolutely affect how we behave and interact with opportunities throughout our lives. Thus, stifling youth's confidence and perhaps negatively altering their beliefs regarding their confidence can have wide-reaching effects on them as they transition from adolescence into adulthood. It is also important to foster true, authentic confidence in youth. Some sport environments inadvertently support growth of false confidence, which can be just as detrimental. False confidence presents itself in youth sport in several ways.

- False confidence is the coach who doubles down on authoritarian coaching practices because they "worked for them" or because "our team is winning."
- False confidence is the athlete who believes they should never come out of the game because they were the best player at a young age without trying.
- False confidence is the parent who feels emboldened to belittle their child after a game because they are certain "tough love" will help their child be successful.

We've heard many stories throughout our communities that highlight the important role confidence plays in a youth's sport experience. Some stories describe kids falling in love with a sport after they acquired enough skill competence to really enjoy participating and competing. Unfortunately, we've also heard too many stories describing coaches or parents unnecessarily hindering kids' confidence by applying a version of authoritarian and old-school tactics to youth athletes. This is especially detrimental given that we believe *real* confidence is a key ingredient to a joyful youth-sport experience.

True Confidence Is Created through the Development of Competence

There is no question, confidence can be fleeting and fragile! Richard (the co-author of this book and not the late father of Venus and Serena Williams) used to race luge internationally, and his experiences include the more extreme version called *natural luge*. When competing in natural luge, Richard needed the confidence to travel down a twisting ice mountain road at over 100 kilometers an hour because any lack of confidence could cause him to hesitate, and hesitating in natural luge could result in serious injury. An incredible amount of practice time was required for Richard to build the confidence necessary to maneuver the course at podium-performance speed while remaining safe. During this practice time, Richard developed *perceived* and *actual competence*, which are important concepts to understand while fostering youth athletes' confidence.

Richard took the importance of preparation from his luge days and applied it in his coaching of all sports. For example, he always ensured the challenge was at an appropriate level so that his athlete could experience success. From there, he increased the difficulty of the task to help increase the challenge and, in turn, increase his athletes' skill. Let's examine what this approach might look like if Richard is coaching an athlete in the natural luge.

First, Richard may ask the athlete to simply navigate the bottom part of the course slowly and safely, with confidence. Then, the athlete can increase the skill by beginning the higher up on the track and thus at faster speeds, with confidence. Once the skills and confidence developed higher up the track, athletes would then progress to racing the full length of the track at extreme speeds.

The skill acquisition referenced in the luge example represents *competence*. To be competent in something means that you're able to complete the task successfully and with an adequate level of mastery or proficiency. There are several competence-specific terms that frequent sport research and literature. Let's review these now, as it's helpful for us to be on the same page as to what these terms mean as well as how they influence the youth-sport experience.

Sport competence refers to an individual's ability to effectively perform various physical and technical skills required in a particular sport. It includes a combination of physical, technical, tactical, and psychological abilities necessary to achieve success in the sport.

The following figure, which we also touched on in chapter 2, illustrates how physical competence (sometimes referred to as *motor competence*) leads to real confidence. Real confidence manifests into *motivation*. When one is motivated, they will practice, give their best, and continue to enhance their physical competence, and the cycle continues. This image, created by Sport for Life, beautifully highlights the necessity that youth engage in sport experiences that focus on their physical competence.[63] In other words, youth deserve to engage in sport experiences where their development is a primary focus. In chapter 9 (page 211), we examine how playing time, specifically the lack thereof, decreases competence, confidence, and motivation in sport. Here, we highlight how prioritizing development (aka competence) will help keep kids in the game!

Physical literacy
is the...

physical
competence

motivation
knowledge
valuing

confidence

...to be
🍁 **Sport for Life**   **active for life**

Figure 5: Physical Literacy[64]

The visual depicts the definition of physical literacy which is, "the motivation, confidence, physical competence, knowledge, and understanding to value and take responsibility for engagement in physical activities for life."[65]

When sport competence (including physical, tactical, technical, and psychosocial) exists, one is more confident and more motivated to participate in sport. But while true confidence can only be earned over time and there are no shortcuts, don't quit on a child who is struggling with building competence (and therefore confidence), because the plight is a worthy one.

A finding that coaches and parents often find fascinating is that confidence can increase in sport even if an athlete's competence is perceived and not actual. *Perceived competence* is the extent to which a person feels they have the necessary attributes to succeed,[66] while *actual competence* in the world of sport is the ability to employ physical skills and patterns to a level where one is able to enjoy physical activity.[67]

Perceived sport competence has been found to play a mediating role in enhancing self-esteem in adolescents over two years, which certainly supports the plight of helping youth gain competence in their motor skills and patterns.[68] Research concludes that children who perceive themselves to be competent in their motor skills and patterns are more likely to demonstrate behaviors such as giving their best effort.[69] As you might imagine, once people try their best in the areas they feel competent in, they will continue to improve. As such, as perceived competence increases, it is likely that actual motor competence increases.[70]

We've seen this in youth we've coached as well as our own kids. Often youth who are improving might still be classified by coaches and teammates as athletes who haven't yet reached proficient levels of sport ability. But the athlete may feel really great about their own improvement. They know they've further developed their current skills and they've also acquired new ones. As such, they perceive themselves to be competent and gain confidence in their abilities because of this improvement (development). This is why we are big believers in having youth practice their skills outside of sport practice and for them to find ways to track their growth while they do so. When Amanda's daughters proclaimed they wanted to improve their field hockey skills, they began practicing in their driveway, backyard, and basement. In doing this, they were able to experience progress quickly, which increased their confidence as they progressed toward mastery. As a result, they are self-motivated to continue practicing for a little bit each evening, as they see how their improved skills make practice and games more enjoyable for them.

Sport competence hasn't just been found to increase confidence in sport. Italian researchers examined perceived and actual competence in sport's role in predicting pleasant psychobiosocial states such as emotion, motivation, performance, and communication. Among 320 youth (160 girls and 160 boys) aged thirteen to fourteen years old, perceived and actual youth-sport competence were the strongest predictors of participants' pleasant psychosocial states.[71]

Now that you have an overview of sport-related competence and understand its role in increasing confidence, let's take a closer look at confidence's important role in the sport experience. For decades, confidence has consistently been identified as a key element that distinguishes successful athletes from unsuccessful athletes.[72] Steven Magness, a world-renowned expert on performance, writes in great detail in his book, *Hard Things: Why We Get Resilience Wrong and the Surprising Science of Real Toughness,* that real confidence cannot be given; rather, it must be earned through increased competence or mastery. Let's pause here to address a related common reality in youth sport.

We have observed time and again early developing youth athletes receiving praise for hitting the DNA lottery, only no one is telling them their early successes are mostly a result of holding the elusive lottery ticket. We've heard them be told they are the best player or watched them receive preferential treatment in the form of playing time or wearing captains' bands simply because they might be faster and stronger at younger ages. Coaches and families who over praise and give special treatment to youth who are more skilled, experienced, or physically strong at these young ages compared to their peers may actually be doing these kids a disservice because these kids are being praised for things that they do not control, such as their DNA. By holding each player to the same high expectation of developing skills they don't yet have, regardless of what they do have, coaches help all youth gain confidence through increased competence. Otherwise, the early developing youth might not see that they have areas to improve and, as a result, may not put in the same effort as their later developing peers. This sets the early developing athletes up for a difficult situation later in adolescence when the later developers begin catching up to them in strength and speed, equipped with a far deeper pool of skills and likely more resilience from the way they were acquired.

Alas, we've all experienced the coach who favors the early-developing youth, and we've certainly heard of coaches favoring their own kid in terms of playing time. We've also witnessed the politically or socially connected parent waving their wand of extra privilege in an attempt to help their child have a leg up on the peers who don't have the same power. While parents may feel frustrated that other kids are unfairly benefiting from either being fast, being the coach's kid, or having calculating parents, we disagree that those kids are being advantaged even though we can understand the frustration. The youth who are being rewarded for being early developers or receiving extra playing time because their mom or dad is coaching the team or kissing up to the coach aren't being incentivized to develop their skills and build actual competence and real confidence. Through time, they may not demonstrate the same work ethic as their peers because they haven't had the chance to experience how rewarding and empowering it can feel to improve and gain opportunities because of effort. Deep down these kids will realize that they didn't earn accolades on their own, and when they experience a growth spurt, or when other kids catch up, or when their parents are no longer able to pull strings, they're less likely to have the confidence needed to persist with joy.

The lesson here is simple and gets back to one of the main points Magness makes in his book. If we want all kids to develop real confidence in sport, it is essential we understand the important role that effort in pursuit of development (competence) plays in this.

The relationship between real confidence and motivation is easy to understand when we think about the principles in our own lives. Think about a time you were trying a new type of physical activity. How did it make you feel? While it depends on what type of sport or activity you were trying for the first time, there is a high probability that you didn't find it to be a lot of fun, and you didn't feel very comfortable in your body. We can relate. When Amanda learned to snowboard in her twenties, surf in her thirties, and compete in Ironman triathlons before she hit age forty, she was well beyond her competitive soccer career. While pursuing these new lifetime sports, she felt uncomfortable, frustrated, and even a bit silly as a beginner. With the benefit of a master's thesis based on a theory in sport psychology and a PhD in teaching and learning in her pocket, Amanda knew this uncomfortable period was a necessity to picking up these new skills. She stuck with it and eventually developed the competence to enjoy these sports. But, in the early stages of learning how to snowboard, surf, and compete in triathlons, she wasn't totally excited to do them. At all. They felt scary and she felt awkward in her body as a beginner. Now, her family surfs and snowboards together, and they typically hop in a short-course triathlon each year for good measure. She shared her experience learning these sports with each of her three daughters, so they could expect the beginner stage to feel uncomfortable and even frustrating when they started. That way, the girls understood that the sticky period wasn't because they weren't capable of acquiring new skills; they were just in the beginner phase.

At this point, you may be wondering if there are certain conditions that can help someone arrive at a place where they are intrinsically motivated, or self-motivated, to participate in an activity while enjoying themselves. Mihaly Csikszentmihalyi, the father of flow theory, set out to determine just that as he pondered what common conditions exist for those who chose to engage in activities for enjoyment.[73] Learning from rock climbers, chess players, dancers, and others, he discovered that people want to be challenged, but the challenges should never be so far out of reach that they seem impossible.[74] Through his research, he introduced the term *flow state*, which is when someone is completely focused, present, and involved in their activities at a certain point of time, as well as deriving enjoyment while doing so. More specifically, Csikszentmihalyi defines being in the state of flow as "being completely involved in an activity for its own sake. The ego falls away. Time flies. Every action, movement, and thought follows inevitably from the previous one, like playing jazz. Your whole being is involved, and you're using your skills to the utmost."[75]

Is flow state possible without sport competence and confidence? Hell no. Flow state is the goal, and it's commonly referred to as being in the zone. Richard Williams clearly understood the level of competence needed that could develop into actual confidence and then motivation. He helped create conditions as Venus and Serena's youth coach that would allow them to experience a flow state. Mr. Williams realized the amount of effort required to gain actual confidence, but he also respected and understood what it took to maintain confidence. Just as we shared in Mia Hamm's quote at the start of this chapter, he realized that once we reach a confident place in sport, we have to continue to nurture that state.

Indeed, confidence can be fleeting, and parents and coaches need to keep this in mind—always. In summary:

- Don't give false praise, as it does not build true confidence.
- Set realistic and high expectations for each athlete with the focus on effort and improvement (development) from their current level.
- Don't give preferential treatment in the form of playing time or roles on the team at younger ages, as you may stunt early developers from acquiring skills while denying other athletes opportunity to develop their skills.
- Understand what the challenge zone is and that it is imperative for youth to practice in the zone if they are to have any chance of experiencing the flow state in sport.

The Challenge Zone

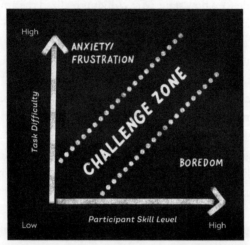

Figure 6: The Challenge Zone [76,77]

A success or mastery rate in sport is the percentage of time athletes are successful. To ensure you understand what a success or mastery rate is, we'll explore it in a soccer setting. For example, a coach asks their athletes to throw a soccer ball high in the air, track it, trap it with their thigh, and in that movement take the ball to the ground and quickly and efficiently take three quick steps to space (away from all teammates) with the ball. In this situation, several things may happen:

- Some athletes may not be able to track the ball properly.
- Some athletes may not be able to trap the ball with their thigh, and thus are unable to take it out of the air.
- Some athletes may be able to perform the task some of the time.
- Some athletes may be able to perform the task proficiently each time.

When teaching skills, coaches can modify conditions in ways that increase or decrease the complexity of the skills. This helps athletes practice in their challenge zone. How do they do that? We're glad you asked. In education, the term known as *differentiated instruction* is used to explain how teachers adjust lessons and assignments to meet the needs of the various learning levels in their classroom. In sport, coaches can also differentiate tasks by considering time, task, equipment, space, and athletes.

How to Differentiate Instruction	
Time	• Increase level of complexity. • Add a time constraint (e.g., You have thirty seconds to complete this task.). • Decrease level of complexity. • Decrease time constraint for some athletes (e.g., you have sixty seconds to complete this task.). • Remove time constraints initially for some athletes.
Task	• Give youth different tasks depending on their current skills. For example, some soccer players may be asked to trap a ball out of the air with their thigh, while some teammates are asked to trap it out of the air with their dominant foot, while some are asked to trap it out of the air with their non-dominant foot. • In small-sided games, some kids may be allowed to take three touches on the ball before sending it to a teammate while others may be asked to take only one touch on the ball, while others are required to take one touch on the ball using only their non-dominant foot.
Equipment	• Vary size of equipment at different ages to increase or decrease difficulty in practicing new skills. For example, the use of small soccer goals in a small-sided game.
Space	• Decrease or increase the playing space. When you decrease space, you create a condition that requires faster decision-making and performing skills under more pressure. Conversely, when you increase space, you increase time for decision-making and players have less pressure from opponents to perform their skill.
Athletes	• Divide teams carefully so that similarly skilled athletes are together.

Coaches ought to differentiate instruction in ways that help athletes experience a 60 to 70 percent success rate. In our example, the soccer player who was able to perform the task some of the time may be the only athlete who would fall into the 60 to 70 percent success rate on their team, whereas another athlete who was unable to track the ball properly might fall well below the 60 to 70 percent rate. This 60 to 70 percent success rate zone is known as the challenge zone. The challenge zone provides an environment that isn't so easy that participants become bored, and it is not so difficult that makes participants feel hopeless.

There are many approaches parents and coaches can take to support this development. Action steps that can help foster youth-sport competence and confidence include:

- Directors deliver coaching development around the relationship between competence, confidence, and motivation.
- Coaches set high expectations related to skill acquisition for all athletes, regardless of their current skill level, in a supportive and caring environment. This way, all youth will gain competence from their development, and this fosters confidence and intrinsic motivation.
- Just like teachers provide progress reports and report cards, coaches can do the same. Report cards should inform parents where their kids are in developing their technical skills and movement patterns as well as tactical knowledge as applicable. These reports should be explained to the kids and information for how kids can improve in the identified areas would be fair and helpful. Directors should work with coaches prior to them completing report cards so clubs are consistent in how they assess and report to families.
- Parents and coaches should define success based on what we learned in chapter 3 regarding goal orientation (see page 53). In other words, praise kids when you see them doing their

best, trying something new, or improving, and avoid over-celebrating things such as goals scored. This helps keep focus on development.

• Coaches and parents should expect mistakes. In fact, before any type of competition this is one thing that you can be guaranteed of. We've witnessed situations where some youth can make one mistake and be yanked from competition while others can make the same mistakes repeatedly and coaches do not even notice. This is due to bias and is really unfair to those who are expected to perform or to sit out. When you expect mistakes, you don't react to them. Kids will then remain calm and learn from their mistakes.

Parents, coaches, and directors are able to position youth athletes on their journeys in ways that introduce, guide, and nurture competence within sport, which leads to true confidence in themselves and their abilities. Facilitating this growth successfully will ensure children thrive within not only their sport environments, but long into their healthy adulthoods as well.

Positive Sport Culture Can Increase Confidence in Individuals and in the Team

As noted, self-confidence is individual, yet it is influenced by external factors such as parents, coaches, and teammates in the sport environment. We've explored how individual perceived and actual competence influences confidence, so let's now examine how team culture can influence individual and collective confidence among team members.

Team culture is the lived attitudes, values, and goals and behaviors of a team.

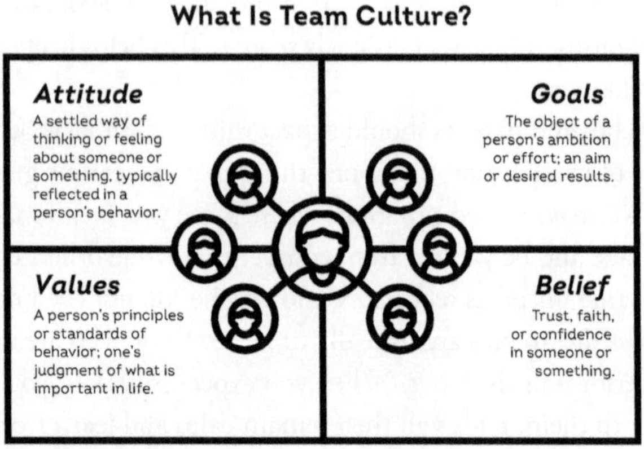

What Is Team Culture?

Figure 7: What Is Team Culture?

Team culture is established due to a combination of coaches', athletes', and parents' attitudes, expectations, and communications. Coaches can set high expectations and mottos regarding culture, but it is up to athletes to buy in and model behaviors that align with these expectations. A positive team culture is most likely when coaches continue to encourage youth to model the attitudes, values, goals, and behaviors necessary for a positive team culture. It is important to note that as youth enter and progress throughout adolescence, parents have a very important role in holding their children to a high standard as it relates to team culture.

Teammates

We argue that when positive team culture is in place, individuals and groups are more likely to compete confidently. We also believe this is where the magic will happen. Conversely, toxic team environments can decrease development, strip perceived competence, and in turn diminish a player's confidence in themself. Just how magical can team culture be in positively influencing performance? Well, to give an example, we'd like to introduce you to a group of youth hockey players from rural Nova Scotia, Canada.

In Canada, U18 ice hockey players compete annually for a AAA National Hockey Championship Title. For girls, the championship is called the Esso Cup, and for boys, it's called the Telus Cup. In 2017, the Cape Breton West Islanders finished their storybook season as the first Atlantic Canadian team to ever win the coveted Telus Cup. Cape Breton Island is a stunningly beautiful island located northeast of mainland Nova Scotia. The Cape Breton West Islanders' home rink is named after Stanley Cup champion and hockey legend Al MacInnis. The Al MacInnis Sports Centre is located in McInnis's hometown—picturesque Port Hood, Nova Scotia.

The 2017 Telus Cup Championship team was made up of a close-knit team of boys from throughout that rural part of the province. As legend has it, the team who represented Ontario at the Telus Cup Championship that same year had more kids try out for the goalie position than the Cape Breton West Islanders had try out for their entire team! As you can imagine, no one expected the Islanders to capture the crown. No one. In fact, this team was thought of simply as a bunch of rural kids who were lucky to even make it to the championship tournament. But the boys on that team had confidence in their own abilities, and they had confidence in each other.

Two of Amanda's nephews, Jacob and Sean Stewart, were rookie players on the Islanders in 2017. Despite the countless odds stacked against them, the Islanders made it to the championship game. It took Amanda about eight hours to figure out how to stream the game held in British Columbia from her home in St. Louis, Missouri. It also cost her about fifty bucks. But this game had the potential storyline worthy of a movie in the making, and, as they say, you can take the girl out of Canada, but you can't take the Canada out of the girl.

In the final game, the Islanders were down two goals going into the third period. A mid-period goal brought them within one, and then a goal with about a minute left in the game tied it up and sent it into overtime. To the surprise of everyone except the players in the Islanders jerseys, the Islanders won with an overtime goal. It is noteworthy that a second-year player, Jacob Hudson, opted not to take the shot in the closing minutes and instead passed to rookie Logan Chisholm who scored the game winner.

As students of sport, we were always intrigued by this story, so we talked to Sean and Jacob about their experiences on this team. They shared how the third-year players on this team embraced the younger players. Instead of being jealous or fearful of their status on the team, the older players welcomed them. The third-year players on the team were coming off two subpar seasons and believed they could do better with the quality of players coming up through the ranks.

For the first time in program history, the team won the provincial crown after losing a tournament mid-way through the season while ranked first in the province. That loss was a wakeup call as the boys reflected, and it was time to put their head down and keep doing the work. Getting along was never a factor as, due to the welcoming nature of the older players, the team was free of cliques and prima donnas. Sean recalls feeling tired doing homework while his parents drove him seventy minutes to practice but getting there and feeling motivated and excited to be with his friends because they were always in such an upbeat environment when together. The older players often communicated that this team could aim high because they've never been on such a skilled or close-knit team before. The younger players believed what the older players were telling them as they looked up to them. The team confidence that was fostered was the key piece of the puzzle of the coveted AAA Midget Canadian Championship.

Coaches

Coaches bear responsibility to build and nurture a team climate that helps structure the collective confidence while building individual confidence among players. We understand that there are a lot of coaches who do not have a background in how to facilitate this, and we really want to help them because we've witnessed the beauty of sport when kids find a home on a team, and it makes them want to develop as players so that they can best serve their team. This experience leads to increased confidence in their abilities, which in turn serves the teams well. The team from rural Nova Scotia was led by coaches who understood this and got it right.

Jake and Sean both explained how the coaches rolled the lines, which means all players experienced consistent playing time with the exception of maybe a couple final minutes in a couple games all season. When no players are benched, they can all continue to develop (competence) and then gain confidence in their abilities. They also coached in ways that did not contribute to a culture of fear. Kids weren't worried about messing up because they knew their coaches understood that everyone makes mistakes. The team did not play with fear, and as a result they were creative and played their best.

Sean's sister, Sara, is also a hockey player. She plays for a NCAA D-1 team that has adopted the hashtag #WePlayFree for their social media posts over the past several years. This team, the Colgate University Raiders, just won their fourth consecutive Eastern College Athletic Conference Championship greatly in part to the environment coaches have established and players have bought into. "Playing free" means players are encouraged to take risks, have fun, and find the play in training and competition. Coaches like Coaches Fargo, Decosse, and Walkland at Colgate understand that a positive team culture breeds championship banners and their hashtag is an overt approach to this time of environment.

When Dr. Beth McCharles, a certified mental performance consultant who works with several Canadian national teams and many elite-level players, coached university soccer in the early 2000s, she had a walk-on try out for the team. A young woman with a fabulous personality and strong work ethic tried out with the team. Dr. McCharles thought she'd fit well into the team philosophy and culture that the staff was trying to build.

At that point, she did not seem to be up to the skill level, however she certainly had what it took to contribute positively to the team culture. Therefore, while being exceedingly transparent, Beth offered her a spot on the team but communicated to her that she probably would not dress or get playing time in the coming year. This proposal created zero promises and allowed the player to make her own choice around her willingness to be "all in." Dr. McCharles shared, "If I tried to convince her to join the team by telling her that she would get playing time or she could work hard and probably move her way up, that wouldn't be authentic communication and perhaps would not have been true.

Dr. McCharles explains, "The great aspect about being transparent is that it also limits any hardship on your mental and emotional state as a coach, and more importantly it limits the malice toward the coaching. So, when the player actually got a chance that year to get on the field due to a number of different injuries there was no fear, there was just an opportunity for her to play at her best. The best part of the story is that she was one of the best players on the field that day, and I believe it was because she had no fear of failure or the notion that she 'must perform.' She went on to help her team because she needed to for her team to be successful. From that day on, she never left the field and ended up being our team captain. The staff created an opportunity for her to grow but not give her false hope in what was to come. Transparency creates a confident environment when we can be authentic in our communication and trust the process."

Amanda's not surprised that Dr. McCharles approached the situation the way that she did. They were college teammates and Beth always led with her heart and with integrity. So, we ask, if the highest levels of youth and college sport can create a culture devoid of fear, and experience the greatest success in doing so, why wouldn't youth-sport coaches want to do the same? If you're not sure where to begin, start small. For example:

- Make practice pairings and groupings intentional and put kids in situations to get to know teammates from other schools or communities. Not everyone comes to a team knowing other kids, and sometimes they find themselves in situations where they are the only one who doesn't know kids.
- Make sure all coaches, athletes, and parents know the team values, philosophy, coaching styles, and preferred way that each athlete receives feedback. In doing so, you will decrease uncertainty while increasing confidence in a group setting which will enhance team unity.[78]

- Tell kids you expect them to make mistakes, as that's when they are challenging their comfort zone. Remind athletes that everyone makes mistakes and not to get angry when a teammate does; rather, they should be supportive of each other and praise the effort.
- When you notice teammates being difficult or exclusive to others, don't be afraid to talk to them about it. In the next chapter, you'll learn about courageous conversations, and such a conversation may be necessary with an athlete or their parents to ensure negative behaviors of teammates stop. We promise you that ignoring them may seem like the best approach at the moment, but it'll hinder the team climate in the short and long term.
- Remind the kids that fun is serious business on your team! You want them to feel joyful when they come to practice and when they compete. Talk to them about what that looks like and how they each can contribute to it.

Parents

Dr. McCharles warns parents to watch what they say to their children so they avoid creating an unintentional, albeit vicious, cycle of self-pity. The more a parent tells their child that "they should be playing," "that they are better than," or "the coaches don't know what they are doing," the more they are creating a narrative in their child that is confusing. She explains that it can also create entitlement and contribute to an individualistic mindset.

When asked how parents can support a positive team culture, Sean and Jake shared that they could help their kids understand the importance of being a good teammate. Teach them to see the opportunity and excitement when teammates who are better than they are as they get older and play at more competitive levels, as they will make them better. Parents should be intentional about teaching their children to be open and inclusive and explain how these things contribute to the overall success of the team and, if appropriate, align with their family's values.

Sure, it didn't hurt that the team consisted of many players who went on to play in the exclusive Canadian Major Junior Hockey League and later on to university hockey in Canada. It also didn't hurt that in nets for the Islanders was Colton Ellis, who at the time of publication was in the St. Louis Blues organization. But lots of teams have talent. Especially Midget AAA hockey teams in Canada. What was special about this team and what propelled it to meet its potential was that the team was confident in their abilities and was willing to train at a level that allowed their abilities to meet the challenge. It is undeniable that the team climate contributed greatly to their individual success.

Richard reflects on how his confidence in the luge was only possible because of the supportive environment where teammates and coaches as well as the loved ones surrounded him and took a positive, effective approach to communication while he did the necessary work of improving his competence. Richard's confidence could easily have been torn down by negative comments, regardless of his abilities. The classic error detection approach taken traditionally by many coaches was often ineffective, because that approach highlights mistakes and mentally reinforces the error. That approach doesn't build on successful completion of skills or tasks and thus, not only increases competence but fails to build confidence.

While a lack of confidence in some sports may not have the potential to lead to serious injury as it can in a sport like the natural luge, it can affect all kids. Researchers have concluded that physical activity levels decrease as confidence in one's physical abilities decreases.[79] Knowing the myriad benefits youth gain from living physically active lives, it's important that confidence is a key goal of all those who work with them in the sport setting. This message transcends many of life's situations where the building of confidence is critical for children to try new things or to enjoy the activities they participate in. Youth are best situated to give the effort necessary to gain competence and confidence when there is no fear of a negative reaction from those around them, when they feel like they belong, and when they feel supported.

And remember to be patient. Confidence is built incrementally through successful repetition and needs to be nurtured. When confidence is secure, the joy of the activity blossoms, whether it is the thrill of the speed of descending a mountain or the execution of a skill to the best of one's ability. This is when, and only when, the love for sport and physical activity is embedded.

Questions to Ask Yourself

Parents:
- Do you compare your child to others on the team? If so, why do you do this? How do you think this could hurt your child's confidence and joy in participating?
- Do you praise and reward outcomes (e.g., goals) that are often not within your child's total control over their effort?
- Do you praise effort and teach kids that their best is all that you're expecting?
- Do you communicate with your child that being a positive teammate is an expectation that you have for them?

Coaches:
- Do you give all athletes feedback on their development?
- Do you plan practices purposefully to try to challenge every athlete based on where their skill level is currently?
- Do you make positive comments when you notice improvement?
- Do you encourage athletes to celebrate each other's improvements?
- Are you willing to take an athlete aside who is behaving in exclusive or inappropriate ways toward a teammate?

Sport Directors:

- Do you educate your coaches and/or parents on how true confidence is developed in youth? If not, how can you do so? If so, are there any additions you can make to your current practice to improve how you do this?
- What, if anything, challenged your current thinking around confidence in youth sport? Did you feel inspired by what you read? If so, how will you apply this information?

Do's and Don'ts

Do's

- Comment on improvement, skill acquisition, and effort so that youth know they have the ability to improve.
- Teach kids the difference between false and actual confidence.
- Modify skills and drills in ways so that every athlete can practice in their challenge zone.
- Plan ways to foster a positive team culture.
- Teach kids the importance of confidence and how if they develop their confidence will improve and that sport will become more enjoyable.

Don'ts

- Compare kids to each other, as kids all develop at different rates.
- Overpraise or give preferential treatment to those who happen to be faster and stronger at earlier ages.
- Require athletes to practice the same skills under the same conditions when they are at different skill levels.
- Ignore negative social dynamics among a team because you aren't sure what to do.
- Place value on wins and losses and thus deny kids the chance to feel proud and motivated by their improvement.

CHAPTER 7

Call the Shots

*The Importance of Communication
on and off the Field*

"Communication does not always occur naturally, even among a
tight-knit group of individuals. Communication must be taught
and practiced in order to bring everyone together as one."

–Coach Mike Krzyzewski

S t. Louis is a soccer town. USA Women's National Team captain
and star center back Becky Sauerbrunn grew up in Ladue, a suburb
in St. Louis's West County. Fans of the USA Men's National Team
cheered on St. Louis born-and-raised defender Tim Ream and forward
Josh Sargeant during the 2022 World Cup. Locals tell us that soccer fever
has always been high in St. Louis, which is highlighted by the fact that
they recently got their own professional soccer team. The St. Louis City
Soccer Club joined Major League Soccer (MLS) in 2023. They play in a
brand-new open-air stadium called CityPark and the city, where Amanda
lives with her spouse and their three kids, is buzzing about the new team.

A new youth league in the United States and Canada preceded the
expansion of the St. Louis City SC MLS team, and this league is called
MLS NEXT. Amanda was speaking with a mom of a player who plays
in the MLS NEXT league as a thirteen-year-old (age modified to protect
anonymity) and shared a story that really (and sadly) surprised Amanda.

Let's call the mom "Lisa" (not her real name). Lisa's son "Dylan" (also
not his real name) typically receives a lot of playing time. All of a sudden,

he didn't play for an entire half. To be clear, this was the first time Dylan didn't play during a half, and it was also the first time that Dylan was benched at all during his time with MLS NEXT. Lisa and her spouse were a bit concerned because their son wasn't sure of why he was benched in the second half. They don't view him as perfect and don't expect him to be given whatever he wants, but they also didn't want the coach messing with his confidence due to the absence of communication and understanding. Playing in this league is a massive commitment for a youth athlete. They spend hours training, doing strength and speed training, and they weren't interested in their son participating in this league and giving up a lot of typical thirteen-year-old activities due to his very full soccer schedule if he wasn't going to get the chance to fully develop with adequate playing time.

That said, they didn't want to be "those parents"—the ones who overreact or place a mark on their son for their being "overbearing" or "annoying." After all, it's such a privilege to even be on a team like this. After this happened a couple more times and after much thought, Dylan's dad decided to write an email to the coach. In the email, he was intentional about making sure the tone was upbeat and not accusatory. He thanked the coach for all he's taught their son thus far. The dad asked what the coach would like to see their son do more so that he could maintain the minutes he was receiving earlier in the season. Since there was a twenty-four-hour rule[80] and the dad emailed the coach only hours after the most recent game ended, he apologized for sending the email but said that it could have easily referenced the previous games that occurred more than twenty-four hours ago. The dad also asked if the coach would please consider making time to talk to his son about the shift in his playing time, as Dylan was beginning to make up stories in his head and believe them to be true.

Within five minutes of sending the email, the coach called the dad. The coach shared that the last few games were exciting, and he admittedly just lost track of subs. Upon being more aware that Dylan didn't play in the second half the last few games, he apologized profusely. He shared that he hates the twenty-four-hour rule, as if he was reminded of this sooner it wouldn't have happened a second time. He said at this age, every player deserves adequate time to develop and that's what this team was about—developing the next generation of MLS players. The coach encouraged the dad to call anytime and for any reason because "it is my job to care for these boys so they all feel valued, seen, and appreciated as important members of this team. To deny parents the chance to solve problems together during such an important phase of the kids' development would be to place sport over the human—something he wasn't interested in doing." The coach assured the dad he would be very communicative with his son, and he later apologized to him and assured him that his confidence shouldn't be hindered at all from the experience. He stated, "I'm a human who coaches. I will make mistakes. But I will never intentionally deny a kid to develop on my team."

The boy felt great after the coach spoke to him at the next practice. He stood tall with his shoulders back while leaving practice. "Coach just made a mistake," he told his parents. "How cool that he simply said he was sorry and encouraged me to talk to him about this stuff anytime?" the boy thought out loud on the drive home.

Amanda thought about this story for days. While this shouldn't be the exception to a parent inquiry, it felt that way because it differed so much from the vast majority of calls she received from parents of club soccer players around the city. Most often, she hears from parents curious what to do when their twelve-year-old consistently finds themselves getting played less than 20 percent of a game, or parents who aren't permitted to ask the coach any questions, or parents who are upset about a coach cursing at their child but unsure if they should complain for fear their child will be punished with time on the bench if they do.

....

The important role that communication plays in creating a collaborative and joyful youth-sport experience can't be overstated. *It's imperative.* And it needs to be fostered and supported by everyone involved—coaches, parents, and by the athletes themselves.

Before we examine what a positive communication practice looks like at the youth-sport level, let's identify some current norms that we believe ought to be challenged and fast. Specific norms that we would love to see eliminated are things like the twenty-four-hour rule, which forbids parents speaking to coaches after perceived incidents, as well as norms that flat-out restrict or forbid parents to communicate with coaches or club directors regarding their children. We are well aware norms that decrease or discourage communication between the adults involved in youth sport were established over the years in response to difficult parents. While we don't wish difficult parents on anyone, we also don't believe that helpful and caring parents should be punished or that their kids are subjected to cruelty or mistreatment due to communication restrictions. If it takes a village to raise a child (as we believe it does), then a system must be in place where the leaders in the village are able to come together in a timely fashion to determine what is best for the child.

A positive youth-sport culture does not forbid parents from speaking with a coach until twenty-four hours after an "incident." Rather, it's one where effective communication occurs before a sporting event so that everyone has clear expectations, and no one is caught off guard by the approach taken. Sport can be incredibly emotional, and temperatures can run high. Simply stated, these are not the times to put kids or their parents in a position they aren't prepared for. And it is a coach's responsibility to share their approach and expectation for how they run teams. Somewhere along the line, society has decided that all parents are crazy and don't know kids, thus no one is permitted to speak to the coach. It might be beneficial to pause and ask why parents or kids might be upset in the first place. Coaches and parents are humans, so both will make mistakes. As such, of course there are times when parents are inappropriate, but policies set up for the lowest common denominator of parents aren't the answer, and they can ultimately decrease the joy kids find in sport.

If you're still on Team Twenty-four-hour Rule, we have a question for you: Were you ever in a classroom where the teacher kept the entire class in from recess due to the behavior of one or two students? Most code of conducts for teachers don't permit them to do this anymore, because it is not fair to punish a group for the behavior of one or two. We don't think it's wise for any child to miss recess, as the child misbehaving is likely the one who needs to move more than anyone, and it's certainly not fair to the classmates who have to miss. Likewise, it's not fair that a common sport policy is to forbid a parent from communicating with a coach until twenty-four hours after a game.

If you're still thinking *Why not? Parents are nuts!*, please read on.

Think about this for a second: If a child has a school-related incident, would parents be okay if the teacher or principal decided that they wouldn't involve the parent until after twenty-four hours had passed? When youth are at the center of a situation, thoughtful and caring adults ought to be able to collaborate in ways to provide the best guidance for the player. We don't condone any angry parent berating an official, publicly humiliating a coach, or, even worse, physically assaulting someone. None of that is fair to kids. At the same time, we can acknowledge that coaches make mistakes and poor decisions from time to time that can lead to short- or long-term psychological trauma to kids. The mistakes and poor decisions we are alluding to are not simply high expectations for a solid effort and respectful behaviors, we are talking about verbal abuse and psychological tactics that rob kids of their confidence and joy or pit them against their teammates. Coaches and parents are humans, and humans are inherently imperfect. It's extremely difficult to imagine parents being totally objective about their child in sport, but it is not fair to assume they are *all* wrong when they want to discuss their child's situation with a coach.

If an eleven-year-old is participating in a tournament and is benched out of the blue, and no one speaks to them or the parents about it, the child and their parents are left in a very precarious situation. Regardless of whether you view it as acceptable behavior to bench a child of that age (we do not think it is, and will die on that sword), no one should be caught off guard with the decision due to a lack of communication. In other words, oftentimes frustration mounts unnecessarily because the coaches, parents, players, and a sport director entered a situation with different expectations. If club directors are going to insert a twenty-four-hour rule, they ought to hold themselves accountable by ensuring that everyone involved in a sporting experience is on the same page in terms of expectations.

For example, when you invite a child to participate in a tournament or on a team, be very clear about playing time policies. Words such as "fair and balanced" are well intentioned but fall short because they are subjective and open to interpretation. We posit they can create more confusion and catch families off guard in certain instances. What is fair? What is balanced? If the most skillful movers miss a good number of practices, is it fair that they get to play 100 percent of the game? Is it balanced if some kids receive 80 percent of game playing time, while others receive 5 percent? We're not answering these questions; we're simply asking them to point out that it's important to be as specific as possible in advance as a coach, and parents should feel comfortable asking for clarification so that they can adequately prepare their child for the possible situations they might find themselves in.

We understand why directors may choose words such as "fair," "balanced," and "similar" when describing playing time; they don't want their coaches feeling overly stressed during competition while trying to manage observing and coaching the players during the game and constantly referencing a stopwatch to ensure exact playing time. We appreciate that balancing both can be very difficult because we've been there. Yet, we believe it's a mistake at best and a cop out at worst to insert rules such as the twenty-four-hour rule when a child who always shows up and does their very best only plays a small percentage of time, because rules like this often work against a youth understanding why they only received a small percentage of playing time. Surprise, confusion, and disappointment with no understanding decreases the likeliness that a youth will have a joyful positive experience. Instead, consider establishing a policy that makes clear what type of communication is permitted when discussing potentially hot topics such as playing time. Words such as "professional," "caring," and "intentional" come to mind as we dream up a draft of such a policy.

In this chapter, we examine different types of communication from varying viewpoints in youth sport. Playing time serves as a good topic to highlight an example of the importance of effective communication in youth sport, but it's certainly not the only example or topic we'll explore in this chapter. Take a look at the plentiful dynamics at play in youth sport:

Who Interacts in Youth Sport?

COACH → CHILD	PARENT → DIRECTOR
COACH → COACH	PARENT → PARENT
COACH → PARENT	CHILD → OFFICIAL
CHILD → CHILD	COACH → OFFICIAL
CHILD → PARENT	PARENT → OFFICIAL

The more aware we become of the countless opportunities we have to connect, understand, and inform within youth sport, the more positively we can influence youth athletes' experiences. Effective, positive communication is necessary for youth sports to be safe spaces for kids to grow, develop, and enjoy the journey.

We are purposeful in our inclusion of the word "effective" when we describe communication in this chapter. "Effective communication is defined as the process of exchanging ideas, thoughts, opinions, knowledge, and data so that the message is received and understood with clarity and purpose."[81] Effective communication is not simply saying what you want to convey, and communication is only effective should the sender and receiver feel satisfied about the interaction. It is important to remember that there are also several communication types; not all of them involve language.

Years ago, Richard was coaching soccer to a group of U13 kids. After one game, he noticed a parent of one of his players did not look happy (non-verbal communications). In fact, they looked so angry that Richard felt compelled to speak to them immediately to determine if everything was okay. Richard approached the parent with a worried look on his face (non-verbal) and asked (verbal) if anything was wrong. The parent quipped with a sarcastic tone, saying, "Everything is just fine, super good," (verbal). Richard observed (with eyes and ears) intently and noticed that their tone and words did not align. So, he asked them again (verbal) if everything was okay. This time, they responded with the same words but in a less edgy tone and a smile on their face.

Due to the cues that Richard picked up, he remained unsettled by their interaction. Later that day, he sent the parent a short text (written communication) checking in to be sure that the child's experience was not a negative one. He quickly received a response in the form of a smiley face and thumbs up (visual communications) emojis, which alleviated his concerns.

It's important that adults understand that awareness of all types of communication helps them in connecting and aligning with athletes, parents, and coaches to ensure youth experiences remain positive and joy in sport is always supported.

Listen to Understand

"You know, you never are able to learn anything when you're the one doing the talking, and I don't know that much about this particular topic," proclaimed Vince Stanec, Amanda's eighty-six-year-old father-in-law, at a

Stanec family gathering during one of Amanda's first visits to her spouse's native St. Louis, approximately two decades ago. At the time, Jim and his three adult siblings were jokingly debating around their parents' kitchen table over American Thanksgiving weekend. Like most siblings, it didn't take long for the volume to rise as they each attempted to complete a full sentence before a sibling chimed in. Much later, when everyone was dispersing, Amanda asked her father-in-law why he didn't offer his thoughts on the topic. The previous statement was his response, and Amanda thinks about it often. It's why she wrestles with discomfort when giving keynote speeches; she knows she could learn far more from the collective wisdom in the audience than in the words she's about to relay. Richard's father gave him similar advice when he was a boy by sharing, "Keep quiet and let people think you're an idiot rather than open your mouth and remove all doubt." Both were highlighting the importance of listening intently and for the purpose of understanding.

Over the years, when we've read about the types of communication and listened to people speak about it, listening is often listed last, if it all. But a major component of communication is the *receiving* of information, not just the expressing. Michael Bungay Stanier's book, *The Advice Trap: Be Humble, Stay Curious & Change the Way You Lead Forever*, talks about the power of staying curious before offering advice as a leader. Grandfathers and authors aren't the only people promoting listening and asking questions. Just look at recent health education in our public schools and their adoption of skills-based health education. Skills-based health education was created in response to what the research has proven: knowledge doesn't change behavior, skills do. This is why some people continue to engage in dangerous or risky behavior even when they understand it's not good for them to do so.

How well one listens will determine their effectiveness in many roles of their lives. People listen to gather facts, to understand, to learn, and for enjoyment or connection with others. Active listening is very useful when working with youth or parents in sport situations. According to the U.S.

Institute of Peace, *active listening* is a way of listening and responding to another person that improves mutual understanding.[82] Dr. Stephen Walker provides tips for active listening in an article he wrote for the *Podium Sports Journal*.[83] These tips include:

- Make eye contact and pay attention.
- Use open posture to encourage conversation.
- Make physical gestures to show that you're listening.
- Provide feedback in a timely manner and consider tone when you give feedback.
- Paraphrase what is said to be sure you fully understand.
- When paraphrasing, consider your body language and tone.

We've heard about a lot of unnecessary disappointment on the part of kids, parents, and even coaches due to an absence of adequate curiosity and active listening in the context of sport. For example, we've heard from parents who feel the sport director wasn't really listening to their concerns on a phone call or feel the coaches don't want to really hear their concerns, they just want to end the conversation as quickly as possible. We've also heard from coaches who wish parents would reach out and ask them questions rather than criticizing them throughout the community. Finally, we've witnessed parents jump to conclusions as they took their adolescent's moment of venting to mean their sport experience is all terrible without asking more questions to get a fuller picture. Wondering how we can all do better, regardless of our role? Here are some things to consider.

Parents, let's start with you. First, ask your child more questions! Parents really need to stay curious when trying to get a full picture of their child's experience at sport. Ask kids if they really want to play the same sport next season or if they need a break. Don't lead them in your questioning, and don't preface the question with things such as: "We've already invested so much time and money into it. I don't know why you'd want to stop." Ask them if they are happy and feel like they belong on their team.

Listen to what they tell you and probe to better understand what you think they are holding back. If they come home from practice one night upset, ask them specifically what went well to help you determine if they are simply having a moment or if things are as bad as your child is portraying. As you're checking in with your child, remind them that their happiness is what you deem most important. Remind them that happiness and joy include a solid effort, as nothing is rewarding if it wasn't earned.

Coaches, we encourage you to always listen to understand and not to respond too quickly. In other words, intently listen to what other people are saying without trying to prepare a rebuttal or response while they are sharing their thoughts. You hold the power to provide young people a positive interaction that encourages them to speak to authority figures throughout their lives. Never quip at a child and tell them it's a bad time and that you're too busy to answer their question. If an athlete comes to you at an inconvenient time, like the beginning of practice when you have a thousand things on your mind, have a default comment prepared that you deliver with a caring tone. For example, "You have something important you'd like to discuss with me, and I am so happy you've come to me. Since I'm so focused on practice right now, I fear I won't be able to listen as intently as you deserve. If it's quick, let's talk after I get the mini game going. If it's long, could you text me after and we can set up a time to talk? I'm happy you've come to me!"

If athletes do not have a phone or parents don't want them texting their coach, simply modify the statement to ask the parent to set up a time for the child and coach to talk. A mom recently told Amanda that when her daughter approached a coach a few years ago, the coach criticized her for speaking with her before practice about something on an individual level. Specifically, she said "I can't believe you're asking me this right now. It's not the time. I'm busy." It really hurt the tween because she simply was trying to gather specific details on how to improve enough to make a particular team. Instead, she walked away feeling annoyed and dismissed at a critical stage of development. Now, there will be people reading thinking, *Suck it up buttercup. You're not the center of the world.* We assure you that sport will still provide ample levels of disappointment and frustration to build resilience, but we know resilience is built in supporting and controlled environments—not environments when people treat you disrespectfully and seemingly out of the blue.

Athletes also need to listen for understanding and to stay curious a little bit longer. When coaches give athletes corrective feedback in a less-than-desirable tone, they should be encouraged to try to find the information that can help them rather than focus on the tone that prompts them not to want to listen. We are asking a lot from kids when we ask them to ignore the condescending tone of an adult. This is why we really dislike when people use comments such as, "They are behaving like a child," when describing a poorly behaved adult. That said, it's a great life skill to search for personal growth. Sport provides youth and coaches ample opportunity to model personal growth through listening and seeking feedback.

It Is How You Say It

Tone is obviously an important part of written and verbal communication. We already referenced tone in this chapter when we shared the story of the dad being cognizant that he emailed his son's coach with a positive, non-accusatory tone. Tone is important and can be set in writing by using a specific greeting and opening sentence, stating the intent of the email, and how one signs off. Tone can either have a reader or recipient of our words perk their ears up or close them off. No one wants to receive an email that is rude, vague, or accusatory, and when speaking about issues that require positive collaboration, threatening and cruel language isn't going to help solve a problem.

Our verbal tone can also result in either someone wanting to listen to us or putting someone on the defensive. Sometimes time is necessary after a situation to find a tone that is necessary for effective communication and, if this is the case, by all means the twenty-four hours or however many hours are required to find that tone. You'll know you've nailed the tone if the person you're speaking with seems receptive and their own tone and body language communicates to you that they're comfortable continuing in the conversation.

The reason why there are so many resources available that highlight key components of verbal communication and its importance is because positive, effective verbal communication is essential to be effective in all areas of one's life—including a joyful youth-sport experience.

Courageous Conversations

Amanda is a big Brené Brown fan. If you were to peek in on Amanda when she's doing daily chores or prepping supper for her family, it is likely that she's listening (or relistening) to one of Brown's books on Audible hoping her family will soak up some of the wisdom. One concept that *Dare to Lead* focuses on is the idea of being courageous in giving feedback. The book explores how it is not unkind to give truthful feedback; rather, it is unkind *not* to do so. Alas, Brown calls on the reader to choose courage over comfort. The first time Amanda read about this, it stopped her in her tracks. How many problems in youth sport could be solved in a caring and loving way if people chose to apply courage and vulnerability in their approach to the problem? Alas, as phone calls came in looking for support in navigating tricky youth-sport situations, Amanda encouraged people to initiate and have courageous conversations.

In the youth-sport context, courageous conversations are conversations that are initiated by someone who is uncomfortable with something in the sport experience; this individual seeks to solve the problem, or at least contribute to a solution, in a way that—as Brown coins it—is generous. As such, if one is generous, they listen to understand, give grace, and are kind in their approach. Courageous conversations aren't venting sessions, and they are meant to involve effective communication so that everyone leaves the conversation feeling better than before it began.

Courageous conversations can help enhance all relationships involved in the context of sport. For example, a parent's sports relationship with their child, a parent's understanding of the coach's approach, the director's relationship with their coaches, etc. Amanda has initiated courageous conversations in the past, and she's also shared the concept with those she thinks would benefit from the idea. The first time Amanda initiated a courageous conversation in sport was at a 10U sporting event. Throughout that season Amanda heard a dedicated mom repeatedly calling to her child throughout each game telling her to "try harder," and shouting things like "come on!" and "let's go." After a couple weeks, Amanda asked "May I have a courageous conversation with you?"

"Sure!" the mom responded.

Amanda was a bit nervous to have this conversation, because she didn't want to come across as a know-it-all who thought she had a right to tell others how to talk to their children (because she knows she doesn't have that right!). Yet, her teacher's heart really wanted to talk to this mom because the little girl's body language looked really defeated on the field. The little girl was trying her best and would look over at her mom with frustration when her mom would try to motivate her from the sideline. The mom didn't mean to hinder her child's development or love of the game, but both were plausible results if this type of sideline communication continued. The tone and urgency in which she was supporting her daughter clearly wasn't working for the young athlete. So, Amanda mustered up all the love and calm in her voice that she could and shared, "She's trying so hard. I'm sorry if I am overstepping, but I understand the research and have to tell you, because I care, that if you continue to cheer for her in this way you are increasing the probability that she will quit this sport sooner rather than later." The mom was (so!) extremely graceful in receiving this feedback from a peer she barely knew. Rather than get defensive, she cheered in a more positive way while complimenting effort and hustle instead of calling out the mistakes. The mom also told the story to other moms in the community who would later call Amanda for advice navigating their own kids' sports journeys. The 10U little girl is quickly approaching high school age and is totally rocking it in sport! She continues to do her best and enjoys success in several sports.

In 2022, a friend of Amanda's shared with her that her son lost his starting position on his lacrosse team as a freshman and had no clue as to why. The mom explained that her son was devastated. As a former athlete, the mom said she wasn't going to talk to the coach because she didn't want to be perceived as a helicopter mom or a nuisance to the coach. Amanda didn't disagree at first, but as the conversation went on, she changed her mind. The mom shared with Amanda that her son no longer wanted to attend practice or games anymore. He wanted to quit. When Amanda asked if it was because he lost his starting position the mom reflected and said, "I think it's more that he has no idea why his playing time has been so drastically cut and that the coach hasn't addressed the change with him at all. He didn't act this way in the past when he didn't start or wasn't the star on a team."

Amanda encouraged the mom to reach out to the coach via email and ask for a time to chat. They discussed how she would let the coach know she wasn't judging; she was just asking that he consider speaking with her son to explain why he lost his position and what he might be able to do to be considered for it again in the future. She let him know that her son would be emailing to ask for a meeting, but she wanted to give him a heads up and would be happy to talk and learn more to see if there was anything she should know about. A few days later the mom followed up and shared how much she loved the concept of courageous conversations as a positive approach to clearing a hurdle in the youth-sport journey. She and the coach talked soon after she emailed, and he was happy to speak with her son. The coach shared what went into his decision and this alone really helped the boy feel better about the situation. What could have resulted in a teenage boy quitting a sport due to a lack of communication ended up being a motivating experience for him with a solution-focused path forward. The boy dedicated time to the gaps the coach identified, and the coach continued to communicate where his thoughts were around his progress.

We read the tweets about how kids are soft if they quit when they don't get what they want in sport, but we disagree. Kids quit when they don't feel *seen* in sport. They quit when they don't feel they are *valued*. Courageous conversations can help keep kids in the game by helping to ensure they know their value.

Richard also initiated a courageous conversation after experiencing something that is common in gyms and on sports fields across North America. One season, while coaching on one side of a practice field, he noticed that fewer and fewer kids were showing up for practice with the team on the other side. The decrease in participants was staggering, and Richard guessed that the trend was due to the coach's behavior. Anytime the coach was annoyed with what a player was doing, they would say the classic "get down and gimme ten." Yep. The coach was punishing their players with exercise by making them do ten push-ups. The coach was using an activity that would benefit the players as a punishment for poor behavior or even for being last in a drill or relay. Why would any coach want to characterize working out (doing conditioning) as a punishment? Don't we coach because we want kids to love being physically active?

Richard considered his options for approaching the coach. He thought about asking the coach out for a coffee, but he didn't really know them very well, and he was worried that wasn't a good option. He decided after a practice he would ask why they punished kids with push-ups, and he would be mindful of his tone so as not to come across as judgmental or confrontational.

First, Richard identified something that he really liked and admired about their practices, and then Richard asked why they were punishing with exercise. The reaction, at first, was confusion because clearly the coach had never thought about it. Like most coaches, they were perpetuating what they experienced as a player. After reflecting, the coach shared they weren't going to do it any longer and the two began talking about other coaching practices. Since then, they've even joined groups to practice together. Richard could have easily not said a word and just focused on his own group of kids. But, for the sake of the kids on the other side of the field, he chose to initiate the conversation, just as Amanda chose to do for a kid she believes has a ton of potential as an athlete and the mom who helped her son understand why he lost his starting position.

We've had additional courageous conversations over the years, some with sport directors around playing-time philosophies for younger ages. We've had courageous conversations with coaches when we've asked them to look our kids in the eye and communicate the reason behind various decisions they've made. Coaches and sport directors have held courageous conversations with parents and players about the players' skill and performance when they place them on teams that don't match the families' desires. Perhaps not all courageous conversations have happy endings, but it doesn't mean they shouldn't happen. Parents should never forget to put themselves in the coach's shoes, and coaches should never forget to put themselves in their athlete's shoes. The intent of courageous conversations is not to be hyper critical or to offer unsolicited advice (we all know how much others love to hate such advice). That said, there must be room in youth sport for a conversation around topics such as playing time for the purpose of understanding.

Suggestions for courageous conversations:

- At the beginning of the conversation, the person who initiated the conversation ought to verbalize their intention for both parties to leave the conversation feeling better about the situation and with more understanding of the experience of the other person.
- Enter the conversations with a curious mind and listen to understand. Ask questions and refrain from being defensive or giving excuses until you have all the information.
- Have these conversations face to face whenever possible. When not possible, use Zoom or something like Zoom. It is important

to have eye contact and demonstrate active listening during these conversations. We find phone calls fall short as a medium in which courageous conversations occur.

Positive, Skill-Specific Feedback

In addition to courageous conversations, the other type of verbal communication that we promote in the context of youth sport is positive, skill-specific feedback, as it plays an essential role in developing joy in sport.

Coaches and Feedback

An example of a coach giving positive skill-specific feedback is, "I like that follow-through. Keep it up!" The communication is positive and encouraging in nature, while at the same time is very focused on a particular skill. Researchers found that when elementary physical education teachers gave boys more skill-specific feedback than girls who received general feedback (unspecific statements like, "Good job!"), the boys had higher skill acquisition even though growth and maturation hadn't yet influenced performance variance. The teachers' intentions were kind—they were trying to be kind to the girls because they know girls drop out of physical activity at higher rates than boys. However, in attempting to be kind, they widened the skill competence gap among boys and girls pre-puberty when strength and size shouldn't account for skill competence variance between boys and girls.

All coaches should set the goal of giving positive skill-specific feedback to each player at each training session or competition. Being overt in instruction will help reinforce the skill and will also uplift the player. But feedback doesn't just influence athletes' skill development, it also influences their psycho-social experience in sport. If you're a youth coach who finds themself belittling a participant for poor behavior or low effort, consider calling home and working with the parents to help improve the behavior. Since adolescents have a heightened weight on the importance of peer relationships at this stage of their lives, it's important that coaches are mindful of this and try to keep things positive and inspiring at training and competition. Belittling is the opposite of positive, and more times than not it will not yield the results you're actually looking for—just ask any teacher.

The dichotomy between positive, skill-specific feedback and general feedback that is negative or neutral in tone is expansive. For example, a twelve-year-old was asked by a coach what position he was playing in a scrimmage. When he responded by naming the position that he had never played before, the coach said "Well, then, play the position." The athlete's dad shared that the coach delivered the message in a tone that was abrasive and uninspiring. As he relayed this story to Amanda, he shared that his son's gut reaction was to quip back. But his maturity is decades beyond his age and so he said, "I'd love to do a better job, but I honestly don't really know what you mean when you say, 'Play the position.'" The child reported that he asked in a kind tone in hopes of not upsetting the coach. The coach then went into detail about positional requirements for success and taught him several important tactical components of the position. The interaction ended up being a very positive one, but one can see how it could have gone south quickly. Expecting all youth athletes to have the EQ of this particular boy is unrealistic, but sharing this story with kids can certainly help them if they one day find themselves in a similar position.

When Amanda's daughter was participating in an interclub field hockey scrimmage, her coach, Casey McGowan, gave her the same skill-specific feedback several times in a row. Then, when her daughter performed the skill Coach Casey was telling her to perform, Coach said, "Okay, I'm going to confuse you now because you did what I was telling you to do, which I should love, but now I'm going to tell you why in this situation you actually shouldn't do that." Coach Casey approached this tactical advice brilliantly. Rather than frustrate an adolescent by simply giving her different feedback without context, Casey educated her on why—in that instance—a different tactic should be applied. Amanda was almost giddy hearing this. *How lucky*, she thought, *my daughter is to have a coach who was putting on a master class of feedback.* To conclude this story, it should be noted that the feedback provided in this instance really elevated her daughter's game in a big tournament shortly after the scrimmage.

Amanda isn't the only researcher interested in feedback's role in youth sport. Researchers out of McGill University in Montreal examined the influence of perceived and preferred coach feedback on youth hockey players' perceptions of team motivational climate.[84] As discussed in chapter 3 (page 53), motivational climate is the psychological environment a coach establishes through the way they plan and implement training, how they set up tasks and rewards, and how they communicate with their athletes. We already learned that athletes, even the most competitive ones, prefer a task-involved motivational climate. Don't mistake this as a warm and fuzzy environment absent of a very high standard or work rate. That's not what it is. A task-involved motivational climate, when established optimally, has an upbeat energy, a high standard for all, and asks all players to do their best all the time. It doesn't include punishing with exercise or berating kids who fall short in a drill. But, back to the study at hand. This study concluded that the thirteen- to fourteen-year-old hockey players who had coaches who provided feedback associated with an ego-goal orientation (e.g., winning and being the best is the goal) defined their experience to be an ego-involved motivational climate (e.g., high pressure, punishment if they lost, etc.). Not surprising, players who had coaches who provided feedback associated with a task-goal orientation (e.g., doing your best and giving your best effort is the goal) defined their experience to be a task-involved motivational climate (e.g., when we compete, we do our very best and then we hold our heads high regardless of the outcome).

Knowing that feedback is strongly related to the perceived climate of the athlete, it is critically important that coaches make time to talk with their athletes about: what type of feedback they feel most empowered by, how they prefer to receive it, and when they prefer to receive it. Then, with this knowledge in their pocket, they can give feedback to specific individuals in specific ways. To summarize the work on feedback and coaches, we present key feedback essentials identified by Dr. Thelma Horn, who is a professor at the University of Miami in Oxford, Ohio, through a meta-analysis of the literature on coaches' feedback.[85] Dr. Horne analyzed current research and theory to identify and discuss four dimensions of coaches' feedback that are relevant to athlete development: content, delivery, degree of growth orientation, and extent of stereotyping. She concluded that those who coach youth should:

1. Provide higher rates of positive and informationally based (skill specific) feedback.
2. Deliver feedback in an autonomy-supportive rather than controlling manner.[86]
3. Use feedback to nurture a growth-oriented mindset (one can develop skills through hard work).
4. Use feedback to create and maintain sport environments free from bias (everyone has the right to develop).

Teammates and Feedback
Teammates should focus on giving positive, skill-specific feedback as well. Since most youth don't know how each of their teammates prefer to receive feedback and since the research is clear that negative feedback can hinder the play of youth athletes, it's really important coaches teach youth how to give feedback and what type(s) of feedback is acceptable if the goal is for everyone to play to their potential in a given game or competition. While this won't require a lot of time to prepare or implement, it is essential, as it can avoid situations where youth are devastated after a game because a well-intended teammate chose adult-version of sport language to call out a peer who bases her sport competence and—sometimes even self-worth— on such feedback.

If a teammate is simply calling out when others do something wrong, one can assume they are not fully understanding the purpose of giving feedback during training or competition. Teammates should communicate clearly and effectively during training, so it becomes habit and also occurs during competition. In invasion-type games such as soccer, lacrosse, ice hockey, field hockey, this might include letting a peer know when there is a player quickly approaching, where an open player is positioned on the field, or if their mark is wide open. Effective feedback can also include positive affirmations such as "great hustle" or "good try" to acknowledge the effort. When a teammate is simply pointing out obvious mistakes such as "get there quicker" or "you need to receive that," it can be counterintuitive to an adolescent who struggles with confidence. That doesn't mean a teammate can't call out a peer when they need to give a greater effort, but the teammate saying it will have had to build a rapport with who they are saying it to in order for that player to want to listen. By acknowledging when their teammates shine, they will help create a trust whereby the critique is heard and valued. The key to this is that adolescents have to be taught this. It's not enough to say "go ahead and call out your peers if they are making mistakes" if you're not also saying "be sure to also tell them what they do well and use a tone that is encouraging and makes them want to be successful."

Two of Amanda's college teammates, Julia Lorefice and Trish MacDougall, were brilliant at this. Both earned All-Canadian status and were phenomenal leaders in addition to exceptional athletes. When Julia or Trish told Amanda that she did something really well or had a great game, it meant so much to her because she knew they meant it. Likewise, when they told Amanda to pick it up a notch, there was a level of motivation that is difficult to describe. Amanda didn't want to let them down because they were simply incredible teammates.

Coaches play an important role in helping to create an environment where such feedback becomes the norm. One activity Amanda loves leading when working on community building within a team at the start of the season is referred to as the "candle circle." Everyone holds an unlit candle in the circle. The coach lights the candle and then lights the candle of the people next to them. This continues until everyone has their candle lit. Amanda then asks everyone to look at the initial light—the coach's. What's happened? It's still shining bright. The lesson in this activity is that when you shine your light on a teammate in the form of positive, specific feedback you are not diminishing your own light. The message is to remind youth that part of their job is to lift up their teammates. Amanda likes to call this investing in the team's bank account. When she drives her kids to sport she asks, "What will you do to shine on a teammate tonight?" or "How will you make a deposit through positive feedback?" The key to this is that youth need to be taught how to give feedback.

When they return from sport she follows up, or she at least tries to remember to. Sometimes her kids text a teammate after and share something they noticed that they did well. Sometimes they tell them in the moment. Teaching kids to demonstrate kindness as teammates should be overt and should never be up for negotiation

Parents and Feedback

Parents should also give positive, specific feedback to kids, but they should *never* do so on the technical or tactical side of the game, and they should *never* coach from the sidelines or stands. Ever. This is important because parents' job is to parent and the coach's job is to coach. For example, "I loved seeing you hustle up and down the ice even though I know you were so tired." Or, "I noticed when Sophie missed that shot you immediately told her to shake it off and that she'll get the next one. That made me so proud to be your mom." Focusing on non-technical and tactical components while giving feedback like this allows you to help reinforce positive behaviors to your child without overstepping your role as the parent.

Amanda's husband Jim loves to tell the story of the time his dad yelled "cradle" to him from the stands at a youth wrestling tournament. Jim, not realizing it was his dad who said it, attempted to cradle his opponent. Jim was unsuccessful and lost a match he should have won. When his coach asked why he would attempt a cradle at that moment, Jim said, "Because

I heard someone tell me to do it." The same thing happens in youth-sport events all across North America. Parents yelling for kids to be in a certain position even though they are unaware of the system or press the team is playing, telling a kid to shoot when there are two kids marking them rather than pass to someone wide open, and we could go on. In other words, parents can unintentionally hinder what a coach is trying to accomplish when they step out of their lane on the sideline. By the way, Jim still gives his dad grief about this thirty years later!

The fact that parent coaching from the sideline is so common may explain why researchers decided to explore the effects of such behavior. Specifically, researchers have explored the effects of parents giving both negative and positive feedback to their children.[87] They concluded that athletes who received feedback based on their effort or improvement perceived their sport environment to be more task-involved. You've already learned in chapter 3 (page 53) that a task-involved motivational climate is one where doing one's best, developing, and reaching a new goal is celebrated. Researchers also concluded that athletes who received feedback based on ego-goals such as winning or scoring perceived their environment to be more ego-involved. As a reminder, that ego-involved motivational climate is one where success is defined as winning or being better than others.

The takeaway from this research is clear: parents or fans shouting anything other than "good hustle" or "good try" or "you got this!" is likely going to be counterproductive to a large amount of the youth participating in the sport, regardless of the level. If you find yourself coaching from the sideline, have a lollipop in your pocket. This practice was made famous at a local level by Peter Tasker, athletic director at John Burroughs School in St. Louis, Missouri. Tasker hands out lollipops to parents who can't help but coach from the sidelines or the stands. It's a not-so-subtle way to let them know there is never an okay time to do this. We love this approach.

Written Communication Plays an
Important Role in the Youth-Sport Experience

It's true that verbal communication ought to be effective and occur in a positive tone. The same can be suggested when referencing written communication among all of those involved in youth sport. Given the reality of how youth sport is set up with kids getting dropped off and picked up and coaches tasked with no shortage of moving pieces before, during, and after practices and competition, most communication between parents, coaches, and directors occurs over email or text.

Current norms around texting and vague messages can leave a lot up to the imagination and hinder the intended tone being delivered. In fact, when written communication isn't thoughtful, it can create anxiety, problems, or even unnecessary drama. It's important parents and coaches alike approach all forms of written communication as essential contributors to the overall youth-sport experience rather than just an item on one's to-do list. Let's examine specific instances where we suggest written communication can be a very helpful tool to ensure a joyful youth-sport experience for all involved.

Communicate to Seek Specifics before Competition

Written communication from parent to youth-sport director/coach is essential prior to travel in club sports—often "pay to play" is criticized, but why should a family of an eleven-year-old pay to travel for their child to "develop" (which ought to be the main goal of this time) and then not have a chance to practice/develop through the competition?

I doubt any adults coaching kids want to put them in situations to loath the sport or the team's culture, but we must be honest about how sometimes decisions are made that do just that. The very clubs that preach love of the game and growing the game can mess up when they forget that every child should have the chance to develop. We talk more about playing time in chapter 9, but we will use the topic of playing time to help illustrate how effective written communication can set coaches, parents, and players up for positive competition in the form of meets, games, and tournaments.

We encourage parents to write to sports directors before a tournament and inquire about things such as playing time philosophy and policies related to playing time. Ask if coaches are aware of both and what was communicated to coaches if they did not follow the established policies. If the club has a requirement for parents to not talk to coaches about an issue until twenty-four hours has passed since the event, determine what steps are to be taken by the parent if the coach doesn't adhere to the playing time philosophies and policies that were shared.

Parents should request sport directors and coaches to quantify what "fair and balanced" and other similar wording means when it comes to playing time. In our opinion, general language like this sets people up for conflict because it's not specific enough. The intention isn't cruel on behalf of sport directors. While we understand the hesitancy to promise exact playing time in minutes—as some parents may be on the sideline with a stopwatch—giving generally the same amount of time to everyone (while asking parents for grace if the coach makes small mistakes here and there) is a better way to go. The language "fair and balanced" falls short of perfection because we've seen coaches abuse it. What part of giving a thirteen-year-old ninety minutes to compete in four consecutive soccer games in a two-day tournament while a teammate gets six minutes each half is fair or balanced if both are giving their all and consistently do so? As such, if you're a parent receiving general terms, ask them to be quantified and explain that the reason is simply to know what you're signing up for. Questioning details about an upcoming tournament related to playing time should be required if it's not offered by the coach and club. Understanding important details help parents prepare their children for situations they might find themselves in.

Communicate When Things Go Right

Did your child come home from a practice or competition with a huge smile on their face because of something the coach did or said? If so, it's okay to pass that on. We know firsthand how disheartening it can be to give so much to a youth-sport experience in the role of coach. While we're always open to criticism, it's nice to hear when things are going well, too. We hear a lot of coaches complain about parents, and we think it's mostly because they only hear from the loud minority of parents who might be displeased. In order to keep good people in sport, it's important we let them know what they are doing well and that their efforts are appreciated. When Amanda fires off an email to thank a coach or director she's also sure to say, "Don't worry about writing me back" as the last thing she wants to do is extend their to-do list. The purpose of these emails or texts is to help make someone's day a little better simply by recognizing their efforts and letting them know how their actions positively influenced your child.

Communicate When Things Go Wrong

It's true that there are times when a coach needs to call a parent to discuss the actions of a child, and there are times when a parent needs to call a coach or director to discuss the actions of the adult. This should be expected and invited, but we believe the best way to approach these issues is to send a formal email requesting a time to talk. Then, we believe it's fair to propose an agenda or outline what it is you'd like to discuss. This way, the other adult isn't caught off guard and can be prepared for the conversation when it occurs. We recommend that if you can't have the post-email conversation in person that you do, at the very least, over a video chat. Looking people in the eyes when discussing things as important to us as our kids is really important. There is a reason parent-teacher nights are never held over the phone! Coaches, don't put off a conversation if a child is distracting the group, or displaying a negative attitude or poor teammate traits as they are likely limiting the team's potential and the overall experience of the players. Likewise, parents, don't put off a conversation if your child consistently senses an unwelcome feeling, consistently comes home from sport looking dejected, or is sharing things with you that are concerning.

Be Consistent in Your Communication

A very helpful tip for all coaches and parents is that *consistency is key!* Be consistent with your communication and make sure that everyone receives the same messaging. One time, Richard was coaching youth soccer with a buddy, and both of them had children playing on the team. Of course, they wanted to do everything right, so they hosted a short parents' meeting at the beginning of the season. Each child had to have a parent or caregiver at the meeting, and that person was to share the information with all adults involved in raising the child. One "do" that they covered in the do's and don'ts list was that the parents weren't to coach from the sideline. They could cheer things such as "nice try!" or "good effort!" but they were asked not to respond with anything technical. During the first game, two spouses who were not at the meeting began coaching from the sideline during the game. Richard looked over and noticed other parents were looking at the parents coaching from the sidelines because they knew they were breaking the team rules. At that moment, Richard left the bench with his co-coach and simply walked over and shared with them that they missed the meeting, and their cheering was encouraged, but only if it wasn't tactical or technical. No coaching. The parents were great about it, and they went on to have a really fun season.

It is likely that Richard could have spoken to them after the game and the season would still have been great. But it was important to him that expectations were clear and consistent. He needed to be seen to be fair! Practicing the same principles with parents as coaches do with athletes fosters a trusting, balanced youth-sport community.

Sometimes when parents are coaching, consistency can be difficult due to the dynamics of coaching your own child, your child's friend, or your friend's child! Depending on the coach, the coach's kid can sometimes be given more seemingly favorable treatment in terms of being rewarded in playing time despite effort given, and sometimes the coach's kid is expected to try harder and behave more responsibly than any other child. It truly depends on the coach and their child and the dynamic. If you are a parent–coach, which many of you are as parents are often the volunteers coaching in our communities, it is important that you are consistent and clear in your messaging.

Conflict Resolution Is a Key Component of Effective Communication

While it is our hope that active listening, clear verbal and written communication, and consistent messaging will result in joyful seasons filled with development and an increased love of whatever sport your child loves or that you coach, conflicts will inevitably occur.

Ideally, courageous conversations will resolve these conflicts, and everyone comes out of the experience having learned something and feeling good about centering the child as they sought a resolution. For this to happen, adults must stay calm, be sure to mention positive things as long as they are being genuine, focus on the behavior or situation and not on the person overall, be clear in what your concern is and why it concerns you, and focus on solutions and moving forward rather than being stuck.

When kids have conflicts with teammates, parents should listen for understanding and ask for particular facts, and then they should ask how the other child might explain the situation if they were present. Doing this helps your child understand there are two perspectives involved. Joining your child in name-calling of another child will not help them to push forward through the conflict. Offering to role-play with your child if they choose to address the conflict through a courageous conversation is another helpful way to model mature and solution-focused practices. Parents should also realize there is a high probability that after a moment of venting, their child may immediately feel better and move on from the situation, so the parent shouldn't dwell on it either.

It will pay dividends to remind your children that conflict is a part of life. How you learn from it, navigate it, and move past it can be one of the magical lessons they gain through sport participation. When these sticky moments arise, remind your child that this experience could be a good story in a job interview one day. Remind them that childhood is magical not just for how youth see the world, but for all they learn in such a short time. Focusing on the humility and growth that comes with personal development through conflict helps to normalize vulnerability in all areas of their lives.

Club hopping (moving from one sport club to another as soon as any form of conflict or disappointment arises) is not an ideal approach if we want sport to teach our children good life lessons. You will know as a parent when the environment is not supportive or predictable (tenents to build resilience), and in those situations it may not make sense to resolve conflict and it may make sense to move on. If your personal philosophies don't align with the environment you're in, it may be time to move on.

There is no doubt in our minds that communication has the power to make or break a youth-sport experience. Coaches, athletes, directors, and parents are human, and humans get tired, stressed, and can quickly feel unappreciated or undervalued. Given its important role in the overall youth-sport experience, we implore all involved to approach sport with positive, effective communication. This involves apologizing when one gets it wrong, thanking those who get it right, and initiating courageous conversations when the purpose is to project joy for all.

Positive, effective communication will undoubtedly set everyone up to have the best possible experience in sport while negative, ineffective communication will do the opposite. We ask that you come back to this chapter before every sports season and to think about it before you email your child's coach with a concern. We ask that coach's think about it before each season and feel inspired to help every participant to feel valued as humans and to always speak to them with respect and kindness.

Questions to Ask Yourself

- Do you listen to understand?
- Do you ask probing questions as you stay curious?
- When you communicate with parents about topics such as playing time, are you clear with families? If not, why not?
- Do you reference effective communication practices with your child as it pertains to sport? Could you find ways to do so that are inspiring?
- As a coach, do you teach your athletes the importance of teammates uplifting each other? Could you?

Do's and Don'ts

Do's

- Hold parent meetings at the beginning of the year if you're a coach and ensure communication is a part of this meeting.
- Seek to develop your own communication skills alongside your child or athletes and tell them you're doing so.
- Anonymously survey kids on their experiences related to communication for the purpose of helping to enhance your coaching.
- Parents should check in with their kids to see if they are still enjoying the sport.
- Know that you have agency and can ask questions as parents without being an overbearing parent.

Don'ts

- Berate kids, coaches, or other parents before, during, or after games.
- Coach from the sideline if you're a parent. Cheering is okay, but keep it positive and based on effort.
- Approach a coach when you're angry or unsure if you can approach a conversation calmly and in a solution-focused manner.

Key Takeaways

- Self-assess your own ability in listening, verbal and written communication, conflict resolution, and non-verbal communication. Set specific goals for improvement, as applicable.
- Parents, when looking for a certain club for your child, ask about their communication policies. Make sure club philosophy and policies align with what you think is best for kids.
- Understand that coaches have a lot of power over your child and that it is very important two-way ongoing communication is celebrated in an attempt to provide a joyful experience for your child.
- Initiate courageous conversations with athletes, parents, coaches, and directors as needed and with the intent that they end with everyone feeling better about the situation than prior to the conversation.

PART III

How to Clear the Hurdles

CHAPTER 8

Go the Distance

Set 'Em up for Success

"By failing to prepare, you are preparing to fail."

–Benjamin Franklin

One day, while writing this book, Amanda's cell phone rang during her reserved writing time. Amanda typically doesn't pick up the phone during protected writing time, but the woman who called is someone Amanda admires very much and who she considers a good friend. The woman has a day job outside of coaching but also coaches several youth-sport teams. Additionally, she's a mom to several active children. After Amanda answered, she could tell right away that her friend was concerned about something due to the tone in her voice, and this was immediately confirmed when her friend commented she was calling for advice.

The overall concern Amanda's friend had was that the cost of the sport experience her child was receiving didn't seem to match the value of what she was experiencing. Her friend's concerns included:

- The coaches didn't seem experienced enough to coach the high-level baseball team her son was on.
- The coaches behaved unprofessionally at some out-of-town

tournaments. For example, they would consume alcohol on these trips and would sometimes show up past the time they asked children to arrive.

- The coaches seemed to treat kids differently (less than) who weren't their child's closest friends on the team or the children of their friends.
- The coaches didn't have any coaching certifications or show any overt interest in developing as coaches.
- The coaches would gossip within earshot of players and other parents.
- The coaches gave neutral, general feedback on their son's player evaluation card. Feedback was minimal.
- Every time this mom would speak to the coach in passing, it felt like the coach would reference the fact that her son was lucky to be on the team and only made it due to his athleticism and despite being low skilled.

The mom called to share that it was time to move on from their club and look for something different; something that aligned more with her coaching philosophy and their family's values. She explained that while the price was high, she was privileged enough to afford it. The issue was that the quality of coaching her son was receiving and development opportunities he was provided fell short of what they were paying.

....

Who doesn't love a good plan? There are few areas of our lives that do not benefit from intentional preparation and planning. Let's start with meal planning. It saves money. It saves time. It leads to meals with more nutritional value. It keeps a hangry human from staring into a refrigerator as if inspiration for a quick and delicious meal will jump out at them. The list goes on. Yet, despite knowing its benefits, many people don't meal-plan and many others fail to do so consistently. Perhaps this is because it's labor intensive and requires discipline and creativity. But ask those who prioritize it, and they will share that they never regret their weekly meal plan practice.

If you're a runner, you can list off the benefits of following a training plan leading up to a run. There are similarities to meal planning in that the guesswork is removed. Your brain is free from wondering what to do because you have a plan that you're following. Whether your desire is to complete your first 5K or qualify for the Boston Marathon, there is a plan for you. What works for one athlete may not work the best for others. The magic is in the plan itself. And while you may not have the expertise to create a plan, there are lots out there to serve as a guide for you to meet your goals.

Moving on from food and running, let's think about the importance of a teacher having a solid lesson plan before they attempt to inspire and reach all the students in their class. It's imperative. Amanda was a teacher and professor earlier in her career and taught ages kindergarten through graduate school. She estimates that to plan for a one-hour student-centered lesson where all learners met all objectives, approximately three hours of planning were required. Not unlike meal planning, lesson planning wasn't something that she always looked forward to, but it was something she always appreciated having once she was in front of students and seeing the lesson's impact. On the days she thought she would wing it, she learned that winging it leads to a bad experience…for everyone. Students were less happy, she was less patient, and learning was far from optimal. The good news is that she learned not to wing it very quickly.

We share these examples of where we plan in our everyday lives to reach our goals and to provide more positive experiences and results to outline how impactful planning can be in creating a positive youth-sport experience. Parents, coaches, and sports directors can all support this approach. Coaches can implement planning into their coaching frameworks to best guide and empower youth athletes, and directors can support coaches by ensuring they have a plan for their teams. Finally, parents can educate themselves on the value of preparation and planning in athletic development, so they are poised to ask questions and have the very reasonable expectation that the practices, clinics, and camps they pay for are well-thought-out, intentional, and enjoyable for children.

Most people raising kids who are interested in youth sports or volunteering with community teams do not have a background in physical education, pedagogy (the art and science of teaching), or child and adolescent psychology, and that is perfectly okay and expected! This does not limit your impact on kids' lives or your ability to support them through their youth-sport journey. Feeling a bit overwhelmed while learning about these frameworks is also normal. We suggest you look no further than the Long-Term Athlete Development (LTAD) model. LTAD was introduced in more detail early in the book (page 23) but deserves mentioning here, as we believe that it's an exceptional framework to help sporting directors, coaches, and parents to have a plan. In familiarizing yourself with LTAD, you will be able to plan and deliver a developmentally and age-appropriate program that is enjoyable, while focusing on each child's individual development needs and pace. As a reminder, LTAD is an eight- to twelve-year plan that categorizes development into three- to four-year stages. Each stage of the LTAD framework has annual plans, which are then divided into phases (training, competition, recovery), macrocycles, and microcycles. Often a microcycle is seven days of training or competition that is made up of a series of sessions made up of workout and lesson plans.

In education, when writing curriculum there is something called *vertical alignment*. Vertical alignment ensures that students are progressing from basic knowledge, to concepts, to application, evaluation, etc. In other words, vertical alignment helps ensure that students aren't being taught the same information year after year and, as a result, other content is missed altogether. This is analogous to what LTAD sets out to do in the youth-sport domain. We would never teach an eighth-grade mathematical concept to a five-year-old, and we shouldn't put a five-year-old in a late middle-school-age activity in sport.

The lesson plan or daily practice plan phase is sectioned into a preparation movement/warm-up phase, activities (skills and tactics), and a cool-down phase. All of the plans within the LTAD model require attention to meet the model's objective related to the stage of development. Of course, whenever training is properly planned it includes a reflection and evaluation phase to determine what was effective and what should be adjusted to enhance the training environment and experience. These are practices that Amanda's friend felt her son was missing from his club team.

We highlighted that conversation for several reasons. Today's world is quick to judge and often fails to get the details before drawing its conclusions. Social media keyboard warriors slam sports parents who switch their child from one club to another without knowing the details when, in fact, switching a child from one club to another can be a wise decision, or it can be a poor decision, depending on the circumstance.

There is benefit to youth who persevere through disappointing experiences. But this doesn't mean we purposefully expose our kids to long-term negative and inappropriate coaching in order to increase the number of hurdles we want them to clear in pursuit of gaining thick skin. The parent who phoned Amanda was focused on what is important: her son's experience and his development. At no time did she say her son deserved to be the star or that she doesn't want him to be challenged. She simply, and rightfully, questioned if she was getting a good bang for her buck. And she was also concerned with her son getting the best possible developmental experience during a stage of his childhood he can't get back once it passes.

There is no shortage of adults complaining about youth-sport costs, and there are many who struggle to fund their children's interests in sport. However, there are also many who are willing to keep paying for it without questioning the value they are receiving. The parent in Amanda's story was being reflective, looking at the big picture, and not following the herd when she didn't suspect the herd was on its way to a beautiful watering hole.

We loathe the price of youth sport as it is exclusive, seemingly by design. But we *really* loathe when families who simply want well-rounded kids who gain personal and selfless benefit from playing sport are investing top dollars in programs that simply don't listen to what the research tells us about kids or about youth-athlete development.

If parents are going to be part of the solution to keeping the joy in youth sport, and we believe they can be, they should ask the exact questions that this mom was asking. Ideally, these types of questions are asked prior to choosing a club. These include questions such as:

- What is your club's philosophy on parent–coaches?
- What parameters do parent–coaches have to operate under in terms of playing time decisions by age?
- What type of behavior should we expect coaches to demonstrate?
- What certifications do you require coaches to have before they work with children or adolescents?
- What is your procedure to report when experiences don't align with a club's promises?
- Is your club open to ongoing and thoughtful communication to help keep our kids in this club?

In this chapter, we point out specific areas that require careful planning to deliver optimal experiences and development to the youth who participate in the sport. Sport is often expensive in both invested money and time, and parents should expect high value. After planning for a quality LTAD experience, club directors can deliver high value when they focus on and plan for coach development in three primary areas:

1. Solid understanding of youth psychology, tactics, and technical elements to the sport
2. Community building among team members and families
3. Preparation and recovery for training and competition (athlete-centered approach)

Club Directors Must Ensure Coaches Are Well Prepared

We often come across tweets and comments by coaches with large social media followings implying that parents should simply be grateful for the coaching their children receive. Such posts suggest that parents should never question coaches and they should always assume the coach knows best. They also suggest that kids should be fully content with whatever level of opportunity they receive during youth sport. These posts may get a lot of likes or even go viral, and we cringe at the fact that those liking and retweeting such posts aren't willing to dive a little deeper. Being grateful to volunteers and expecting that they take their volunteer role seriously aren't mutually exclusive positions. Holding volunteers who work with impressionable youth during a critical phase of psychological development to a high standard does not make a parent crazy. It makes them *parents*. Club directors must ensure coaches are well prepared prior to the start of any season under the guise that while coaches ought to be appreciated, minimal expectations of coaches should be high, even if the coaches are volunteers.

Sharing and Expecting Best Coaching Practices

Before any coach gets too far into the Xs and Os of a specific sport, we suggest they first spend time reading about best practices when instructing youth in physically active settings. We recommend additional and equal time is dedicated to understanding some key components of adolescent development. While we recognize a lot of coaches wear multiple hats—parents, professionals, etc.—and perhaps are volunteering, this information will enhance their knowledge base in the parenting space and likely would interest them.

Ideally, club directors or coaching recruiters should have an efficient way to read about best practices in delivering physical activity to youth. A lot of this information comes from quality physical education space, but there is a lot of overlap between this and a lot of coaching development courses. We spoke about specific, positive feedback in the previous chapter (page 174). Positive, specific feedback is a best practice for coaching kids in sport or teaching them in physical education. Other examples of best practices include non-exclusion games. This does not lead to kids becoming soft or unable to handle any disappointment in life, despite that people love getting quick likes or clicks by disseminating such comments. On the flip side, it allows kids to continue practicing.

For example, growing up playing soccer, both Amanda and Richard participated in their fair share of juggling contests. Meant to be fun and offer a bit of competition, there is nothing inherently wrong with juggling contests. But, if the opening activity of every soccer practice is a juggling competition, it is likely that the following will occur: the top jugglers will get to juggle while on display for their teammates to observe while those who really need to practice their juggling skills will be sitting and watching to see who wins. What happens in this instance is that the opportunity to practice (develop) is removed. To help maintain the opportunity to practice, simply deliver the juggling in a task-involved motivational climate (Remember learning about this in chapter 3?). In this instance, tell the kids you're going to time them for sixty seconds and you want them to keep track of how many juggles they can get in total. If the ball drops from their body, they don't have to start over in their count, they just keep counting the juggles based on where they left off. Then, have them remember their total score. After asking them to reflect on what they did well and what they could try to do better, repeat for another sixty seconds. Then, ask who beat their score in the second round. In setting up the juggling exercise in this context, everyone has an opportunity to be challenged and to develop their skill, yet those who are beginners with the skill can still *win*, as they can potentially improve the most the second round. Here, effort, personal best, and development are what is celebrated.

In some sports, people end practice with a penalty shot contest. We've seen this happen in ice hockey, field hockey, soccer, and other sports. Again, it's meant to be upbeat, competitive, and model a game-like experience.

When it happens at the end of every practice, the same thing occurs. Some get multiple chances to develop while others get very limited chances. This is easily fixable by having several other nets set up so if they miss, they simply move on to the other station and continue to practice. In this instance, the winner is the last person remaining at the initial net. Thus, competition is not removed and those who are most competent on that day are still declared the winner, but the opportunity to develop for all remains.

Moveable grid games are games played within a number of square or rectangular grids set up in a row. These grids can range in size but we'll say they are 10 x 10 yards so you have a visual. We love using moveable grid games because they maintain a high level of competition and an upbeat tempo while keeping the focus on the development. In moveable grid games, players and their teammates in the game move clockwise if they are declared the winners at the end of the specified time, and they move counterclockwise if they lose. In the event of a tie, an overtime minute can be added or rock, paper, scissors can be used to declare the winner. These drills are excellent examples of how to maintain opportunity to practice, competitiveness, and game-like conditioning. Other excellent examples are smaller-sided games for younger youth and not moving to large fields until as long as possible.

Physical development isn't the only area in which best practices can enhance experiences and development. We often hear coaches request that players put themselves into groups of three or four as the coach rushes to set up the cones for the next activity. What coaches often miss are cliques shunning individuals to other groups or shy players holding back and then not finding a group on their own. Rather than having the opportunity to get to know kids they might not go to school with, carpool with, or know from previous years, some kids continue to feel like an outsider while others stick close to those they already know. In order to help kids feel included and to facilitate connection, coaches can try to set up cones prior to practice (we realize this isn't always possible) and then call out conditions for groups to randomize them. An example condition could be: "Form a group if your birthday is in the first four calendar months." There are endless ways to group kids that are not performance related. Then as the next small-sided game commences, the kids are in different groups and have the chance to get to know new kids. Overtly teaching young kids that everyone on the team is of equal value and importance is really important, as is telling them no matter their skill or speed, if they aren't an inclusive teammate, they are failing to do their part for the team.

Safe Sport

If you're a parent reading this book, you likely registered your child for sport due to the plethora of benefits you believe that sport can provide your child. These benefits include enhanced physical and social health, resilience, and time management skills. When these things are gained from sport, we can all celebrate! But the reality is that sometimes sport—when done wrong—can harm our kids, and unfortunately it has harmed many. As such, it is absolutely essential that directors require all coaches and those who serve in the background of youth sport to complete safe-sport training to help protect the physical, psychological, and social health of all participants. Abuse awareness and prevention are necessary to keep kids safe and a reasonable expectation given the lofty fees associated with youth sport in North America. Background checks are essential and ought to be one of the minimal requirements to volunteer with youth.

In Canada, "Safe-sport training was developed to help anyone involved in sport—whether you have direct contact with athletes or work in the background—to promote physical, psychological, and social health, in line with the Universal Code of Conduct to Prevent and Address Maltreatment in Sport."[88] The Coaching Association of Canada (CAC) provides a no-cost safe-sport training that meets the minimum standard required by Sport Canada to all of its funded organizations.

In the United States, abuse awareness and prevention courses were created and are provided by the U.S. Center for SafeSport.[89] The U.S.

Center for SafeSport creates their courses to help all involved prevent abuse in sport, to recognize abuse in sport, and to respond when abuse is recognized in sport.

As a coach, and even a volunteer coach, it is your responsibility to become trained in safe sport. As a parent, it is your responsibility to ask directors if coaches are safe-sport certified and to feel inspired to share online safe-sport training sessions with directors in partnership with getting coaches certified. There is no way a youth-sport journey can be joyful if it is not safe.

Sport-Specific Skills and Tactics

Most sports have national federations that create and disseminate excellent coaching development certifications and resources in addition to overseeing all sport governance related to the sport at national and elite levels. Example national federations include Canada Soccer, USA Soccer, USA Field Hockey, Hockey Canada, USA Wrestling, etc. The issue is not that these resources do not exist; rather, it's that coaches aren't often required to earn a certification to coach at certain clubs. Some sports require all coaches to take at least a beginning coaching course offered through the national federation, while others do not. In the event that a national federation does not require coaches to complete a level 1 coaching course before coaching, sport directors can make this a requirement at the club level and would be wise to do so.

Amanda's two oldest daughters have developed a passion for field hockey in recent years, and Amanda helps coach the club's kindergarten group. Since she didn't play field hockey, she took it upon herself to register and complete the USA level I field hockey coaching course. She was thrilled with this experience. She learned some priority tactical messaging that USA Field Hockey wanted to see during the early stages of development, learned basic skill cues for coming skills, and learned the coaching philosophies encouraged throughout this book, such as prioritizing development. Amanda also discovered that enjoyment over winning or other short-term gains was not only validated, but it was also requested by USA Field Hockey. Since becoming certified as a level 1 coach, Amanda references the resource when planning weekly practices. If national federations are investing in delivering quality sport programming including coaching development resources and certifications, it's up to directors, coaches, and parents to help ensure the information is trickling down to those working directly with kids to keep them in the sport due to the quality sport experience they are receiving. In other words, when choosing a sports club for your child, parents can ask if their coaches are required to complete coaching certifications. Coaches can ask directors to cover any associated costs for such development even if it's not required.

Skill and tactical coaching development is really essential to help youth progress through the stages of the Long-Term Athlete Development (LTAD) model. It helps educate well-intended parents who are willing to step up and coach their kids and their peers on how to coach that particular age of the athlete. Oftentimes, these parents will be people who haven't played the sport very much or at all or who played the sport several decades ago and the sport has evolved so much that they are no longer well versed in the sport. There is no shame for a coach to need to learn new things or to coach a group who may even be more skilled than them; however, they have to be prepared in order to be effective.

We share these few categories to help club directors, coaches, and parents identify some best practices that will help add value to the youth-sport experience. We believe that youth sports should enhance lives and that a parent is not overbearing to expect clubs to prioritize these areas of coach development. If a volunteer doesn't have degrees in physical education or isn't a developed coach, they may not think of these simple ways to develop every child. Thus, clubs are setting well-intentioned people who are willing to serve their community up for failure in many ways when failure is defined as kids not wanting to play the sport due to the lack of fun or opportunity to develop.

Community-Building Is Essential for a Positive Sport Experience

Another area that, when prioritized, will serve every club well is community building. When coaches build positive, supportive, and joyful communities, players and their families will feel as though they belong to something special. When we talk about community building, we want to be clear that we do not mean hokey team-building activities that do little to nothing to create meaningful connection. Rather, community building takes time, is well-thought-out, and is absolutely worth the time. To help us make our point, let's think about the following two scenarios:

Scenario A

Coach is excited to work with her new team. She's nervous because an important tournament is scheduled in a month. She's a new coach in the area, and the girls are all joining this team from a variety of other clubs. While she knows it's important to get to know the players, her priority is making sure they are in tournament shape in terms of skill and fitness. Ice breakers can wait, because she gets a vibe from the club director that, with the talent on this team, results are important to the club.

Scenario B

Coach is excited to work with her new team. She's nervous because an important tournament is scheduled in a month. She's a new coach in the area, and the girls are all joining this team from a variety of other clubs. She knows it's important to get to know the players and for the players to get to know each other; her priority for her first month is helping the girls feel physically and emotionally safe while they improve and get to know each other. She works with the girls to build a list of non-negotiables in terms of team culture. Examples that emerged were: no cliques, making sure the girls make an effort to form different groups and work with different partners in various drills, no gossip or snarky behavior toward one another, etc.

Coach felt great about her plan for the first month and she has the support of the club director. Both know that teams that love each other are more likely to win big championships rather than teams that are too focused on internal competition within the team.

We argue that in order for youth to have joyful experiences in sport, they must feel as though they belong. If your child doesn't have a sense of belonging within a club, you're not a crazy parent for exploring other options. In fact, researchers at Stanford University created The Belonging Project—a broadly engaged, multidimensional effort to promote emotional health and personal well-being through connection with the communities of their campus and beyond—as a result of the clear evidence that those who are in distress and feel disconnected from a larger community are more likely to experience poor health outcomes, including impulsive or self-harmful behavior.[90]

Given the natural heightened levels of impulsiveness in an adolescent brain, adults should be making every effort to provide inclusive spaces that foster belonging. If you're wondering how the hell to foster a sense of belonging among a group of kids, we're thrilled you asked.

- Coaches can ask their players to make an effort to get to know everyone on the team. This is a huge request by the way, and it takes effort, particularly in larger communities where kids may not go to school with the kids they play sports with.
- Parents can ask their children to shine their light on at least two different teammates every time they go to practice or a game. Examples of doing this include calling out a positive comment to a teammate who demonstrates a clear improvement, or who learned a new skill before others, or who attempted something very difficult. Parents should be certain to follow up at the end of practice with their child to see who they shined their light on and how they did so.

- Ongoing and clear communication is essential. Check in with folks! Directors and coaches are encouraged to ask families periodically if they are happy. Ask specifically if their child feels as though they belong.
- Have players stand in a circle at the end of every practice and game and ask each player to give a positive compliment to a teammate. This type of practice can help youth feel seen by their peers. A special shout out goes out to Coach Dawn Callahan who is the varsity field hockey coach at Parkway West High School in St. Louis, Missouri. Coach Dawn's use of this tactic helped Amanda's kids feel welcomed and to meet new friends while playing in Coach Dawn's middle school program.
- When coaches notice players being exclusive or unkind to a teammate, don't be shy to talk to them. Ask them why they did what they did, what they could do differently, and how a more uplifting approach would not only make everyone feel better, it would positively contribute to the team's culture. Conversely, when coaches or parents see beautiful examples of inclusion, they can make an effort to compliment the behavior.
- All sport directors can have a one-question survey at the end of season and ask parents and athletes to rank on a five-point scale how much they felt they belonged to the team and the club. An open-ended space for suggestions is also encouraged to help gather ideas or to understand the lived experience of the kids in the club.

It takes a very skilled coach to correct such behavior in ways that don't shame an adolescent as that's not the intention. The intention is that players recognize their role in creating a community of belonging. We love to share with adolescents that goofing up and testing boundaries is their job, just as it's our job as adults to give them appropriate feedback on their behavior.

> "A DEEP SENSE OF LOVE AND BELONGING IS AN IRREDUCIBLE
> NEED OF ALL PEOPLE. WE ARE BIOLOGICALLY, COGNITIVELY,
> PHYSICALLY, AND SPIRITUALLY WIRED TO LOVE, TO BE LOVED,
> AND TO BELONG. WHEN THOSE NEEDS ARE NOT MET, WE DON'T
> FUNCTION AS WE WERE MEANT TO. WE BREAK. WE FALL APART.
> WE NUMB. WE ACHE. WE HURT OTHERS. WE GET SICK."
>
> ~BRENÉ BROWN

We suspect investing in a culture of belonging will leave people perceiving that their child is in the right place. And, directors, if you're working with coaching to create such a culture, you should educate potential families of this fact. If you're a parent who is able and willing to pay for club sport, belonging is a topic worthy of research when choosing the club who will receive your payments. It's impossible for kids to have fun in sport when they feel like an outsider in a group, and a lack of fun is the number one reason kids quit sport.

Safe Training and Injury Prevention in Joyful Sport

The final area that we identify as of critical importance when thinking of high value in youth sport is related to athlete safety in the context of injury prevention. Amanda's friend Ann once called her when her son was nine years old and scheduled to play seven basketball games in one weekend. Ann shared that he was curled up in a ball and didn't want to go play basketball when only several months prior he was extremely passionate about it. His game schedule was clearly not age appropriate, and it was creating feelings of burnout. Amanda shared with Ann that it was also worrisome given the load on a growing body. Seven hours of physical activity throughout a weekend certainly can be good for kids, particularly if they are outside doing a combination of riding bikes, climbing trees, and playing tag. But, when all seven hours involve the same movements in a single sport setting, it sets kids up for overuse injuries.

Erica Suter, author of the *Strong Female Athlete: A Female Athlete Guide to Reduce Injury, Improve Performance, and Increase Confidence* works with growing girls in age-appropriate ways to prepare their bodies for the load they receive in competitive sport. Suter shares, "For parents looking for the right club and coach for their child, it is important to ask the coach their philosophy on load management and recovery. Most youth athletes play more than ten months of organized sport per year, which is dipping into the realm of overtraining and overscheduling. A coach who promotes recovery and takes care of the physical development of the child is a coach to seek out and hold onto. Parents must be direct and clear and hold coaches accountable. After all, they're the ones paying, so the coach must have the best interest of the health of the child in mind and be well versed on child development and the stages of growth and maturation."

By now, you are fully aware that kids play sports to have fun. No one is having fun when they are too injured to participate or are (unfortunately) choosing to participate while injured. Quality youth-sport experiences are led by adults who prepare in ways that acknowledge overuse injuries and burnout are real. While we recognize that strength and conditioning coaches who specialize in youth development likely aren't coaching local teams, we can also learn from them.

It's no secret that youth sports are costly in terms of finances, time, and energy. Who your child spends a great deal of time with during their formative years should never be a decision made lightly. Parents, it's okay to question your investment and coaches and directors who have kids' best interests at heart will welcome you to do so. While no one should feel entitled or expected to develop into a professional athlete as a result of youth sport, we should all agree a reasonable minimal expectation is an overall positive experience for kids. We think that if every participant in youth sport is treated with respect, feels a sense of belonging, and has the opportunity to develop that parent and caregivers will be more than pleased with the return on their investment. Youth sport should support and nurture kids and provide ample opportunities for personal growth and development. This development should occur while collecting beautiful memories and ought to leave them with a belief that they can overcome challenges.

Questions to Ask Yourself

- Is my child enjoying their sport experience?
- Is my child receiving an opportunity to develop?
- Does the coach help teach the kids how to be inclusive and supportive teammates?
- Is this club, team, or coach creating a culture of belonging?
- Do the coaches invest in their own learning and does their learning come to life in their actions?
- Am I surveyed about my child's experience in the sport?
- Is my child asked about their experiences in the sport?
- Are coaches supported by the director?
- Does the director hold coaches to high expectations?

Do's and Don'ts

Do's

Parents:

- Check in to make sure that sport environment your child is in brings them joy and develops their skills and love of the sport.
- Ask questions before choosing the club for you.

Coaches:

- Seek development opportunities and don't be shy to ask

directors or clubs to fund them.

• Focus on a culture of belonging and building community so that every participant feels seen and valued.

Directors:

• Make a list of expectations that you think families should have if they register with your club. Ask if that list matches what you provide and adjust accordingly.

• Model a growth mindset in your approach. Be reflective, plan in detailed ways, and adjust as needed to ensure a high value comes with the high price tag of youth sport.

Don'ts

Parents:

• Feel bad for questioning where your money is going.

• Keep your child in a situation that is stealing their love of sport and that is not age appropriate.

Coaches:

• Assume that coaching the way you were coached is the best way to coach.

• Don't create an overly competitive environment at ages and stages of development that will stunt improvement and steal joy.

Directors:

• Assume that mediocre understanding of adolescent psychology, coaching in physically active settings, or creating a culture of belonging are easy or on the minds of most coaches who sign up to coach at your club.

• Do the same thing year after year unless numbers are growing at incredible rates.

Youth Sport Season Planning Checklist

Pre-Season Checklist	
O	Coaching Development: LTAD
O	Coaching Development: Technical and Tactical
O	Coaching Development: Adolescent Psychology
O	Coaching Development: Safe Sport
O	Coaching Development: Training and Competition Physical Safety/Overuse/Injury
O	Coaches and parents understand LTAD
O	Coaches complete equivalent to level 1 coaching courses in the sport they are coaching. These are often inexpensive and offered online. If funds prohibit volunteers from completing the course, organizations should cover the cost. This should be non-negotiable.
O	If safe sport is not a component of the coaching course, coaches should also complete a safe-sport training.
O	Mandatory parent/caregiver meeting
O	Understanding of how to prepare the body for training and competition and how to recover properly.
In-Season Checklist	
O	Community Building
O	Ongoing Reflection: Physical Safety/Overuse
O	Ongoing Communication: Document and Identify Themes
Postseason Checklist	
O	Survey re: Injuries/Burnout
O	Survey re: Enjoyment
O	Survey re: Practices and How They Align to LTAD
O	Survey re: How Coaching Behaviors Align or Don't Align with Literature in Adolescent Psychology

CHAPTER 9

Put Me in, Coach

Prioritize Development over Winning

"Your moral imperative as a youth coach is to make sure
the kid leaves practice having had the time of his or her
life playing the sport."

–Anson Dorrance, head women's soccer coach,
University of North Carolina, on
The Reformed Sports Project podcast

The quote that kicked off this chapter was shared on Nick Buono-
core's *The Reformed Sports Project* podcast. Amanda was invited to
be a guest on the podcast to talk about the importance of building up every kid to help them take ownership and feel empowered in
their sport journey. In preparation, she decided to binge-listen to previous episodes during the eight-hour round-trip journey from St. Louis to
Kansas City where she presented at a U.S. youth soccer conference. She
was a bit nervous when Anson Dorrance was introduced, because she is
always nervous when those who coach the most elite athletes offer advice at
the grassroots level, especially if that someone is named Anson Dorrance.

When Amanda graduated from undergrad and her college soccer days
more than twenty-five years ago, she embarked on a career of teaching and
coaching. At the time, a lot of soccer coaches would read about Dorrance's
methods at the powerhouse, powder-blue Chapel Hill program and try to
apply them to girls during their middle and high school years.

Why should parents and youth coaches think critically before taking
the advice elite college and professional coaches offer and applying it to

youth? In research, there is something called *external validity*. External validity is the ability to form conclusions from a population and apply them to others while expecting the same results. Even though Amanda didn't understand the concept of external validity until graduate school, she felt uneasy about applying the same coaching methods that were documented as contributing to the UNC Chapel Hill women's soccer program's success to a JV soccer team. For example, too much competition within a team could hinder team results during the delicate stages of adolescence, and the competitive cauldron could run a lot of kids out of the sport if applied too early to players who are not as developed in the Long-Term Athlete Development (LTAD) model.

Luckily, approximately thirteen minutes into the episode Amanda was put at ease. While sharing the importance of teaching competitiveness and fostering an ultra-competitive environment, Dorrance criticizes youth coaches and parents who are overly competitive. Yes, you read that correctly. Anson Dorrance—the creator of the competitive cauldron at the dynasty UNC women's soccer program—said that there are far too many overly competitive parents and youth coaches.

What are overly competitive parents and youth coaches? In our opinion, these are the adults around youth sport who:

- Don't really realize the children they coach are NOT professional athletes.
- Are in a hurry to rank kids based primarily on size, speed, and strength.
- Are narrow minded about altering these rankings as kids continue to develop and mature physically at different rates.
- Focus on short-term results rather than development of each player on the team.

How is an overly competitive youth coach or parent easily identified? They are typically the ones who will choose to bench players—also known as those who will "shorten their bench"—or are the parents who are completely comfortable with some members of the team being benched.

Dorrance suggests that the only time that wins should factor into things such as playing time are at the Olympic development level for around fourteen years of age or older. Let's break that down for those of you who aren't familiar with the soccer landscape in the United States. The Olympic Development Program (ODP) is the high-performance talent identification program for highly skilled youth soccer players in the United States. The purpose of ODP soccer is "to identify and provide opportunities for high-potential players, facilitate their development, expose them to the next level of their chosen pathway, and motivate their pursuit of excellence."

At this point of the podcast, Amanda activated the cruise control feature of her minivan so as not to drive too fast due to her excitement. She was so excited and relieved that Dorrance was sharing this message to the masses. He pointed out that the mission of the youth-sport coach "is to make sure the kid is having the time of his or her life and that they can trust adults to protect them, to keep them safe, and to make sure they are enjoying life."

If someone with twenty-one NCAA D-I championship titles encourages parents and coaches not to let youth sports get too competitive too soon, shouldn't we at least consider it?

....

It wasn't long after Amanda heard Dorrance on *The Reformed Sports Project* podcast when someone called her from a tournament because their daughter was benched in a sporting event. By "benched" we mean that the child played about two to three minutes in each of the two halves of the game. No one spoke to the child about it or explained why she was benched. In fact, no adult even acknowledged it. Nope. The parents were left with a disappointed child who asked, "Don't they know we're kids? I mean, I'm eleven."

Look, we understand that life isn't fair, and people can't always get what they want. We also understand that sport can be a terrific place for youth to learn about perseverance and humility. But is it necessary to teach kids this lesson when you invite them to a tournament and then do not play them or talk to them about it? Moreover, when sporting clubs have rules in place that forbid parents to discuss the situation with the coach until after twenty-four hours have passed, the child is not the center of the experience; one is left to wonder how to approach a situation like this in a tournament setting.

In chapter 7 (page 157), we told you about a former athlete who had a ninth-grade son who was confused as to why he lost his starting position and curious why the coach didn't communicate with him. Like that mom, this one who called Amanda from the tournament did not care if her child was a shining sports star. Nah, she loves her kid because her kid is a good human not because of her potential in sport. She called because she couldn't understand why an adult version of sport—or, as Dorrance would call it, an overly competitive version of sport—was placed on an eleven-year-old (and several of her teammates). After recognizing that she had to sign a form at the start of the season saying that she would not speak to the coach for twenty-four hours, the mother felt confused and annoyed at how to respond since there was another game in fourteen hours. After brainstorming with Amanda, the mom tabled her negative feelings and focused on being a supportive and uplifting parent. She would email the coach when the tournament was over to schedule a courageous conversation but, for now, being present for her child was the number one goal.

Often, stories like this one are shared as black-and-white situations. But any reasonable person who is involved knows these issues are much more nuanced. For example, these coaches are awesome people who taught the child a lot about the sport. They planned thoughtful practices, and the good they did for the child will never go unnoticed or unappreciated. The girl looked up to them as role models and cared for them very much. The mom shared that she respects them for their countless positive traits and has no desire to vilify them or be angry with them because she disagrees with them about the topic of playing time or with the twenty-four-hour no-communication rule.

We will never know for sure why a few kids on this team, like many youth-sport teams across North America, consistently didn't get the same opportunity as others. But if we were betting people, we'd place our money on one word: **fear.**

Fear of losing the game. Fear of trying something different. Fear of upsetting kids (and their parents) who normally get to play 90 percent of the game. Novelist Karen Walker-Thompson gave a phenomenal TED Talk about fear called "What Fear Can Teach Us." In it, Walker-Thompson shares a part of *Moby Dick* to help illustrate how even though we all have both logical and creative parts to our brain, the creative side can sometimes overpower our logical or scientific side and lead to unintended bad consequences. In *Moby Dick*, the captain of the whaleship *Pequod* found himself and fellow whalers in three lifeboats after a whale hit *Pequod* and caused it to capsize.

Rather than choose one of two options that would most likely lead him and his crew to safety, the captain chose the third option, which was the route farthest away. The captain knew that this third option would only be a plausible one if specific winds aided the lifeboats. Yet he chose this option because option one led to an island that had vivid rumors of cannibalism, while option two led to an island in a location where massive storms were feared.

In other words, the captain made a choice to head to the third island, located farthest away and the option that came with the most risk, because the images of cannibalism and a capsizing lifeboat were so vivid that they overpowered the most logical choice.

As Walker-Thompson points out in her talk, we've all been there. I mean, who among us hasn't flown and experienced imagery of the plane crashing? Despite the fact that traveling by plane is statistically safer than traveling by car or train, many of us have a detailed visualization of crashing with the onset of turbulence, yet we don't report these feelings when getting in our cars each day. This is a simple example of how the artistic part of our brain can quiet the scientific part of our brain.

The point of sharing the thesis of the TED Talk is to help you understand that while fear can teach us positive things, such as leaving a situation when your intuition tells you that danger could be near, it can also overpower logic and lead us to make decisions that don't make sense and can be damaging—decisions such as benching kids age seven to age fifteen and denying them the chance to develop while stealing joy from sport.

It is difficult for us to imagine that youth coaches who bench kids want to hurt them. It is far more likely that the coaches benched kids because they were scared to lose the game. It is likely they didn't have faith in the players they benched, and they haven't been asked to really think critically about the playing time issue. Coaches have communicated with us over the years that sometimes they feel pressure from a sport director to win while others fear parents will take their kids to another club if the team doesn't win a championship. While these reasons may not excuse the act of benching youth in sport, it does help to explain it.

Theodore Roosevelt's quote, "It's not the critic who counts," hangs in the main hallway of Amanda's house. Every family member must pass it multiple times a day to get around their home and out the front door. It's hung there to remind her and her family not to be overly critical of those we come in contact with. Not our teachers. Not our bosses. Not our coaches. Not our colleagues. It's easy to be a hyper critical person of those serving in our communities, so Amanda hung this to help remind her and her family to navigate the world's challenges with empathy and understanding.

Amanda shared with the frustrated mom that a few activities could help her and her child move forward in the tournament. First, she suggested they zoom out from the experience and identify all the positives that the coaches have taught the child. She reminded the mom that the coaches are volunteers who weren't certified educators who gained competence in child psychology and pedagogy through formal training, and to remind her child of this. The mom was also encouraged to validate her daughter's feelings. I mean, the kid totally had a right to feel pissed off.

This story ended well as the playing time issue was regulated the next day and the child, with supportive parents, was able to put it in her rearview mirror. But it could have gone much differently and literally resulted in kids quitting because, in case you didn't know this (inserting sarcasm here), eleven-year-olds play sports to play not to sit on a bench.

We hope this chapter helps clear murky waters around playing time in youth sport. As with all chapters in this book, we aren't trying to vilify coaches who demonstrate practices we don't agree with. If you currently grant some kids a lot more opportunity to practice their skills in competitive situations than others, we don't want you to feel judged. We want you to reflect and invite you to be open to a different way that could positively influence all aspects of your team, ranging from fun to development to success. We hope that readers will become uncomfortable with terms such as *starters*, *role players*, and *bench players* when they are normalized at the youth level, as somewhere down the line our own opinions shifted from feelings of comfort to discomfort with these terms.

In this chapter, we examine various issues around playing time and how benching kids can—at best—hurt them, hinder team chemistry, and hinder team results and—at worst—how it can lead to kids quitting sport altogether. We'll also explore how kids who are not benched can be stunted when large playing time disparities at the youth level occur. On the other hand, we imagine what a youth-sport experience would look like when the focus is on development and fostering love of the sport for each participant, and how all can thrive when fully supported by caring and knowledgeable coaches and parents. The impact this can have on individuals extends far past their adolescent and teenage years—it changes how they think about themselves, challenges, and opportunities through adulthood.

Disadvantages to Rewarding Early Developers

Coaches and directors sometimes reward early developers over late developers, and this can hinder the development of players who fall into both of these categories. In this book, when we use the term *early developers*, we are discussing a group of children who are fast and strong at the young ages—they are physically *more* developed. The term *late developers* is applied to those children who are slower and not as strong—they are physically *less* developed during the early years of sport participation. This appearance of early and late development can also be due to age difference within the age category. Depending on when the age cut off is for a particular activity, kids can be up to twenty-three months older than others. Most coaching education courses advise against playing time disparity and against playing early developers more than late developers during the early years of sport participation. However, as we've explained, coaching education is often not required at the local youth levels. And, even when coaching education is required and shares sound messaging, it is not always applied by the youth coach.

Let's look to education to help illustrate the absurdity of benching late developers over early developers. For example, imagine a fourth-grade class is divided into two groups. The teacher tells some of the ten-year-olds that they have forty minutes to complete a math assessment, while the other group has ten minutes to complete the assessment.

An *assessment* is a task that determines the child's understanding of the material covered, and its purpose is to help guide the teacher's instruction. A math quiz given in the middle of the unit is known as a *formative assessment* and helps the teachers to identify what material needs to be revisited and who might need extra support with certain concepts. Assessments parallel sport in the form of games, meets, and competitions because youth have the opportunity to demonstrate their skills and game sense in such authentic environments. But let's get back to our fourth-grade math class.

Those grasping the unit material easily are placed in the forty-minute group, while those struggling a bit are placed in the ten-minute group. The students who are assigned forty minutes to complete the math assessment are reassured when they are told that they can use their books as a resource. They are also encouraged to look over their work and to fix any mistakes they find while doing so. Students in the forty-minute group are also told that if they answer most of the material correctly, they will receive an extra five minutes to complete the next assessment.

Conversely, the students in the ten-minute group are told that if their assessments aren't perfect at the end of ten minutes, they will only get five minutes to prove what they know on the next assessment. They are not permitted to use their books as a resource and will not have time to review their work because they will be rushing to complete the assessment. Also, they know that if they make mistakes, they might get less than ten minutes to complete the next assessment.

Have you caught on to the insanity yet? Of course, educators would never put youth with lower confidence in a testing situation that is more challenging and includes more constraints. However, this is exactly what coaches do when they give late developers far less time to practice their skills in authentic environments, such as games, meets, and tournaments, than early developers. Early developers can hone skills and take chances without risk of being pulled, while late developers are expected to be perfect or else they will be yanked from the game. We are well aware that math class is not a sport, but either way, a ten-year-old is an early adolescent and conditions must be age appropriate no matter the domain.

The only thing that is assured in sport at all levels is that mistakes will happen. No youth should feel nervous about making a mistake because the consequence will be that they'll get even less opportunity in the future. The benefit that early developers often gain due to much more playing time gives them an additional advantage than just being fast and strong at young ages. While this might not seem like a bad thing to those of you pondering, *Why not develop those who are faster and stronger?*, many do not realize that during and post puberty, all bets are off as to identifying who will be the fastest and strongest. If you chase the late developers out of the game, you're decreasing your pool of players by neglecting those who very well can become the fastest and strongest later.

You actually don't want your child to peak in fourth grade. Early developers who are recipients of maximum playing time may lead them to believe they are better than their peers who aren't getting played much at all. In other words, they haven't really earned the confidence they carry. We've mentioned Steve Magness, author of *Do Hard Things* and a world-renowned expert on performance, previously in this book when we share his definition of true or real confidence. Magness explains that false confidence can lead to an array of problems and can hinder true confidence from being developed. It should be noted that giving preferential treatment to early developers increases their likelihood to develop false confidence. For example, when early developers finally do meet adversity—because every athlete will at some point—they may not be equipped to handle it because they haven't had to confront challenges or disappointments in sport up until this point.

In our own experiences, we've watched an early developer sob after a game because they weren't the chosen person to take a penalty shot. We've watched players stomp their feet when they are subbed off. And, we've coached kids or observed kids pout when they aren't placed in their favorite position. We suspect you've observed some of these behaviors too, all the while the late developers are expected to be grateful for any opportunity at all to be *team players* and to cheer from the sidelines. Keep in mind that these double standards and expectations are often placed on children and adolescents, which only makes it more disturbing.

Richard was an early developer and can speak from experience how it stunted his long-term athletic development as a soccer player. His early gift was his speed, something Amanda is still waiting to receive as a gift, but given that she's pushing fifty years old, it's unlikely to happen. His youth soccer experience consisted often of a coach yelling for teammates to "send him," which meant long balls were lofted down the field for Richard to receive and then finish by scoring. Richard was a youth soccer scoring machine. He never had a need to develop a great touch on the ball or any creativity in his decision-making. He knew his role and he did it. He did it well, even earning an all-star conference scoring title while in college. Although his speed was fast enough to earn him a professional tryout in the North American soccer league, it is also what ended his career and professional soccer aspirations. Because Richard was so fast as a kid, his skills and self-described lack of decision-making ended his soccer career. His passion, his drive, his work ethic, and the fact that he would run through a wall for any coaches weren't enough to overcome the gaps in his development.

Now, let's compare that to Canadian soccer great, Alphonso Davies. Davies, for those of you living under a rock, is the best soccer player ever to come out of Canada on the men's side. In a recent FIFA World Cup profile of Davies, who holds the record as the fastest player in the top level in Germany, it was shared—unsurprisingly—that Davies was the fastest youth player on the fields in Edmonton, Alberta, where he grew up playing soccer. His coach frustrated him because he refused to apply the "send him" coaching tactic to Davies's team. He requested that Davies play with the ball, engage his teammates, and demonstrate creative decision-making. Davies is now a global icon partly because his youth coach placed his development above him scoring goals and winning games.

We believe that rewarding early developers with playing time does not encourage them to hone their skills as much as if they received equal playing time to their peers. As such, those late developers who choose to keep plugging away instead of quitting sport due to a lack of playing time will often pass their early developer peers during puberty. We're not alone in our thoughts. Dr. Colin Higgs, professor emeritus from Memorial University, Newfoundland, conducted a meta-analysis (an examination of many studies) of related literature, and he has extensively presented on the sport-related concept: the black box of puberty. The black box of puberty was aptly named because it starkly represents the fact that predicting one's athletic ability or potential after puberty cannot be done accurately before puberty or in its early stages. Dr. Higgs's conclusions[91] are as follows:

1. Early developers have an age-group competition advantage in sports where size, speed, and strength are important. Mesomorphs (those who have more muscle and modest amounts of body fat) on average are the earliest to experience adolescent growth. This can lead late developers to drop out of sport since they are generally smaller and weaker, and sport can be more challenging for them during the early adolescent years.

2. Late developers who don't quit out of frustration when they are compared to and treated differently than their early-developing peers will linger in the "skill-hungry" Learn-to-Train stage of Long-Term Athlete Development (LTAD) model for a longer duration than early-developers. (See page 23 for a full description of the LTAD model.) This allows them to hone skills for a longer period of time. Dr. Higgs speculates that the longer, slower adolescent growth spurt may be less disruptive to skill adjustments required by changing limb length than the generally shorter and faster growth spurt of early developers.

3. Late developers who stay in the sport through adolescence often overtake their early-developing peers in the long run. As a result, with the loss of dominance toward the end of adolescence, early developers may drop out of sport later in adolescence. They aren't used to not being the star or one of the go-to players, and they haven't gained the resilience due to always being preferred to their late-developing peers up until this point.

4. Regarding gender differences, late-developing males are more likely to drop out early in adolescence and early-developing males drop out late, while early-developing females are more likely to drop out of sport than their late-developing peers. This is likely because when males gain weight and muscle,

the added strength is perceived as beneficial to their sport participation, and often this is true; whereas when females experience rapid changes in development such as weight gain, breast development, and wider hips, it is not perceived as helpful for sport participation, and often this is also true.

Lauren Fleshman, a fifteen-time NCAA All-American and five-time NCAA champion, is the author of recent bestseller *Good for Girl* where she chronicles issues females face as athletes in a male-created and male-dominated space like sport. We strongly recommend that everyone reads this book to learn about how the onset of puberty affects female athletes. In fact, coaches and parents alike would benefit from understanding this seldom discussed but incredibly important body of research.

Supporting Development with Tiered-Teams and Training Levels

Early vs. late onset of adolescence is not the only issue that is worthy of exploration regarding the topic of playing time. Youth coaches and sport directors sometimes perceive the variance in skill, strength, and speed to be far greater than it actually is within a team. With the exception of school-based teams during the early years, most teams are tier based or leveled. In other words, players are placed on teams through a series of tryouts where participants go through a series of stations and small-sided games. Sports that have tier-based teams likely include soccer, basketball, lacrosse, field hockey, volleyball, ice hockey, etc. Leveled sports are those that have objective measures in place to place the child in the appropriate environment. Leveled sports include individual sports, such as swimming and gymnastics.

The reason tiered-teams and leveled-sports exist is to give participants a positive experience that strikes the perfect balance of challenge and success or proficiency. Related to motivation, youth are in the best environment to develop, all other things being equal, when they experience a perfect blend of challenge and success. If kids aren't challenged, they are not motivated, and if they are challenged at inappropriately high levels, it can leave them feeling unsuccessful and frustrated, which will also stunt motivation. So, we agree tiering teams is the most logical way to set kids up for a positive learning environment, and it's important for all levels and tiers to be on the development continuum.

Parents and coaches should support the environment where their child can experience this sweet spot of 80 percent success rate. This means that quantifying rules and systems should be in place to inform where youth athletes are placed. When Richard worked with a tennis organization, a leveled sport, they followed this rule of thumb. If a player wins four in a row, they should move on to the next level, but if they won two and lost one, or won three and lost one, they should stay at their current level.

Tiered teams should be chosen in an objective setting. It is really important that as much subjectiveness is removed as possible. At the St. Louis Lady Cyclones hockey club, unbiased evaluators (individuals who do not coach or know the players) observe the girls' tryouts, and their data is used to form the teams. No parent–coach is permitted to participate in the evaluations, and coaches are assigned teams after the teams are chosen. Additionally, kids are given pinnies to wear over their practice jerseys and asked to remove any name tags from helmets. We endorse this approach, as it results in youth being placed in the most appropriate environment for them to develop with others of similar skill and experience.

Sometimes people will "club hop" (move from one club to another) if their child does not make the highest tier team because they want their child to compete at the highest tier. Depending on the size of one's town or city, there may be enough options to make this happen. While sometimes a club switch is the best thing to do for a child due to an uneducated and misinformed coach or toxic team culture, other times it is not the answer. Switching clubs can be short sighted, as a lot of benefit can come from their child gaining confidence and developing as a leader on the second team. Before club hopping, parents should ask themselves why they are doing it. Do you truly believe they were placed on the wrong team, or are *you* disappointed that your child didn't make the top team? If it's the latter, we suggest that you step back and consider that being the strongest and most experienced player on the second team might lead to a better experience and higher confidence than being the least experienced and skilled player on the top team. While it's impossible to determine which is best for a player on the "bubble," it's important that parents don't assume the top team is the best team for development or enjoyment.

Once tiers or levels are determined, every youth participating should receive equal time to develop. Anson Dorrance asks naysayers, "Why wouldn't I want to develop every soccer player that I recruit to North Carolina?" Great question! If you haven't watched a UNC Chapel Hill women's soccer game recently, you really ought to. You will notice that Dorrance subs up to seven field players at a time. That's not a typo. *Seven.*[92] You'll also notice that the formation or shape players take on the field varies throughout the game depending on what players are on at a given time. Dorrance explains that he makes sure everyone gets time because it is his duty to develop each player that he has recruited. He rightfully questions college coaches who recruit players and then choose not to play or develop them, just as we question youth coaches who pick a team and then choose not to develop all players.

When you focus on developing the entire team, you are not only increasing the team's chances of success due to a more all-around competent team, but you are also building team chemistry. You are preventing unnecessary cliques between those who play a lot and those who receive little time to play at all. In an environment like this, the team is more likely to remain the focus rather than individual accolades.

Objectivity and Team Selection

Maya Angelou famously said, "When you know better, you do better." We share this quote here to reinforce our no-shame approach. If you're not choosing tiered teams objectively or if your athletes' playing time is skewed within a tiered team, you're not alone. It would be naive of us to say that you could simply start changing philosophies around tryouts and playing time and your life will be smooth sailing from here on out. We're aware that people don't like change, and that sometimes adults really want to prioritize winning championships over development at the youth level and this can lead to short-sighted actions.

But if you would like to try something different and gently propose or shift your current club's approach, we suggest that you consider the following actions:

1. Hold a club-wide meeting prior to tryouts in your tiered sport and let everyone know what criteria kids will be assessed on and that data will be collected by unbiased (non-parents, non-coaches) professionals. If this isn't possible, do the best you can, and be clear as to who will be collecting data during the assessments. Moreover, make sure that every child is aware of what they are assessed on so that they are prepared. It's not a valid tryout if some kids know the testing parameters in advance and are able to prepare differently than others.

2. Once teams are chosen, at your pre-season meeting with parents present Dr. Colin Higgs's research on the black box of puberty to parents. Inform them why having bench players and starters doesn't make sense in keeping kids in sport. Educate them on the fact that pre-puberty performance is not a good predictor of post-puberty performance. Explain why all athletes who make the team will receive near equal playing time unless they are being selfish teammates, and in those instances, conversations will occur between parents, their child, and the coach.

3. Let parents know you understand competitiveness and would
   love to win too. Assure them that, with you as the coach,
   winning will be more likely due to the rapid development of
   all due to a team effort toward development and increased
   confidence among every athlete. Simply state that fear of losing
   will not drive decisions that hinder development.

When players are given equitable opportunities to develop in youth
sport, both the individual and the team are positioned for long-term
success. Playing-time decisions shouldn't have to be made at youth levels
until increased emphasis on performance sets in well into adolescence.
When coaches choose to develop all players and give players equitable
opportunity to develop, player development and team chemistry are both
enhanced. Giving some players more time or less playing time at young
years clearly puts an overemphasis on winning when player development
should be prioritized.

When coaches play kids close to equal amounts of time, not only
will it be more enjoyable for all involved, but players will be more likely to
reach their technical potential, and teams will be more likely to perform,
tactically, at higher levels. It also eliminates an unnecessarily toxic sporting
environment for kids who aren't yet old enough to navigate a situation
like that. You're not benching one child; you're stunting your team in the
moment and in the future.

People have asked us what to do about playing time because *parents
want to win* and *they want their child in a successful club*. We suggest these
parents sign up for their own sporting competition to help alleviate their
competitive drive rather than put it on kids. We also hear a lot of coaches
say, "Well, if these kids are tough, they'll be resilient from the bench." That
sounds great, but resilience is not built from unpredictable and uncon-
trollable environments. Resilience is actually gained from predictive and
controlled settings led by supportive and caring adults, so benching a child
out of the blue doesn't just steal joy, it fails to build resilience.[93]

Together, we can choose to let kids enjoy their childhood even when they are competing in sport. When we understand that the youth-sport experience is a marathon and not a sprint, we can foster joy for everyone involved in youth sport. When we give kids close to equal time to develop, we will have fewer complaints, happier kids, more joyful coaches, more grateful parents, and—we argue—teams that are better positioned to reach their potential.

Questions to Ask Yourself

- Why do you justify benching kids if you do?
- Do you apply the adult version of sport when it comes to playing time to youth? If so, why?
- How will you, as a parent, address a coach or director if your child is benched without warning and no one communicates to them about it?

Do's and Don'ts

Do's
- Enter every practice, competition, season to develop each child. Development > Wins unless in unique high-performance situations as youth enter their high school years.
- Recognize that skill variance is not as great as many believe if a team is picked on skill and competes in a certain tier (e.g., AAA Ice Hockey, ECNL soccer, Pool A in field hockey, etc.).
- Understand that a culture of development does not equate with a culture that is not competitive.
- Don't think you're an obnoxious parent if you feel something is wrong when your child is being benched. Your child is in fact, a

child. Kids play sports to have fun, and it's not fun to be on the bench when you are twelve years old.

Don'ts
- Over-reward early developers (speed and strength).
- Think, just because you have a child who experienced a team that benched kids that it's okay to do so as a coach.
- Be in a hurry to rank kids in their skills or abilities. Recognize that development takes time and that growth and maturation play important roles into the timing and speed of development.
- Approach a coach or club director about a child's playing time in a way that is rude or confrontational, as it is important to model professionalism and respect.

Action Steps

- Ask sport directors and coaches about their playing time philosophy before your child tries out or before you pay fees for a season or a tournament. Be certain that the topic is out in the open so that you know what you are signing your child up for.
- Revisit chapter 7 (page 157) and evoke a courageous conversation with a coach if your child is being purposefully overlooked in competition or games.
- If you encourage your child to have their own courageous conversation with the coach, be sure to give the coach a heads up. Coaches are human and could be defensive if caught off guard. Let them know your child is going to be brave and address this with them and ask that they don't dismiss them.

CHAPTER 10

Get ahead of the Game

*Make Informed Decisions
for Young Athletes*

"The most common way people give up their power
is by thinking they don't have any."

–Alice Walker, author of *The Color Purple*

Delaney's Journey

Delaney has always had a knack for volleyball. She has benefited greatly from opportunities as a result of being an early developer, because Delaney was faster, stronger, and bigger than most of her peers. Delaney's parents played some sport growing up, but, like most North Americans, their sport journey ended upon completion of high school. Now, in sixth grade, twelve-year-old Delaney, who was committed to community club volleyball, asked her parents if she could keep playing on the school basketball and soccer teams with her friends from elementary school who she rarely sees anymore because they aren't in class together.

Her parents reach out to Delaney's club volleyball coach, because if she did school basketball it would mean that she'd miss club volleyball periodically, although she would still make most of their practices. Coach responded that while not ideal, he would support this as long as she didn't miss any games or tournaments.

When the school basketball schedule arrived, her parents were concerned. There were more conflicts with games and tournaments than they imagined. Due to gymnasium space, she would have school basketball on the weekends and not just after school. Although the school coach, a teacher at the school, understood that Delaney had other commitments, she just asked that Delaney come to some of the games and practices so that she felt part of the team; otherwise, she felt it was fairer to give the spot to someone who could commit more time.

Delaney and her parents sat down to talk about what could happen if she goes forward with the school basketball team, something Delaney really wants to do because she loves her friends and club volleyball has suddenly become more demanding in terms of time and intensity. For example, they are now driving to other cities for competitive tournaments on more and more weekends. The girls on the team were also scared about their performance, knowing they would get in trouble from the coach, plus teammates get upset with each other when someone makes a mistake. The volleyball club coach has told Delaney's parents that if she misses more than one or two sessions every two weeks out of six to eight practices and games, her spot may go to someone else. He also told Delaney and her parents that her participation would result in her missing additional strength and conditioning that he has arranged for the team—something that undoubtedly would be hard for her to make up.

Delaney's parents encouraged her to reconsider participating in the school sports. They made some calls and realized that no one else on the club team was trying to squeeze in a second sport, even if the second sport requires much less of a time commitment and zero travel. They reminded her of her goals for the sport and that she was on track to getting to do something they didn't do—play sport post high school. Did she really want to throw that away? Delaney responded that she was just a twelve-year-old kid who liked both sports, and while she was pretty good at volleyball, she couldn't see how taking a day off here and there to play basketball would hinder her volleyball goals. She wondered why her parents didn't seem to want her to just have fun with her friends.

There are several ways this story can play out...

Option 1
Go with the Flow

Delaney thought about her parents' stories of regret for not working harder in sport, and how they wished they'd done what was needed to play at the collegiate level. While yes, her volleyball teammates and coaches do take volleyball very seriously, that's simply because they want to be great, and there is nothing wrong with wanting to be great. Delaney thought about kids she goes to school with who are accomplishing amazing things in their sport of choice and how common it is for kids to specialize and take sport seriously at a young age. She wondered why she would even consider stepping back despite her coach's honesty that she could lose her spot on such a high caliber team.

So, she told her school friends that she decided not to participate in school sports so that she could continue to stay on the top volleyball team at the top club in the area.

Over time, she dreaded going to volleyball practice and games and found herself feeling jealous when her classmates shared stories about the fun they had on the weekends doing typical kid stuff. Delaney told herself that she made the right decision, but internally she questioned her choices. She longed to have time to hang out with her friends and hated the long travel days to tournaments.

By the time she was in grade nine, she was surprised that kids who were just joining the club scene after years at the recreation level were replacing girls she grew up playing with. Some of her childhood teammates quit, as they were not growing taller and not matching the physical stature of their opponents. In other cases, players were getting burned out with chronic aches and pains while new players were bouncing in, fresh and excited to come train. Delaney's confidence began to decrease, and she was playing well below her potential. As a result, her role on the team changed, and for the first time she was not the key player. Her whole identity was that she played volleyball, and she began beating herself up inside for failing to perform and hold her spot. While words were never shared, Delaney could see disappointment in the eyes of her coaches and also her parents. Delaney couldn't understand what happened. She listened to her coach. She listened to her parents, who themselves listened to parents of older girls or other girls on her team.

Delaney found herself in the counselor's chair asking for advice on how to tell her parents that her dreams of playing collegiate volleyball had changed. She loathed going to practice and games and wanted to pursue other interests during the remainder of her high school experience. Delaney was certain that volleyball was no longer her goal post high school.

Option 2
Do What's Best for Your Family

Delaney called the volleyball coach's bluff and did what she knew in her heart she wanted to do, with full support of her parents. She chose to play school basketball in addition to her club volleyball. Her parents trusted their daughter and chose to give her agency in her own path, even though the other parents warned that Delaney may regret it. While Delaney's parents didn't have the opportunity or natural gifts to play sports at the university level, they decided that their own experience should in no way influence their decisions as parents. Sport was supposed to be fun, and their daughter was a tween who deserved to spend her childhood extracurricular activities at experiences that she chose and that were joyful to her.

Delaney did experience consequences by the volleyball coach for choosing to continue playing school basketball. Playing time decreased, and she began to feel a bit like an outsider socially on the team because she sometimes missed practices and extra optional sessions that would get added to the calendar. Delaney realized she absolutely loved going to basketball, but that volleyball seemed to make her sad. She asked her parents if she could join a different club team, one that maybe wasn't as well-known in the community but one that "cared if kids had fun." While they secretly worried if Delaney was wasting her natural talent, her parents followed their daughter's lead a second time and found her a new club led by a coach who cared deeply about the overall experience and well-being of every participant. Meanwhile, after she switched volleyball teams she started to open her mind to the idea of experimenting with other sports. It seemed all the girls playing field hockey were really close and loved their coach, so she wondered if she should try it. Since everyone told her how "fast" she was she also thought that maybe she should go out for track.

Several years later, Delaney asked her parents if she could re-focus her time and energy primarily on volleyball. She continued to develop and thrive, and she noticed in PE class that she was excelling over kids who have been playing with her previous other club for years. Her former club coach stopped coaching because she didn't coach kids past middle school, but Delaney's parents helped her find another coach who coached girls at a higher level who celebrated multisport. The new coach assured Delaney it would be okay to miss periodically since Delaney also wanted to play high school basketball and run track, and the coach asked that she promise to communicate if her schedule was too busy or if she ever needed to rest her body or simply take a day off to catch up to feel more organized in school.

Her parents, who were criticized by some peers when Delaney stepped back from volleyball because she was on such a strong team, felt really proud that they listened to their daughter and didn't let their unrealized dreams or short-term fear cloud their decision-making for their child. While Delaney was the only player on that sixth-grade club team who switched clubs and played a lower level to allow for a multisport experience, she was thriving in school, socially, and in sport.

....

Delaney is a young girl who found herself having to make a sport-related decision not unlike many youth throughout North America. Delaney's story could have covered a variety of topics other than when to specialize in sport, such as: which level of sport kids should play, how taking a break from a sport can impact the youth in the short and long term, the necessity (or not) of traveling for youth sport, and the list goes on. We used one example to illustrate that sometimes, even if the group has the best intentions, following them down a particular road may not be in the best interest of your child, the kids you coach, or even your family.

We believe that most coaches, sport directors, and parents want what's best for kids. All kids. In all sports. But making decisions when navigating the broad range of emotions that may accompany a youth-sport experience can sometimes make seemingly easy decisions really difficult.

And let's be real. Decision-making in sport is further complicated by the fact that the current sport system is a mess. One doesn't have to look far to learn about sexual and emotional abuse in youth sport and related cover-ups. Sport can be toxic, as some kids feel their only value to coaches is based on performance. The pressure to perform can be so great it can take a toll on kids' mental health. In other words, it can beat kids down. Yet, youth sport can also be uplifting and empowering, and indeed, it changes many kids' lives for the better. The key to making wise sport-related decisions, in our humble opinion, is to avoid generalizations. We want to empower you to cancel out the noise along the way when it's masking what you know in your gut—as coaches, parents, directors—to be what's best for kids.

We need to resist the pack mentality. We're looking at you—parents, coaches, and sport directors. A pack mentality is when a group of people make decisions without a lot of thought or planning simply because there may be a consensus. Some say that adults make decisions on behalf of youth in sport with short-term results prioritized over a long-term journey or experience, and sometimes this is true. Who's to blame? We suggest it always depends on the situation and that gross generalizations are going to fall short of solving problems every single time.

We're asking coaches not to subscribe to the idea that *all parents are crazy.* We see your tweets and all the likes they receive by other coaches when you articulate that you, indeed, do think that current parents are going to be the demise of the world. We're also asking parents not to believe for one second that *no coach wants what's best for kids.* We are fully aware that there are some ill-intentioned coaches and misguided parents in our midst, but most parents and coaches just want youth to have a positive experience in sport that allows them to gain valuable skills.

As such, it's time to…

- Value youth athletes as humans first and athletes second, and remember that the person is always more important than the performance.
- Cancel the noise that places things and people ahead of kids in the decision-making process.
- Avoid making decisions out of fear.
- Avoid making decisions with short-term results being prioritized over long-term experiences and development.
- Stop vilifying groups of people, while at the same time holding coaches, directors, and parents to high standards of care and conduct.

This book set out to be a joyful read that is realistic, practical, and in touch with the current realities sporting directors, coaches, and parents are facing. Most of these realities require deep reflection and ought to only be explored with the human being—the child—at the center. As such, throughout this chapter, we identify several trending topics in youth sport and encourage you, as either parents or coaches, to think critically and collaboratively about how you approach the decisions for the youth involved rather than joining the pack mentality we alluded to earlier.

Parents: Trust your gut, as it's likely telling you what is best for your child. We're not saying protect your child from healthy doses of adversity or struggle in sport. Absolutely not. But if something feels off to you in your child's sport experience, there is a high likelihood that something is off. Always ask yourself, *Is this age appropriate?* If the answer is *absolutely not*, then you know you need to speak up.

Coaches: We're asking you to look at the kids that show up to learn from you as human beings who are in the thick of some key developmental years of their existence. Don't just look at them as athletes. We know you want the best for them, so be sure your actions and behaviors toward them align with your values, and help them reach their potential in all areas of their lives.

One only has to listen to a good amount of parents and youth coaches talk about youth sport to understand there are a lot of myths that exist in the youth-sport space. Unfortunately, these myths far too often lead to a fear-based pack mentality among those charged with making decisions on behalf of kids. We explore some of these myths in an attempt to put your mind at ease so that you will feel inspired to make decisions from a youth-centered vantage point.

Trending Myth #1
Youth must travel for competition and exposure.

If coaches or directors tell your child that to participate at a more competitive level, they must commit to more frequent and ongoing travel at ages twelve and under, you don't have to do it. Give your child permission to say no. Hell, give *yourself* permission to say no. Your reasons for not wanting to join a different league might be related to finances, unrealistic time commitments, having multiple children in sport, or simply because you planned for a life that protected time for family bike rides and other outings. Don't believe that your child can't hop off a current path and continue developing on one that parallels or diverges from the kids they played with in the past. While it may be true that traveling makes sense as kids reach age thirteen or fourteen, it is unlikely that it makes sense at age ten and eleven. Your child still has the option to play at more recreation levels while exploring other interests. Even if youth are able to play at the highest level, they can *choose* not to.

But everyone else chose the team with more travel. Am I hindering my child?

While there may be valid reasons why sport travel is a good option for your child and family, knowing for sure what the best choice is will remain unknown until unique variables are identified and explored. For example, your child may be hooked to a less mainstream sport such as speed skating where travel may be necessary for competition. Or, perhaps you live in a more rural area and travel is necessary for any sport participation at all, which surely would be a good reason.

What we don't want parents and coaches to feel is pressure or fear when making sport-related decisions for their kid or the kids that they coach. Parents tell us they feel pressure for their child to play at a more competitive level because that's where exposure to college coaches exists. There very well could be truth to this, as indeed college coaches are attending certain showcases for recruiting purposes, but keep in mind only 7 percent of high school athletes go on to play college sports, and approximately only 2 percent of them get a scholarship.[94,95] According to the Next College Student Athlete (NCSA) for-profit company that connects high school student–athletes with college coaches, only 0.3 percent of high school student–athletes receive a full athletic scholarship for their college education.[96] Knowing those odds, does that make the most sense for your child and your family? If your child is a gifted talent, trust us, coaches will find them.

Parents aren't the only ones feeling pressure. Club directors and coaches report choosing traveling leagues and out-of-town tournaments and showcases because they say that's what the parents want. Several explained to us while researching this book that a lot of parents like to be able to take their kids to these events, as it helps make it fun for their kids, and they hope it'll keep them involved in the sport. We responded that if sessions and team chemistry is fostered enough, they won't need travel to foster love of the sport. They can love the sport here at home. As well, coaches and youth-sport directors bear some responsibility in educating parents rather than caving to their wishes if their knowledge and experience tell them what the parents are seeking is not in the best interest of youth.

Earlier in the book we introduced you to Amanda's niece, Sara Stewart. To refresh your memory, Sara plays for the Colgate Raiders women's ice hockey team. In her 2023 rookie season, Sara was named first-team all-star forward in her conference tournament. In the following season, Sara's sophomore year, the Raiders earned a berth to the coveted Frozen Four, which includes the top four teams in the country battling for a national championship. Sara grew up in Antigonish, Nova Scotia, just as Amanda did. Nova Scotia is a rural province in a rural part of Canada. Hence, not a lot of recruiting happens there compared to more populated provinces such as Ontario or anywhere in the United States. However, during COVID-19, Sara was recruited despite not traveling to college identification clinics (sport clinics that college coaches host on their campus as a way to view potential athletes without having to travel to them) and summer camps. Her games were streamed online, and hard-working coaches will find kids like Sara. Sara didn't have to move away for exposure, and she is thriving athletically and academically at one of the top college programs in North America. Is she extremely talented? Yes. Has she dedicated an incredible amount of time consistently over the years toward her development? Absolutely. Did her journey include supportive and loving parents who didn't pressure her? For sure. Does she absolutely love playing hockey and does it bring her joy? One hundred percent. Did she play multiple sports as a kid? Of course! Not every young player will reach this level; in fact, few will. We're just sharing this story so that families out there with kids like Sara don't feel scared or pressured into doing what everyone else is doing when it doesn't make the most sense for their family.

To further support the fact that parents do not have to feel they need to say yes to every clinic and showcase tournament, we want to introduce you to another niece of Amanda's. Rhyah Stewart also grew up in small-town Canada. She participated in cross-country, track, and hockey and recently committed to the defending national D-I champion Wisconsin Badgers. Rhyah is also a member of Team Canada's U18 hockey team and additional proof that you can be identified without attending every event in an expensive destination. While most kids will not grow up to play in top-five D-I athletic programs, nor should that be our goal for our children, it is important that stories like Sara's and Rhyah's are shared so that parents do not feel that saying yes to every trip is a requirement.

There are times that travel may make perfect sense for your child or team, and other times when it makes no sense. But the key is that you understand that in each instance it'll depend on the kid, all that they juggle, their academics, and the culture of the team. This, like all myths in this chapter, is not a *this* or *that* issue, and it is an issue that can only be determined with more facts and truly knowing the individual at the center of the decision.

Trending Myth #2
Year-round play is needed to maintain a spot on the team.
If you're a parent and your peers' kids are choosing to play sports year-round, or if you're a coach adhering to the "more is more" mentality, we ask that you pause and give this topic some more consideration before jumping on the bandwagon.

Sometimes, easy choices can present themselves as complicated. Kids are often told that if they choose a path that differs even slightly from the current one traveled by the team, they may lose their roster spot or their starting position or be moved to a position on the field they don't like to play. For some families, hearing this is all they need to hear in order to refrain from taking a season off or a break from the sport. For others, they might struggle with the decision, because although they heard the potential negative consequences, they view sport as a longer journey and want to switch sports with the seasons. Others might be insulted, as they took potential consequences more as threats and wonder if the club and/or coaches have their child's best interests at heart.

We presented evidence in previous chapters for multiple-sport participation and breaks from sports during the calendar year to reduce injury and burnout and potentially increase skill and physical activity behaviors over time (page 81). Additionally, take a long look at who is encouraging you to sign up for year-round sports. *Is it a coach who is making a salary off your registration fees, or is it a facility that needs your registration fees to keep the lights on? Is your child a human or a revenue source?* Before you permit your child to let go of other activities to commit to a sport year-round, it's important to ask yourself questions like these. To the directors or coaches who look around and notice that all their competitors are asking participants to commit for a full year at a time, educate your club's families about why you build breaks into your club's calendar.

Parents should be certain to ask the club director their philosophies regarding year-round play prior to registering their child for the club, and coaches should ask club directors similar questions. It's important that everyone is on the same page and that this is communicated effectively with families. Some sport clubs have multiple seasons with longer (four-plus weeks) breaks woven into their calendar. If your child absolutely loves the sport, they will find ways to practice on their own during the break, and if they aren't rushing off to further their development, it is likely they need that break. Either way, if we had a dollar for every time a parent told us their child burned out of competitive sport, we'd be sipping margaritas under a palm tree somewhere tropical. It's time we step back and let the less-is-more approach keep more kids in the game.

Trending Myth #3
The grass is greener on the other side.

There is definitely a time to switch clubs, but it is not just because you notice other people are switching. You'll know if your child is in a negative sport environment. They won't want to go, they'll share examples of how they are spoken to in inappropriate ways, they won't feel like they belong, and they won't be smiling or may even feel like the coach will never give them a chance.

If your child is truly not receiving a fair chance to show that they can perform, it may not be the best environment for them. Knowing the difference between when your child could benefit from putting in some extra effort to improve their skills *and* when a coach has their mind made up and you can't see them ever giving your child a chance isn't always an easy delineation, although sometimes it is.

We both have children who have benefited greatly in the long term because somewhere along the way a coach (or several) underestimated them, sometimes repeatedly. With our support they hunkered down, worked harder, and were able to develop despite the hurdles being set out for them on their team. They were able to reflect and see how their experience hurt in the short term but actually helped propel them in the longer term thanks to a perfectly sized chip on the shoulder. Admittedly, it may not have turned out this way if we, as parents, didn't work in sport or study youth development through sport. We were able to help guide them, remind them of their strengths and reasons to be confident, and were honest about the areas that needed growth if they didn't want to be considered as someone that couldn't be counted on. Our kids wanted to develop and contribute and thus we were happy to support them as they worked to fill gaps. While we weren't always comfortable when our kids experienced something negative due to an adult version of sport, we did what we could to support their development for the purpose of protecting the joy of sport. As a reminder, joyful sport absolutely includes hard work.

Specifically, we stepped back as parents and asked ourselves some key questions. Were the coaches who perhaps played some eleven-year-olds 85 percent of a game versus playing others 15 percent good people who we felt were doing their best? Mostly, yes. Were they teaching our kids a great deal along the way, despite the (sometimes plentiful) feelings of disappointment? Absolutely. Do we think the coaches were correct to make choices with such large discrepancy in playing time? Hell no! However, we pointed out the positives to our kids to help keep their mind from zooming in only on the disappointment, and we reminded them this wasn't personal. Very few of their coaches to date have been formally trained educators or coaches with certifications related to adolescent development. Sometimes this is very evident and other times it's not evident at all.

We have witnessed different families jump ship from one club to another, and we do not judge because we don't have the facts. In our opinion, there are times to change clubs and then there are times when it makes no sense at all. It's okay to wade in some murky waters for a while if your child is emotionally and physically safe where you are. It's also okay to work with the club to try and make the experience better for all kids. Chances are, the other local club that might look more attractive from the outside has its own plethora of challenges. The grass isn't always greener, and you may just be better off where you are.

Like all myths in this chapter, the situation to switch clubs will depend entirely on the specific facts and conditions of your child's experience. If several teammates jump ship for something else, maybe that's the best decision for them. Maybe it would be a terrible decision for your child. The easiest way to determine the best club for your child is to choose the club where they have the most joyful experiences. If they are having fun, they will be more motivated to play and, through play, they will develop and improve and gain confidence.

Trending Myth #4
Parents should never speak up when
they think something is wrong or unfair.

We've been asked to sign parent consent waivers in the past, and we certainly understand why they exist. Far too many youth-sport headlines are dedicated to the poor, even abusive behavior of parents on the sidelines. We've observed parents yelling at officials, banging on plexiglass at hockey games, and even yelling at kids. We've heard them speak poorly about a coach who is—more often than not—doing the best they can. This type of behavior is shameful and has no place in youth sport.

Yet, hot takes on youth sport shouldn't put all parents under the same umbrella. We believe strongly that coaches and directors should actually encourage communication from parents when they are concerned for their children's well-being, just as parents should reach out to and speak to teachers and principals when it pertains to school.

Parents: If you know that an adult version of sport is being placed on your child and it's creating anxiety and feelings that are not age appropriate for a youth to experience at the hand of a coach, you must question it. It's your job to support your child at all phases of childhood and adolescence, yet it's important that parents recognize the difference between anxiety levels that can hinder a child's mental wellness versus a child venting to a parent in a way that actually helps them to move on from the experience in a helpful way.

In an episode of her podcast *Ask Lisa,* Dr. Lisa Damour explained to her listeners that adolescents collect trash "quasi-bad or bad experiences" periodically throughout their day, which they have to set aside in the moment to be polite, productive, and good students. A trash experience might be a child feeling left out of a group social gathering or perhaps disappointment through sport, like when they fell short of reaching a goal they set for a personal best time at swimming. But, as the "trash pile" grows, it's important that they have some place to dump it. Any parent of an adolescent is acutely aware that they are often the "fortunate" recipients of this trash, even though it doesn't feel lucky at the time. It should be reassuring to learn that an adolescent venting about the annoyances throughout their day to a supportive parent helps them to move on from it and go about their day, yet that doesn't make it any less confusing to then delineate when their child is experiencing a normal day that consists of good and not-so-good experiences versus when they are in a bad situation. Perhaps the best suggestion for parents in this instance is to refrain from an impulsive need to swoop in and fix what the child is complaining about.

Let's be super clear here.

We are *not* suggesting you complain to coaches when your child communicates the bad parts of practice or training.

We are *not* suggesting you complain to coaches every time your child is frustrated.

We are *not* suggesting you rant if your child isn't recognized by the coach as the top player on the team.

We are *not* suggesting that you speak rudely, publicly, or impulsively to a coach or sport director.

So, when do you speak up?

It's not always clear cut or black and white. For starters, ask your kids about the good. After they unload all that annoyed them about the coach or a teammate(s), ask them what went well. Ask them how they uplifted a teammate. Ask them if anyone shined their light on your child. Then, celebrate that. But, if in ongoing data collection (aka: listening to your kid), you feel that things are just off and this is being validated through your own observations at competition, it may be time to speak up in the spirit of collaborating to resolve the issue.

You speak up when—after gathering as much information as possible—your intuition tells you it's necessary.

If you feel your child is experiencing conditions that are clearly inappropriate or unnecessary in your mind, send a formal email and request a time to chat just as you would make an appointment to speak with a teacher who you felt was treating your child unfairly or inappropriately.

For those who say that following this suggestion means every parent will then harass coaches because every parent believes their child is perfect, we have a question for you: Have you ever talked with parents? Most of us are quick to point out areas for growth in our own kids. Unfortunately, an ongoing theme in our lives is that people call us for advice because they are afraid to speak out to coaches or directors because they don't want their child to be punished in any way. In some instances, coaches are using abusive language, in other situations, kids are being punished with decreased playing time for missing a practice for another extracurricular commitment, and in others coaches are benching kids at 10U and 12U levels and parents are scared to question why.

This isn't okay.

There has to be a magical middle between those who complain too much and those who fail to protect their children from inappropriate and borderline abusive sport conditions. That magical middle is what we ought to aim for.

- **Coaches** will make mistakes.
- **Parents** will make mistakes.
- **Directors** will make mistakes.
- **Youth** will make mistakes.
- **Referees and umpires** will make mistakes.

If we all check our egos and collaborate in ways that we preach to the youth we coach and raise, we will be much better off. If a club or coach is not willing to discuss your child with you or wants to paint you as a crazy parent for having a concern, we're thinking they aren't in the business of developing kids through sport.

You have agency as parents. We promise you that you'll never regret waiting twenty-four hours if you're upset and can't find the words in a professional manner, but we also appreciate that not everyone needs twenty-four hours, and in the event of a tournament, a lot more damage can incur within the twenty-four-hour window because it is likely there are additional games scheduled in the upcoming twenty-four hours.

When one considers this book's subtitle *A Positive, Collaborative Approach to Youth Sport*, it's no surprise that we are asking the adults to positively collaborate in ways that help kids protect the joy. The days of generalizing girl athletes, boy athletes, parents, and coaches should be long gone. Every situation is different, and we're all likely to provide kids with the best experience possible when they keep each child at the center and think deeply about their specific needs based on their personality and overall well-being. If we look at what the parents next to us on the sideline or in the bleachers are doing and let that guide our actions, we may not be keeping our own child's best interests at the heart of our decisions.

Questions to Ask Yourself

- Do you sometimes make decisions for your team based on what you think you should do, because that's what other coaches are doing?
- Do you sometimes make sport-related decisions for your child because that's what you see the parents of their teammates doing?
- Why is it that you fear your child will be punished if you ask good questions?
- Do you think it's fair to tell parents they have to wait twenty-four hours to talk to a coach, regardless of the situation or setting?

Do's and Don'ts

Do's

- Understand that every child and every coach is different and that one size does not fit all when it comes to youth sport.
- Trust your instinct.
- If sport is hindering your child's well-being more than it is enhancing it, it's time to switch course.
- Get all the facts before you get angry as a parent.
- Ask kids what is going well after you provide them space to share what it is bothering them.

Don'ts

- Make sport-related decision for your children based out of fear.
- Follow the masses when you don't believe they are traveling on the wisest path.
- Communicate with coaches, sport directors, or officials impulsively or rudely.
- Blindly sign parent waivers if they are speaking to the lowest common denominator of parent.
- Assume as coaches that parents are all unreasonable.

CHAPTER 11

How You Play

It's about "Fun"

"Having fun is not a diversion from a meaningful life,
it is the pathway to it."

–Martha Beck

I n 1998, soon after Amanda graduated from St. Francis Xavier University, she moved to Richmond, Virginia, to teach and coach at a K–12 school called The Collegiate School. Amanda soon realized that Collegiate, as the school is commonly referred to, is a special place. Upon first glance, people might marvel at their facilities or the beautiful, mature trees that frame the campus. But like most exceptional schools, brick and mortar have nothing to do with the magic that exists within. Collegiate's superpower is its incredible faculty and staff.

Amanda's colleagues were kindhearted teachers and coaches who loved to think and laugh. Many had decades of experience. At twenty-one years old, Amanda thought she won the lottery. She found herself immersed in thoughtful discussions about coaching philosophies and teaching best practices while eating lunch and when the colleagues socialized outside of school. Her friend group consisted of legendary coaches and department heads in their seventies, young parents juggling raising young kids and leading championship programs while also being exceptional teachers, and a group of younger faculty who weren't far removed from their college experience. They all loved kids, they all loved sport, and they all loved being educators.

These deep lunchtime and Saturday-morning-run discussions awoke a deep curiosity within Amanda. It prompted her to immediately enroll in a part-time master's program. She likely would have worked at the school forever had she not been offered a full scholarship to complete her PhD at nearby University of Virginia after five years of working at Collegiate. While formal education is important and words can't adequately express all she gained from graduate school and her time as a professor, she really learned how to think and the necessity of humility and was inspired to think deeply thanks to her loving, thoughtful, and nonjudgmental colleagues at Collegiate.

And it's a good thing, too. Because although Amanda was very nice to the kids she taught and coached, she's not too proud to admit that early in her career, she demonstrated a lot of behaviors she and Richard warn you about throughout the book. For example, one time she stated matter-of-factly that she didn't just make her girls and boys soccer teams run if someone was late, she would run with them. As if her joining in on the running excused the antiquated coaching tactic of punishing with exercise. When a thoughtful older colleague looked at her and asked, "Stewie (her nickname at the school), have you asked any of them why they are late?"

Amanda felt like a total dumbass as she paused, and then, while looking at her colleague, said "Oooohhh…that might be a better idea, eh?" They both laughed, and it was at that moment Amanda began coaching more like she taught her students in health and physical education and less like the way she was coached as a college student–athlete.

Up until this time, Amanda was a nice coach. But, as the title of her master's thesis, "Nice Is Not Enough," suggests—nice was not enough. What was necessary was more than niceness; Amanda had to learn how to establish sports conditions where kids could thrive. And so, she set out on a path of learning. While many questions have been answered, she admits she has more questions than answers.

For the past two decades, thanks largely in part to her thoughtful colleagues at Collegiate who taught and coached from a human-centered approach, Amanda has been pushing for more education-like conditions in the sport domain.

....

Throughout this book, we share positive approaches to coaching and parenting that can combine to protect the joy kids experience in sport in an attempt to increase the amount of individuals who participate in sport throughout their lives. If you have misstepped periodically, we'd like to think you're in good company as we certainly have! Many of us were or are nice to the kids we coach, but, we default to mimicking the coaching we received as kids, both the good and the bad. None of us set out to intentionally steal kids' joy.

As the old saying goes, "When we know better, we do better."

As such, we've adjusted our practices throughout our careers and have no plans to stop being reflective coaches and parents. The traditional coaching practices that we've moved away from are perhaps ones you've normalized at some point. The fact that so many of us were on the receiving end of traditional coaching behaviors while we were punished with exercise or made to pick up the equipment when we lost a drill may explain why we are often too slow to identify them as inadequate when our own children experience them. It may also explain why, when we step up to coach in our communities, our well-meaning efforts sometimes fall short. Alas, as Amanda tells her kids, explaining behavior isn't enough to excuse behavior.

If we pause to reflect on the specifics of these traditional coaching practices and sport conditions, it's kind of surprising that more of us didn't quit sport at early ages. For example, Amanda recalls a youth coach yelling from the sidelines "You suck! You're absolutely terrible!" She also recalls a peer being taunted for reporting physical abuse he received at the hands of the community's long-time hockey coach. Rather than everyone protecting her friend, many blamed the ninth grader when the coach was released from his coaching duties. Richard and the other rookies were exposed to hazing upon making the local midget AAA hockey team. Coaches knew what was going on and even enabled hazing as they left the dressing room so the veterans could haze the younger players as they had been hazed as rookies. The joy-stealing cycle of abuse repeated itself under the guise of "team building."

In some ways, the youth-sport landscape has clearly evolved. Fortunately, it is far less common to hear coaches yell expletives from the sidelines; anti-hazing policies have been created, and there is much less tolerance for coaches who physically abuse their athletes. Yet, it's also important to recognize that parents do call us for advice on how to respond to the microaggressions and verbally abusive tactics their kids are receiving in sport from coaches or teammates. And none of us should be surprised by this. As we wrote this book, headlines were written followed by details describing maltreatment and abuse in pro-leagues, college, and national sports teams. Often, abuses are covered up and the perpetrators of the abuse move on to get other jobs in the sport. Many instances of abuse go unreported due to a level of normalization that happens at the youth level, and there is a fear that if one speaks up, they will be kicked out of the sport or denied opportunity because they are viewed as "difficult."

Getting It Right

It is often said in the world of coaching development, "Don't be a kid's last coach." While this is admittedly a very low bar to aspire to, it certainly drives home the message that coaches have a great deal of power in determining if youth continue participating in sport. When we hear this tagline, we're quick to add, "Don't parent in ways that drive your kids out of sport." No one wants to be a youth's last coach, and no parent wants to be the reason their child loses interest in sport.

A more positive spin and a marker that we use when we coach in our own communities and when we create coach development resources is that we aim for every participant to love the sport more at the end of the season than they do at the beginning of the season. If sport clubs really want to know if they're getting it right, they should examine registration numbers from one season to the next, as it is a real indicator of the experience the child had. Additionally, survey the kids on the last day of practice and ask them if they want to play again next season.

Parents, consider this as your reminder that you play an equally powerful role in this. That is, your actions and comments will significantly contribute to whether or not a sport experience is a joyful one, just as your kids' coaches do.

In the opening of this book, we shared our motivation for writing it. There is an apparent need to help parents, sport directors, and coaches navigate common issues in sport that seem to be hindering youth, parent, and coach experiences throughout the youth-sport journey. Coaches sometimes feel frustrated with parents; parents sometimes feel confused how to handle old-school coaching practices; and sport directors want to get research to coaches and parents in ways that are digestible and positively impact kids' experiences.

Yet, the very people who reach out for support are often resistant to change.

When we proudly wave the flag that states the number one reason kids play sport is to have fun, what keeps them in it is because it's fun, and what drives them out of sport is when it's no longer fun, we're inevitably met with skepticism. Specifically, when we share the critical importance of fun, it is sometimes internalized by others' as, "We don't care about kids developing and winning in sport." But, as we will explain, that couldn't be further from the truth.

The reality is, fun is serious business when it comes to youth sport. And, thanks to Dr. Amanda Visek and her colleagues at George Washington University, we now have a brilliant framework to summarize what fun actually is. Fun is synonymous with athlete development, and it most certainly is not a bad word.

Fun Maps

Dr. Visek is the lead researcher of a more recent formidable body of youth-sport research that clearly defines what youth describes as fun in the youth-sport setting.[97,98] Dr. Visek and her team surveyed coaches, parents, and youth athletes and asked them to share examples of what fun looks like to them in a sports setting. Eighty-one statements, or fun determinants, were gathered during this first phase of the research.

Examples of statements shared at this initial phase of research include statements such as, "One thing that makes playing fun for players is playing well together as a team," and "One thing that makes playing fun for players is trying our best." Participants were then asked to arrange the eighty-one statements into groupings that made sense to them, and to come up with a name that described each grouping. Participant groupings resulted in eleven themes, or fun dimensions, and example group names include: positive coaching, learning and improving, and games.

Next, participants were asked to rank the groupings in order from, "This is the most contribution to a fun sport experience," and "This is least contribution to a fun sport experience." The eleven fun dimensions are listed in order from participants' perceived greatest to least importance in contributing to making sport fun for players.

1. Being a good sport
2. Trying hard
3. Positive coaching
4. Learning and improving
5. Game-time support
6. Games

7. Practice
8. Team friendships
9. Mental bonuses
10. Team rituals
11. Swag

Youth identified that being a good sport, trying hard, positive coaching, and learning and improving are things that make the biggest contribution to a fun sport experience, while team rituals and swag were the lowest contributors. These eleven ranked fun dimensions, along with the eighty-one determinants of fun, are known as *fun integration theory,* or *Fun Maps.* A key takeaway from this body of work is that all eleven dimensions contribute to fun, therefore they should be built into all sport programs.

At this point, we suspect that at least a few of you reading this right now are feeling skeptical. Perhaps you're thinking things such as:

- Well, that's cool that some view fun as being a good sport, but girls are so different from boys.
- Yeah, but my kid plays elite club sport, and their coaches wouldn't rank these items the same way.
- This may be well and good for young kids, but it isn't applicable to my 16U elite travel team. I mean how come high performance isn't even mentioned?

Dr. Visek and colleagues were met with questions like these. Therefore, they ran some additional statistical analyses on their data. Unshocking to us, but perhaps surprising to some, the researchers concluded that youth felt very similarly about what fun in sport looked like regardless of sex, age, or level of sport played. When the researchers analyzed the eighty-one determinants of fun, one thing is for certain, almost all of the participants agreed on what fun is. What hopefully will really give the skeptics pause is that clear conclusion that FUN = athlete development.

In other words, the research suggests that what we've presented throughout this book will help enhance kids' experiences in sport, whether they are on a non-cut kindergarten youth soccer team or the top 16U travel soccer team in your community.

The eleven dimensions of fun derived from four sources of fundamentals:[99]

1. **Contextual:** games and practices
2. **Internal:** developing, trying hard and mental bonuses
3. **Social:** team friendships, team rituals, being a good sport
4. **External:** positive coaching, game-time support, and swag

Presenting Dr. Visek's key findings as well as additional research in youth sport via these four sources of fundamentals is helpful for those who care deeply about seeing research findings presented in actionable tasks for parents, coaches, and youth-sport directors.

Contextual sources contribute to a fun sport experience.

As Peter Parker's (aka: Spiderman's) Uncle Ben said, "With great power comes great responsibility." We couldn't agree more. Coaches and sport directors are primarily responsible for planning and delivering an environment that promotes fun in practices and games. In chapter 9 (page 211), we examined why playing time disparities should be minimal at best for youth in sport. Research states that receiving playing time, getting plenty of touches on the ball or puck, learning new skills, and using new skills learned in a game situation all contribute to fun.

In chapter 3, we defined goal orientation theory (page 63) and how when one defines success as developing and improving, all participants are more likely to do their best. We advocated for small-sided games in practices to increase the opportunity to acquire and hone skills, and small-spaced competition for younger athletes when they are still little and full-sized fields, ice surfaces, and courts don't accommodate their pre-pubescent and early adolescent strength and skill.

If parents force their kids to play on teams where they aren't getting the opportunity to develop, research suggests they are putting their kids in a situation where fun will be decreased and that this may lead to their quitting sport. It is important that parents resist any urge to convince a child to play on a team that doesn't meet the criteria for a fun sports experience.

Richard recalls a time when his son played lacrosse, and after playing for approximately five years, he asked his parents to travel to a nearby town to find a team to play on. He describes his son as a late-developing average-skilled lacrosse player on a bantam (14U) team that won some games and lost some. They were by no means a powerhouse team. Richard's son played on the second line, and the second line got a lot less playing time than the first line. The three men coaching the team knew lacrosse well, and one even had professional playing experience. During one game, Richard noticed that the second line, once again, was not getting played very much, and the third line was getting played even less. Richard, aware that his son wasn't the strongest player on the team, continued to watch the game and felt excited when the second and third lines got their chances, and he was proud of their efforts.

As the game went on, Richard's son's team found themselves winning by seven goals. When the second line was put back out, they drew a penalty within fifteen seconds. Richard was gob smacked when the coaches opened the gate for the first line to return to the floor for the power play and motioned for the second line to return to the sideline. Richard noted that in this instance the dads coaching placed their three sons on both the first line and the power play.

After the game, Richard asked his son if he was bothered by the limited playing time, and his son simply shrugged his shoulders as he said, "That's just the way it is with this team." When the season ended, Richard and his son were hanging out one day when his son brought the topic of lacrosse up with his dad. Richard's son shared with him that he'd like to try a different sport next summer season. The joy of playing lacrosse had faded away. An important footnote to this story is that the team eventually folded because they could not fill the roster; the second- and third-line players all found other sports that were more fun.

Far too often, the coaches speaking out about toughness in sport respond to stories like this one that "kids are soft" or that "kids just want instant gratification," but this line of thinking falls extremely short and is ignorant to what is really happening. The research is clear that kids play sports to have fun; it's hard to have fun when you're not playing.

What kid joins a team and gives their time and effort at practice to watch others play? Again, we're talking about kids, not professional- or national-team level sport, which are the only levels of sport we think should be titled "elite."

Other coaches justify benching kids by saying their own kids got benched before. To this we respond, just because another coach got it wrong doesn't mean you have to. To you coaches out there shortening your bench in games, ask yourself why you carry the roster size you do. If you want a smaller roster, take a smaller roster. But if you keep kids on your roster, develop them. Let them play. Let them have fun. (See chapter 9, page 211, for the benefits of providing equitable playing time and opportunities for development.)

Developing players, as we explored throughout the book, doesn't just come from playing time in games. A small-sided games-based approach to practices provide lots of opportunity to practice skills in authentic situations. They also provide an upbeat and fast-paced environment. Thus, the context coaches provide during practice are also big contributors to athlete development and fun.

If coaches aren't providing a fun experience at practices and games, it's time for parents to seek other options for their kids. Don't let club names or team levels influence your ego; find a place for your kid where they can thrive and have a blast with their peers.

Internal sources contribute to a fun sport experience.

Somewhere along the line, fun has been wrongly mistaken for slacking off or doing things that aren't productive in the context of sport. Indeed, fun has almost become a bad word among some in sport circles. Yet, the research explained in chapter 3 (page 53), specifically the research on goal orientation theory and how athletes, coaches, and parents ought to define success for optimal enjoyment and development, is confirmed by Dr. Visek's more recent work.

- Doing one's best is fun.
- Learning new things is fun.
- Developing (improving) is fun.

Amanda and her spouse Jim will never forget the first time they took their oldest to her first soccer game. Their daughter, Scottie, looked so damn cute in her green jersey, miniature shin guards, and neon yellow Nike cleats that a neighbor passed down to her. They were shocked to hear two parents literally shout, "Remember, we're heading to the toy section of Target if you score a goal!" to their daughter. At break time they said, "Don't forget, no ice cream or trip to Target if you don't score."

This four-year-old was being taught to perform for an external reward, even though the research tells us that individual effort and the process of learning new things is described as fun by youth-sport participants. Did the bribing seem to work? Yep. Their little one ran hard, took the ball off her teammates' feet, and dribbled straight to goal...several times. While Scottie chased a butterfly, her teammate did what she needed to do in order to later go to Target and the ice cream shop.

Richard can also recall numerous stories of external rewards, such as his son's teammate on the novice (U12) hockey team. One particular kid had parents that lived in two separate homes and were remarried. So, there was no shortage of parents and grandparents watching him play, and such support is lovely. It became evident that at eleven years old, he was earning twenty dollars per goal, but of course nothing for an assist.

Coaches reading this book are likely able to make accurate guesses as to which kids are bribed to gain points, as they were typically the ones who weren't passing or celebrating teammates' achievements. Parents also know which of their peers are bribing their children, and it's shocking to us how much it occurs. When parents intervene in this way, they have what's needed to post the points earned by their four-year-old on social media, but they unintentionally stunt their overall development in several ways.

First, we're not exaggerating to say that the little four-year-old soccer player literally refused to play after she scored a couple goals. Her work was complete. She was getting her ice cream and trip to Target. The eleven-year-old hockey player who played with Richard's son led the team in shots at goal but lagged behind in passing, which ultimately limited his development and achieving a place on the higher-level teams that he aspired to join.

Fun in sport can't be bought.

We're not trying to be overly critical of excited parents who love their kids and show it through some external rewards for performance, but if we may make a suggestion, it would be to celebrate the effort and not the outcome. It's most likely that they think their kids will have more fun if they score goals. But aren't adults the ones who say, "Kids these days! They always need instant gratification!"? Adults can't criticize kids for their seeming desire for instant gratification while at the same time bribe them with external rewards based on what we want them to do.

Encouraging kids to stick with things, even when they feel challenged, can help them experience the most joy. When Amanda asked her kids if they had any examples of when sport became more fun due to an effort they gave, Scottie, now age thirteen, responded, "Mom, come on. You know the answer to this one."

Indeed, Amanda did.

A couple years ago, Scottie wasn't satisfied with her position within her field hockey team. She communicated to her parents that she wanted to improve her skills to a level that would ensure she would not be over-looked; she wanted the coaches to view her as someone who can positively and effectively contribute to the team. Scottie analyzed the end-of-season report card her coaches thoughtfully completed and used it to identify her current strengths and areas for growth.

Scottie decided that she would dedicate some time to her current strengths to keep them sharp, but that she would focus more on the things her coaches told her she should improve on. Scottie took on extra chores to contribute to the cost of camps and used her free time to improve her skills, speed, and strength. She approached D-1 All-American Mia Duchars at a field one day and asked her if she would work with her and her younger sister, Kassie. Fast-forward six months, and coaches and players alike were commenting to Scottie and Kassie how much they improved.

When asked if they have more fun playing field hockey than they did two years ago, Scottie and Kassie explain that while field hockey used to be fun because they enjoyed learning new skills, it became more fun because they're now able to apply the skills confidently in a game setting or in small-sided games at practice. Now they want to get even better because they perceive their coaches and teammates to appreciate their contributions. Chapter 3 (page 53) explains this perceived competence, confidence, and motivation relationship that Scottie and Kassie referenced in their response, and their thoughts certainly illustrate the *internal sources of fun in the sport* Visek's participants mentioned.

Youth athletes need to understand that it's a gift to get fit, not a punishment. Similarly, it's a gift to sweat and to get a good sleep, as all contribute to making sport more enjoyable. It's also a gift to improve. When parents shift their thinking from celebrating points to celebrating effort and development, more kids will feel good about their status when they put in time to improve. When helping your child set goals make sure they are along the lines of "I will do my best at every practice and game" and "I will communicate effectively at each practice and competition," as these are attainable and connect back to the internal fundamentals Visek writes about including trying one's best and developing.

Coaches also need to be sure they aren't praising points and goals over effort, development, and demonstrating creative decision-making. Highlighting development to kids can be a huge validation to their efforts and will only help inspire them to keep improving. The more coaches praise development and improvement among a group, the more likely the group will understand that if they improve the coach will notice and this is a good thing!

Social factors contribute to a fun sport experience.

Sport is more fun, without a doubt, when kids get along with and are accepted by their teammates. Sometimes, extra effort needs to be made on the part of coaches to help facilitate such relationships. It is very difficult to create a positive sport culture during the adolescent stage of development when a sport environment is overly competitive. When kids are competing for playing time or when cliques emerge on the team, fun is surely sucked from the sport experience.

In our experience, there are coaches who work diligently to build team trust among teammates and those who ignore issues as they percolate. The latter should never happen. When a list of non-negotiables are created *by* team members and for team members, it provides a common language for everyone to aspire to. For example, *No player will ever be excluded or feel alone in practice or game situations or at team outings* is a solid example of a non-negotiable.

Dr. Visek's work concludes that being supported by teammates and receiving help from teammates is a more important contributor to a fun sport experience than specific team rituals. No one is expecting a group of kids on a team to be very best friends, but we suggest that all members of your team understand that they'll be more likely to win championships when everyone feels like they belong and are important members of the team.

If coaches struggle with deciding on how to foster an inclusive vibe, they should once again seek out a coach who all athletes seem to admire or a local favorite teacher. Sport directors need to listen intently to parents who report that their child feels like an outsider on a team and find ways to work with coaches to help them build a cohesive group.

Coaches aren't the only ones responsible for enhancing team chemistry. Parents should make every effort to raise kids who attend practices and games with the mindset of improving the overall team chemistry by making a "positive teammate deposit" at the bank. We're not surprised if you haven't heard this term before, as it's one Amanda made up on the fly one night driving her girls to practice, and since then it's been a common theme during season. Specifically, Amanda reminds her daughters before practice to "shine their light on their teammates" and discusses with them what this means and what it looks like in action.

"Shining your light on a teammate" means to compliment teammates when they are naturally thinking something positive about their teammates. For example, if a teammate makes a great shot in practice, tell them you thought they did an awesome job. If a teammate hustles their tail off in a drill, let them know you admire their efforts and to keep it up. It's important to remind kids that these compliments don't always have to align with productivity on the field; with this direction, kids will be more likely to rally behind teammates who may still be learning skills others have mastered. They can always compliment someone's effort or kindness, regardless of their skill level.

Amanda tells all youth athletes and coaches to be intentional about sharing positive thoughts as they enter their mind during practices and games. When she picks her own kids up from practice, she asks them two questions after they finish saying what it is, if anything, they want to say to her first:

1. Did you have fun? What was fun about it?
2. How did you shine your light on a teammate(s) or
   what sort of positive teammate deposit did you make?

If at pickup she hears one or more specific examples as to why practice wasn't fun, she simply says, "That's a bummer," followed by, "Are you able to zoom out from that experience and tell me about a cool interaction you had with a teammate or coach?" Sometimes parents want to jump in and react or fix a problem that's not even really there. The "problem" may have been a ten-second exchange with a teammate or coach who was having a bad day. We tell them to resist the urge to respond. This is where the "unnecessary communication with coaches" may come into play. A negative exchange is not a bad practice, not a bad game, and certainly not a bad day. It's a bad moment and teaching our kids that bad moments are a part of life—and that it's okay to be bummed by them but that it's also okay to get over it quickly—is a lesson that will serve them well throughout their lives.

By encouraging youth to shine their light on their teammates, you help them understand how to be active contributors to the team environment. They shouldn't just expect others to create a positive and upbeat environment. Imagine the ripple effect if every kid went to sport with the objective to shine their light on a teammate at every practice or session. A community of belonging will more likely be established, and kids can feel seen and appreciated by their teammates.

External sources contribute to a fun sport experience.

We certainly aren't suggesting that we ought to bribe kids to perform in sport when we acknowledge that external factors do contribute to a fun sport experience. Rather than toys from Target or ice cream trips, we're eluding to external factors such as positive and supportive coaching, effective verbal and nonverbal feedback, game-time support in the form of safety to take risks and make mistakes without fear of being benched or yelled at, and—although to a lesser extent—even *swag*. As, of course, don't forget that swag gives a group a sense of team and a sharing of unique branding, and it also builds social connection and builds a team environment.

Examples of positive supportive coaching in Dr. Visek's research mentions things such as, "One thing that makes playing sports fun for players is when a coach treats a player with respect," and "One thing that makes playing sports fun for players is when they are getting clear, consistent communication from coaches." And while we've seen our fair share of examples of players being disrespected by coaches in youth sport just as Richard's son was during his lacrosse experience, we've also seen plenty of examples of when such respect is front and center.

How many times do parents and kids arrive at practice to see the coach busily setting up cones to ensure the drills are all done to perfection? While we applaud the intent, unpublished research shows it is best to use that arrival time to engage the players and their parents. Coaches should check in with the kids on how their day is going; noting kids' mood and energy levels can help provide the best environment of development during that practice. That interaction goes much further than a drill for not only their enjoyment of the training session but also in improving performance.

Amanda mentioned her incredible friend and colleagues from Collegiate at the beginning of this chapter. One of these individuals is Bill Rider. Bill is now a retired teacher who served as math department chair and long-time soccer coach. These days he spends his days drinking strong coffee, mountain biking, and volunteering at a local middle school in Richmond City Public Schools in Virginia. Bill, or Rider as the kids called him, knew his players well and cared about them deeply. He showed his love for his players in multiple ways. For example, Bill had a rainbow pride flag on the back of his car in the late nineties and when one of the kids asked him why he had that he responded, "If anyone I teach or coach is gay or lesbian, I want them to know that I am here for them and support them."

But Bill's ability to show love and support for every kid he coached didn't stop at demonstrating his allyship.

For example, during the first spring season Amanda coached with Bill, she was caught off guard when Bill instructed a couple of grade eleven girls to skip practice and go home. Collegiate had a really strong soccer team and were aiming for a state title. Amanda was unsure why he'd send several players home without really even talking much to them before doing so, until she better understood the realities that these high school juniors were facing. Amanda vividly recalls the weary looks on their faces brought on by copious amounts of schoolwork, college visits, and club sport demands. Bill interpreted the looks to communicate something like, "I have AP (Advanced Placement) exams going on right now, and being at this practice is making me feel unhealthy levels of stress given all that I am trying to juggle."

Rider looked at them and asked, "Would this time to handle your responsibilities be more helpful to you and make you feel better about everything than staying for today's practice?" The look of relief on the faces of these young women is something Amanda will never forget. "Thank you, Rider," was all said after they fought the tears of gratitude, turned around, and made their way home.

Rider had perspective. These were great kids who were managing long days. He personifies lifelong learning and grasped the indisputable findings from sleep research before it became a mainstream understanding. Rider looked at Amanda and simply said, "Everyone just needs to be seen for all they're doing once in a while. We don't need them here today if they are exhausted and stressed; that's only going to get them injured. They need to know we love 'em. They'll come back tomorrow fresh and ready to go."

He was right.

Rider then proceeded to tell the rest of the team why he told the girls to go home. He shared that their health is most important to us as coaches, and sometimes a break is better than pushing through. Amanda was twenty-two years old and had never heard a coach say anything remotely this caring up until that point. And she had some really good coaches growing up! She heard teachers talk like that, but not when they served in a coaching role.

Rider also worked with the local soccer club and made an arrangement whereby kids would miss one club practice a week and one school practice a week. This policy would ensure that kids weren't going to double practices, which would increase likelihood of injury and decrease sleep due to academic responsibilities in the evening. He was a respected former D-I soccer player who also coached club soccer for years, so he had the street credit to pull this off; admittedly, this would be really challenging to do today with a lot of soccer clubs. Amanda's two oldest daughters' teammate, we will call her Sophie, was recently benched at club soccer because she missed a couple "optional" practices for ice hockey playoffs. Sophie is twelve years old, and this is 2023. Rider was making sure this didn't happen to kids in 1999.

Other examples of how Rider exemplified being a supportive coach was when kids played multiple sports. Collegiate's starting center-back at the time, Jamie Whitten, was known throughout the community as a fabulous human being and a really strong field hockey player. Sometimes Jamie would miss our soccer games because she was traveling for high-performance field hockey training. Rider simply communicated with the team that she would never be punished for this because she gives her all when she's at soccer. He told the team that he supports all their goals and won't make them apologize for having them. Jamie, now Jamie Montgomery, went on to win several NCAA D-I national championships in field hockey at Wake Forest University and played on the USA national team and at the time of writing this book was the head coach of the Richmond Spiders women's Soccer team. Jamie shared with Amanda a couple years ago that when she thinks back to playing soccer at Collegiate, the word *fun* immediately pops in mind.

Those of you reading this who are fans of the Olympic style of wrestling will recognize the name Tela O'Donnell. If you know Tela, you love Tela. She has a magical spirit and would give anyone the shirt off her back, but beware, she could also rip your head off with her bare hands. If you're Amanda's neighbors—who went total fangirl mode one time when she attended a neighborhood gathering with Amanda and her spouse—you might know her from the reality TV show, *Alaska: The Last Frontier.* Tela, now Tela O'Donnell Backer, is a trailblazer in wrestling. She recalls the critical importance of an accepting and supportive coach, as she shares a story about her first wrestling coach in her TED Talk, "Grappling with Gender Inequality."[100] Tela's coach, Coach Wolf, introduced nervous middle school Tela as a new teammate on her first day of practice. Tela had to petition the school board for permission to wrestle at a time where it was extremely uncommon for a girl to compete in the sport. Nerves soon subsided thanks to Coach Wolf's supportive and inclusive approach to coaching. Tela went on to have a decorated wrestling career that included competing in the Sydney 2004 Summer Olympic Games, and she works with the nonprofit Wrestle Like a Girl to help grow wrestling and provide girls' specific resources for the long-time male-dominated sport.

Those of us who have had caring coaches, worked with them, or worked diligently to be them don't need a robust research study like Dr. Visek's to convince us that a supportive and caring coach can increase joy in sport. But the reality is, it's pretty cool to see the research as a way to operationalize change and to convince the naysayers.

We love seeing coaches smile when kids try new skills in games and don't quite pull it off—knowing that the coolest part is that they took the risk and went for it. That type of sport climate, one devoid of fear and repercussion, helps increase the fun in sport.

When Amanda began her coaching career, it is true that she was nice. It is also true that she thought she was being a supportive coach by hopping on the line and running sprints with her soccer team when someone came late to practice. She didn't yell or berate her athletes, and she likely subconsciously hoped to earn their respect by doing the fitness alongside her team members. But, by observing, reading, reflecting and staying humble, she soon realized that the title of "supportive coach" wouldn't be earned until she was willing to ask questions and actively listen as laid out in chapter 7 (page 157). Amanda's pretty certain she's not the only one who wishes more coaches were developed to understand that when one focuses on development, a more enjoyable environment is established for all. Luckily, times are changing as some organizations are taking fun seriously.

In 2022–2023 the U.S. Tennis Association (USTA)[101] conducted a study in partnership with Dr. Visek to determine exactly what fun looks like to youth tennis players. The USTA took the novel approach and asked kids what they wanted in their tennis experience and what fun would look like to them. More than 100 youth participated in the study, and they identified 120 determinants of fun, which were then categorized into six FUN factors. Participants reported that for a fun tennis experience they want to: play more matches so that they can have more touches on the ball, have positive coaching (which included less talking), work hard and learn new things, develop mental strength, stay active, and demonstrate sportsmanship. These examples are the six FUN factors identified in the research. At the time of publishing this book, the USTA is applying the findings from this research and building these six FUN factors into their coaching development and programming. It is critical for other sport organizations, coaches, and parents to know what fun looks like to kids, and that kids most definitely do not view fun as goofing or slacking off. If sports want to successfully attract kids to be active and to participate in their local clubs, it is indeed time to take fun seriously.

If you find yourself thinking that you're not buying what this book is selling and you'll continue to coach using traditional methods or berate your child when you don't perceive them to be trying their best, that you still hold to punishing kids through making them exercise, it may be time to step away from youth sport. The stakes are too high. If winning is what you are solely focused on, perhaps you can sign up for a local pickleball league and fill your time with that.

In Amanda and Richard's combined decades of studying, volunteering, leading youth sport–related projects, changing national sport systems, and raising our own kids, our passion for joyful youth-sport experiences has only grown. Why else would we have dedicated our careers to helping coaches and sport directors apply research and sport frameworks in ways that best meet the needs of kids? We believe with all our heart that sport has the power to enhance lives, and that everyone can gain benefits from sport if their sport journey is an overall joyful one. We don't doubt that bridging the divide between research and practice will inevitably help amazing community members better meet the needs of the individuals they serve in youth sport.

It is our sincerest hope that during the time you took to read this book you feel empowered to:

- Initiate courageous conversations with coaches as necessary.
- See every child or youth as a full human and don't mistakenly place their value on their sport performance.
- Set or demand a supportive and caring environment for their development.
- Question norms that place short-term success in the form of

wins over development.
- Spread the profound research that concludes FUN in sport = development in sport.
- Follow your child's lead in terms of determining what sport(s) or level of sport works best for them.
- Listen to concerned parents with an open heart.
- Shine your light on the countless incredible volunteers, coaches, and sport directors who provide caring spaces for your kids to thrive.

In closing, we leave you with Kobe Bryant's Mamba Mentality, which is applicable to all of us—parents, coaches, sport directors, and youth in sport.

MAMBA MENTALITY

"IT'S A CONSTANT QUEST TO TRY TO BE BETTER TODAY THAN YOU WERE YESTERDAY AND BETTER TOMORROW THAN YOU WERE THE DAY BEFORE."

KOBE BRYANT

Sport can use more humility at the youth-sport level. We all need to look in the mirror frequently and question current actions for the purpose of personal growth. Kids deserve it. Kids deserve to experience joy while participating in sport.

Questions to Ask Yourself

- Before reading this book, did you think fun was equal to development?
- Did Dr. Visek's research surprise you at all?
- Do you coach today like you did when you first started out?
- Do you ask sport directors if your child will experience a fun environment if they participate in their club? If they say yes, do you ask what fun looks like to them?

Fun Sport Checklist: Parents

This checklist was created based on Dr. Amanda Visek's fun integration theory and Fun Maps research. The version below is written for parents and can be used to help determine if a youth is in a fun sport experience for their child. If a parent notices that not many items are being checked off the checklist, it may be time for them to explore other sport options for their child on another team, at another club, or in another sport.[102]

Physical	
O	Is my child receiving playing time and competing?
O	Is my child being active for most of the practices?
O	Is my child having fun at practices and games?
O	Is my child getting adequate touches on the ball (or the equivalent in their sport) to improve?
Verbal	
O	Is my child receiving positive and specific feedback?
O	Is my child receiving encouragement for trying new things?
O	Is my child being asked questions to promote their critical-thinking skills rather than just direct instruction?
O	Is my child participating in sports where the officials are making consistent calls?
Emotional	
O	Do the coaches actively listen to my child?
O	Is my child in a psychologically/emotionally safe learning environment?
O	Is my child experiencing conditions that foster confidence?
Environmental	
O	Does my child attend well-organized practices that include small-sided games and drills?
O	Does my child participate in safe training conditions?
O	Does my child get to compete against teams that are evenly matched?

Fun Sport Checklist: Coaches and Sport Directors

This version is written for coaches to self-assess their current coaching practice or for sport directors to use to facilitate coaching development with their staff. If a coach notices that not many items are being checked off the checklist, it may be time for them to consider coaching development in various forms. If sport directors determine they need to set more parameters for coaches to better support their pursuit of establishing a fun sports environment, they should prioritize doing so immediately.[103]

Physical	
O	Are my players receiving similar playing time so that all can develop?
O	Are my players being active for most of the practices?
O	Are my players giving me feedback that shows me they are having fun practices and games?
O	Are my players getting adequate touches on the ball (or the equivalent in their sport) in order to improve?
Verbal	
O	Do I give my players positive and specific feedback?
O	Do I give my players encouragement when they try new things, even if they are not successful?
O	Do I ask my players questions to promote their critical-thinking skills rather than just direct instruction?
Emotional	
O	Do I actively listen to my players?
O	Am I intentional about establishing a psychologically and emotionally safe learning environment for *all* players?
O	Do I speak to and treat my players in ways that allow them to develop confidence?
Environmental	
O	Do I provide well-organized practices that include small-sided games and drills?
O	Do I provide safe training conditions for my players?
O	Do I schedule games that are evenly matched?

Chapter 2: Game-Day Strategies

1   "Long-Term Development Stages," Sport for Life, April 2023, https://
     sportforlife.ca/long-term-development/.
2   R.H. Barnsley, A.H. Thompson, and P.E. Barnsley, "Hockey Success and
     Birthdate: The Relative Age Effect," Canadian Association of Health, *Physical
     Education and Recreation (CAHPER) Journal* 51 (1985): 23–28.
3   J. Baker and A.J. Logan, "Developmental Contexts and Sporting Success:
     Birth Date and Birthplace Effects in National Hockey League Draftees
     2000–2005," *British Journal of Sports Medicine* 41 (2007): 515–517.
4   RH Barnsley, AH Thompson, and P Legault, "Family Planning: Football
     Style, the Relative Age Effect in Football," *International Review for the
     Sociology of Sport* 27 (1992): 77–78.
5   Jim Grove, "Relative Age and Developmental Age: Is Your Child Getting
     Shortchanged?" Active for Life, February 1, 2016, https://activeforlife.com
     /relative-age-and-developmental-age/.
6   Activate, "Physical Literacy," accessed June 2023, https://phecanada.ca/
     professional-learning/physical-literacy.
7   Dr. Colin Higgs, Richard Way, Dr. Vicki Harber, Dr. Paul Jurbala, and
     Istvan Balyi, "Figure 5: Physical Literacy Cycle," *Long-Term Development in
     Sport and Physical Activity 3.0,* (Sport for Life, 2019): 22, https://sportforlife.ca
     /wp-content/uploads/2019/06/Long-Term-Development-in-Sport-and-
     Physical-Activity-3.0.pdf.
8   Dr. Colin Higgs, Richard Way, Dr. Vicki Harber, Dr. Paul Jurbala, and
     Istvan Balyi, "Figure 3: Sport for Life Rectangle," *Long-Term Development in
     Sport and Physical Activity 3.0,* (Sport for Life, 2019): 13, https://sportforlife.ca
     /wp-content/uploads/2019/06/Long-Term-Development-in-Sport-and-
     Physical-Activity-3.0.pdf
9   Eveline A. Crone and Ronald E. Dahl, "Understanding Adolescence as a
     Period of Social-Affective Engagement and Goal Flexibility," *Nature Reviews
     Neuroscience* 13 (2012): 636–650.

10 D. Stanley Eitzen and George H. Sage, *Sociology of North American Sport* (Boulder: Paradigm Publishers, 2009).

11 Adriana Galván, "The Need for Sleep in the Adolescent Brain," *Trends in Cognitive Sciences* 23, no. 1 (2019): 79–89.

12 "Executive Control," Merriam-Webster Online, accessed April 2023, https://www.merriam-webster.com/dictionary/executive%20control.

13 "The Teen Brain: 7 Things to Know," National Institute of Mental Health, accessed April 2023, https://www.nimh.nih.gov/health/publications/the-teen-brain-7-things-to-know.

14 Megan M. Herting and Xiaofang Chu, "Exercise, Cognition, and the Adolescent Brain," *Birth Defects Research* 109, no. 20 (December 2017): 1672–1679.

15 Andrew M. Watson, "Sleep and Athletic Performance," *Current Sports Medicine Reports* 16, no. 6 (2017): 413–418.

16 Johns Hopkins Bloomberg School of Public Health, "The Teen Years Explained: A Guide to Healthy Adolescent Development," Center for Adolescent Health, accessed April 2023, https://www.jhsph.edu/research/centers-and-institutes/center-for-adolescent-health/_docs/policy-briefs/mental-health/Teens_Sleep.pdf.

17 Ruthann Richter, "Among Teens, Sleep Deprivation an Epidemic," Stanford Medicine News Center, October 8, 2015, https://med.stanford.edu/news/all-news/2015/10/among-teens-sleep-deprivation-an-epidemic.

18 Laurence Steinberg, "A Social Neuroscience Perspective on Adolescent Risk-Taking," *Developmental Review* 28, no. 1 (March 2008): 78–106.

19 Daniel Siegel, "Dopamine and Teenage Logic," *The Atlantic*, January 24, 2014, https://www.theatlantic.com/health/archive/2014/01/dopamine-and-teenage-logic/282895/.

20 National Institute of Mental Health, "The Teen Brain: 7 Things to Know," revised 2023, https://www.nimh.nih.gov/health/publications/the-teen-brain-7-things-to-know.

21 "What Is the CASEL Framework?" CASEL, accessed April 2023, https://casel.org/fundamentals-of-sel/what-is-the-casel-framework.

22 Diagram adapted from: "What Is SEL?" Social Emotional Learning Alliance for Massachusetts, accessed April 2023, https://sel4ma.org/about/what-is-sel/.

23 All SEL competency definitions in table are credited to: "What Is the CASEL Framework?" CASEL, accessed April 2023, https://casel.org/fundamentals-of-sel/what-is-the-casel-framework.

Chapter 3: Score

24 This child's name was changed for anonymity, but it is written about a twelve-year-old boy who plays soccer.

25 A "late developer" is someone who is smaller, slower, or less physical based on growth and maturation. It also could be someone who has joined the sport later than others, so they are behind in skills and tactics.

26 Ian Janssen and Allana G. LeBlank," Systematic Review of the Health

Benefits of Physical Activity and Fitness in School-Ages Children and Youth," *International Journal of Behavioral Nutrition and Physical Activity* 7, no. 40 (2010); M. Alexandra Kredlow, et al., "The Effects of Physical Activity on Sleep: A Meta-Analytic Review," *Journal of Behavioral Medicine* 30 (2015): 427–449; Martin Camiré and Kelsey Kendellen, "Coaching for Positive Youth Development in High School Sport," in *Positive Youth Development through Sport* (New York: Routledge, 2016); Rhiannon L. White and Andrew Bennie, "Resilience in Youth Sport: A Qualitative Investigation of Gymnastics Coach and Athlete Perceptions," International Journal of Sports Science & Coaching 10, no. 2–3 (2015); Seunghyun Hwang, Moe Machida, and Youngjun Choi, "The Effect of Peer Interaction on Sport Confidence and Achievement Goal Orientation in Youth Sport," *Social Behavior and Personality: An International Journal* 45, no. 6 (2017): 1007–1018; and Robert Weinberg, "Goal Setting in Sport and Exercise: Research and Practical Applications," *Revista da Educação Física/UEM* 24, no. 2 (2013): 171–179.

27   Stephen Silverman, Amelia Mays Woods, and Prithwi Raj Subramaniam, "Task Structures, Feedback to Individual Students, and Student Skill Level in Physical Education," *Research Quarterly for Exercise and Sport* 69, no. 4 (1998): 420–424.

28   Joëlle Carpentier and Geneviève A. Mageau, "When Change-Oriented Feedback Enhances Motivation, Well-Being, and Performance: A Look at Autonomy-Supportive Feedback in Sport," *Psychology of Sport and Exercise* 14, no. 3 (2013): 423–435.

29   C. Ames and J. Archer, "Achievement Goals in the Classroom: Students' Learning Strategies and Motivation Processes," *Journal of Educational Psychology* 80, no. 3 (1988): 260–267.

30   Jose Antonio Cecchini et al., "Epstein's TARGET Framework and Motivational Climate in Sport: Effects of a Field-Based, Long-Term Intervention Program," *International Journal of Sports Science and Coaching* 9, no. 6 (2014).

31   Self-determination theory suggests that all humans have three basic psychological needs—autonomy, competence, and relatedness—that underlie growth and development. Autonomy refers to feeling one has choice and is willingly endorsing one's behavior. The opposite experience is feeling compelled or controlled in one's behavior. Competence refers to the experience of mastery and being effective in one's activity. Finally, relatedness refers to the need to feel connected and a sense of belongingness with others; University of Rochester Medical Center, "Our Approach: Self-Determination Theory," accessed June 2023, https://www.urmc.rochester.edu/community-health/patient-care/self-determination-theory.

32   *Pedagogy* is a term that refers to the art, science, and profession of teaching. In other words, how teachers teach in theory and in practice. Pedagogy includes various aspects of teaching such as: teaching styles, assessment, and reporting.

33   Parents looking to educate themselves on adolescent psychology and development should consider reading *Dr. Lisa Damour's Untangled: Guiding*

Teenage Girls through the Seven Transitions into Adulthood and *The Emotional Lives of Teenagers: Raising Connected, Capable, and Compassionate Adolescents*, as well as Dr. Daniel Seigel's Brainstorm: *The Power & Purpose of the Teenage Brain.*

34   Katherine a. Yaeger and Susan Bauer-Wu, "Cultural Humility: Essential Foundation for Clinical Researchers," *Applied Nursing Research* 26, no. 4 (2013): 251–256.

35   We recommend the following books for expanding understanding on race and equity: Crystal M. Fleming's *How to Be Less Stupid About Race* and the Mica Pollock–edited *Everyday Anti-Racism.*

36   *Parasport* is sport for individuals who live with a disability(ies). Some parasports are modified versions of traditional sport, while others are created specifically for individuals with disabilities. Examples of parasports unique to individuals who live with disabilities include: sledge hockey or goal ball.

37   Amanda J. Visek, et al., "The Fun Integration Theory: Towards Sustaining Children and Adolescents Sport Participation," *Journal of Physical Activity and Health* 12, no. 3 (2015): 424–433.

Chapter 4: Where Are the Multisport Players

38   According to *Oxford Dictionary*, the term "elite" means a select group that is superior in terms of ability or qualities to the rest of a group or society.

39   "Building Blocks of ADM," American Development Model, USA Hockey, accessed April 2023, https://www.admkids.com/page/show/910837-building -blocks-of-adm.

40   Boris Popovic, et al., "Evaluation of Gross Motor Coordination and Physical Fitness in Children: Comparison between Soccer and Multisport Activities," *Environmental Research and Public Health* 17, no. 16 (2020): 5902, https:// www.mdpi.com/1660-4601/17/16/5902.

41   "Meta-analysis" is a term used to describe a study that looks for similar findings among a plethora of related studies.

42   Arne Gullich, et al., "What Makes a Champion?" Early Multidisciplinary Practice, Not Early Specialization, Predicts World-Class Performance," *Perspectives on Psychological Science* 17, no. 1 (2021): 6–21, https://journals .sagepub.com/doi/pdf/10.1177/1745691620974772.

43   E. Paul Roetert, et al., "Skill Transfer through Multi-sport Play: A Tennis and Hockey Example," *Coaching & Sport Science Review* 29, no. 85 (2021): 5–8, https://www.researchgate.net/publication/356439227_Skill_transfer _through_multi-sport_play-A_tennis_and_hockey_example.

44   Robin S. Vealey and Melissa A. Chase, *Best Practice for Youth Sport: Science and Strategies for Positive Athlete Experiences* (Champaign, Illinois: Human Kinetics, 2016).

45   Keith A. Kaufman, "Understanding Student–athlete Burnout," NCAA Sport Science Institute, accessed October 2022, https://www.ncaa.org /sports/2014/12/10/understanding-student–athlete-burnout.aspx.

46   Jean Côté, et al., "The Benefits of Sample Sports during Childhood," *Physical*

and Health Education Journal 74, no. 4 (2009): 6–11, https://www
.researchgate.net/publication/236002408_The_Benefits_of_Sampling
_Sports_During_Childhood.

Chapter 5: Good Game

47 Morgan's Message, homepage, accessed October 2022, https://www
.morgansmessage.org/who-we-are.

48 Cailin Bracken, "Cailin Bracken: A Letter to College Sports," *USA Lacrosse*
magazine, April 8, 2022, https://www.usalaxmagazine.com/college/women
/cailin-bracken-a-letter-to-college-sports.

49 NIL (Name, Image, Likeness) is a policy adopted by the National College
Athletics Association in 2021 permitting collegiate athletes to make money
through things like personal appearances, endorsement deals, and autographs,
among other approaches.

50 World Health Organization, The Global Health Observatory, "Health and
Well-being," accessed October 2022, https://www.who.int/data/gho/data
/major-themes/health-and-well-being.

51 Sometimes wellness can include up to nine to twelve dimensions of health;
Global Wellness Institute, "What Is Wellness?" accessed December 2022,
https://globalwellnessinstitute.org/what-is-wellness.

52 J.B. Kirby, J. Coakley, A. Stanec, T. Ferguson, and E. Comeaux, *Humanizing
Sport: Best Practices Guide to Support Student-Athlete Mental Wellness and
Resilience for Anyone with an Athlete in their Life*, Recommendations Report,
True Sport, 2023, https://truesport.org/wp-content/uploads/TrueSport-
Recommendations-Report-Humanizing-Sport.pdf.

53 Ibid.

54 Dr. Chapman presented this at the True Sport Student–Athlete Mental
Wellness Conference in Colorado Springs, Colorado, in November 2022 at
the U.S. Olympic & Paralympic Museum.

55 Greg Johnson, "Mental Health Issues Remain on Minds of Student–athletes,"
NCAA News, May 24, 2022, https://www.ncaa.org/news/2022/5/24
/media-center-mental-health-issues-remain-on-minds-of-student–athletes
.aspx#:~:text=The%20data%20indicated%20rates%20of,first%20year%20
of%20the%20pandemic.

56 Braden Brown, Jakob F. Jensen, Ty Aller, Logan K. Lyons, and Jennifer L.
Hodgson, "NCAA Student–athlete Mental Health and Wellness: A
Biophysical Examination," *Journal of Student Affairs Research and Practice* 59,
no. 3 (2022) 252–267, https://www.tandfonline.com/doi/full/10.1080/194965
91.2021.1902820.

57 *Body duality* is the competing demands on a female athlete of society's
definition of beauty (form) and what their body needs to be able to do to
perform (function).

58 Vincent Gouttebarge, et. al, "Occurrence of Mental Health Symptoms and
Disorders in Current and Former Elite Athletes: A Systematic Review and
Meta-Analysis," *British Journal of Sports Medicine* 53, (2019): 700–706.

59 Courtney C. Walton, "Addressing Mental Health in Elite Athletes as a Vehicle for Early Detection and Intervention in the General Community," *Early Intervention in Psychiatry* 13, no. 6 (2019): 1530–1532.

60 Mark F. Riederer, "How Sleep Impacts Performance in Youth Athletes," *Current Sports Medicine Reports* 19, no. 11 (November 2020).

61 P. J. Clough, K. Earle, and D. Sewell, "Mental Toughness: The Concept and Its Measurement," in *Solutions in Sport Psychology*, ed. I. Cockerill (London: Thomson, 2003): 32–43.

Chapter 6: There's No "I" in Team

62 Robin S. Vealey, "Chapter 5: Confidence in Sport," in *Handbook of Sports Medicine and Science: Sport Psychology*, ed. Britton W. Brewer (Hoboken: Wiley-Blackwell, 2009).

63 Sport for Life, *Developing Physical Literacy: Building a New Normal for all Canadians*, 2019, https://sportforlife.ca/wp-content/uploads/2019/09/DPL-2_2021.pdf.

64 Dr. Colin Higgs, Richard Way, Dr. Vicki Harber, Dr. Paul Jurbala, Istvan Balyi, "Figure 5: Physical Literacy Cycle," *Long-Term Development in Sport and Physical Activity 3.0*, (Sport for Life, 2019): 22, https://sportforlife.ca/wp-content/uploads/2019/06/Long-Term-Development-in-Sport-and-Physical-Activity-3.0.pdf.

65 Physical Literacy, "What Is Physical Literacy," May 2014, https://physicalliteracy.ca/physical-literacy/.

66 J. Kremer, A. Moran, G. Walker, and C. Craig, "Self-efficacy and Perceived Competence," in Key Concepts in Sport Psychology (Rosemont: SAGE Publications, 2011): 86–90; D. Castelli, et al., "Chapter 3: The Relationship of Physical Fitness and Motor Competence to Physical Activity," in *Journal of Teaching in Physical Education* 26, no. 4 (2007): 358–374.

67 Fleur McIntyre, Helen Parker, Paola Chivers, and Beth Hands, "Actual Competence, rather than Perceived Competence, Is a Better Predictor of Physical Activity in Children Aged 6–9 Years," *Journal of Sports Sciences* 36, no. 13 (2018): 1433–1440.

68 Stefan Wagnsson, "Participation in Organized Sport and Self-Esteem Across Adolescence: The Mediating Role of Perceived Sport Competence," *Journal of Sport & Exercise Psychology* 36, no. 6 (2014): 584–594.

69 R. Ryan, et al., "Self-Determination Theory and the Facilitation of Intrinsic Motivation, Social Development, and Well-Being," *American Psychologist* 55, no. 1 (2000), 68–78.

70 Human Kinetics, "The Link between Perceived and Actual Motor Competence," accessed May 2023, https://us.humankinetics.com/blogs/excerpt/the-link-between-perceived-and-actual-motor-competence.

71 Laura Bortoli, et al., "Competence, Achievement Goals, Motivational Climate, and Pleasant Psychobiosocial States in Youth Sport," *Journal of Sports Sciences* 29, no. 2 (2011): 171–180.

72 D. Gould, M. Weiss, and R. Weinberg, Psychological Characteristics of

Successful and Non-successful Big Ten Wrestlers," *Journal of Sport Psychology* 3 (1981): 69–81.

73 J. Nakamura and M. Csikszentmihalyi, "The Concept of Flow," in *Flow and the Foundations of Positive Psychology* (Dordrecht: Springer, 2014): 239–263.

74 Jeanne Nekamura and Mihaly Csikszentmihalyi, "Flow Theory and Research," in *Oxford Handbook of Positive Psychology*, eds. C. R. Snyder and Shane J. Lopez (New York: Oxford University Press, 2009).

75 Catherine Moore, "What Is Flow in Positive Psychology?" Positive Psychology, January 8, 2019, https://positivepsychology.com/what-is-flow/.

76 School Physical Activity and Physical Literacy, "Movement in the Primary Grades: Confidence and Motivation Components of Physical Literacy," accessed May 2023, https://schoolpapl.ca/wp-content/uploads/2020/08 /Confidence-and-Motivation-Sep-2020.pdf.

77 The foundational information is from: Mihaly Csikszentmihalyi, *Finding Flow* (New York: Hachette Book Group, 1997).

78 This suggestion was provided by Dr. Beth McCharles, certified mental performance consultant.

79 F. Aanesen, et al., "Gender Differences in Subjective Health Complaints in Adolescence: The Roles of Self-Esteem, Stress from Schoolwork, and Body Dissatisfaction," *Scandinavian Journal of Public Health* 45, no. 4 (2017): 389–396; M.S. Tremblay, et al., "Systematic Review of Sedentary Behaviour and Health Indicators in School-Aged Children and Youth," *International Journal of Behavioral Nutrition and Physical Activity* 8 (2011): 98–120.

Chapter 7: Call the Shots

80 A twenty-four-hour rule in sport is a rule that a lot of sport clubs enforce. Parents aren't permitted to communicate with the coach until twenty-four hours after an incident occurs that prompts the parent wanting to communicate with the coach. The rule is assumed by sport clubs to provide a necessary "cooling down" period for parents before they talk to the coach. An unintended consequence of this rule is that it doesn't allow for positive collaboration in instances of multiple games on weekends and/or a tournament situation. In other words, when a hiccup in a sport experience could be addressed it sometimes is engulfed.

81 Coursera, "What Is Effective Communication? Skills for Work, School, and Life," June 15, 2023, https://www.coursera.org/articles/communication -effectiveness.

82 United States Institute of Peace, "What Is Active Listening?" accessed May 2023, https://www.usip.org/public-education-new/what-active-listening.

83 Stephen Walker, "Relationship Building Skills—Active Listening," *Podium Sports Journal*, April 15, 2007, https://www.podiumsportsjournal .com/2007/04/15/relationship-building-skills-active-listening/.

84 Jonathan Stein, et al., "Influence of Perceived and Preferred Coach Feedback on Youth Athletes' Perceptions of Team Motivational Climate," *Psychology of Sport and Exercise* 13, no. 4 (2012): 484–490.

85 Thelma S. Horn, "Examining the Impact of Coaches' Feedback Patters on the Psychosocial Well-Being of Youth Sport Athletes," *Kinesiology Review* 8, no. 3 (2019): 244–251, https://journals.humankinetics.com/view/journals/krj/8/3/article-p244.xml.

86 "Autonomy-supportive coaching includes such practices as (a) providing choice for athletes, (b) providing a rationale for tasks and limits, (c) providing non-controlling competence feedback, (d) avoiding controlling behaviors such as criticisms, controlling statements and tangible rewards for interesting tasks, (e) acknowledging the athlete's feelings and perspectives, (f) providing opportunity for athletes to show initiative and act independently, (g) providing non-controlling feedback, and (h) avoiding behaviors that promote athlete's ego-involvement." J. Douglas Coatsworth and David E. Conroy, "The Effects of Autonomy-supportive Coaching, Need Satisfaction and Self-Perceptions on Initiative and Identity in Youth Swimmers," *Developmental Psychology* 45, no. 2, 320–328.

87 Lael Gershgoren, "The Effect of Parental Feedback on Young Athletes' Perceived Motivational Climate, Goal Involvement, Goal Orientation, and Performance," *Psychology of Sport and Exercise* 12, no. 5 (2011): 481–489.

Chapter 8: Go the Distance

88 Safe Sport Training, accessed May 2023, https://safesport.coach.ca/funding-partners.

89 U.S. Center for SafeSport, "Safesport Courses for All," accessed May 2023, https://uscenterforsafesport.org/training-and-education/safesport-courses-for-all.

90 "The Belonging Project at Stanford," Stanford Medicine: Department of Psychiatry and Behavioral Sciences, accessed May 2023, https://med.stanford.edu/psychiatry/special-initiatives/belonging.html.

Chapter 9: Put Me in, Coach

91 Dr. Colin Higgs provided an overview of his research related to the black box of puberty with the authors.

92 The soccer substitution rules in the U.S. college system are different from most places in the world where the rule indicates fewer (often up to five for an entire game) subs than seven.

93 Harvard University: Center on the Developing Child, "Resilience," accessed May 2023, https://developingchild.harvard.edu/science/key-concepts/resilience/.

Chapter 10: Get ahead of the Game

94 National Collegiate Athletic Association, "Estimated Probability of Competing in College Athletics," accessed September 2023, https://www.ncaa.org/sports/2015/3/2/estimated-probability-of-competing-in-college-athletics.aspx.

95 The Reformed Sports Project, "The Truth about the College Scholarship,"

September 9, 2022, https://reformedsportsproject.com/blog/f/the-truth-about-the-college-scholarship.

96 NCSA College Recruiting, "Full Ride Scholarships and How to Get Them," accessed September 2023, https://www.ncsasports.org/blog/full-ride-scholarships.

Chapter 11: How You Play

97 Amanda J. Visek, et al., "The Fun Maps: A Youth Sport Scientific Breakthrough," *Olympic Coach* 25, no. 4 (2015): 39–42.

98 Amanda J. Visek, et al., "The Fun Integration Theory: Towards Sustaining Children and Adolescents Sport Participation," *Journal of Physical Activity and Health* 12, no. 3 (2015): 424–433.

99 Ibid.

100 Tele O'Donnell Bacher, "Grappling with Gender Inequality," TEDxAnchorage, March 29, 2022, video, 16:49, https://www.youtube.com/watch?v=7TVHNn-hwGc.

101 Research study was shared by the United States Tennis Association at the International Physical Literacy Conference in New York, New York (2023).

102 Adapted from: Rugby Ontario, "FUN: High Performance vs. Community Sport & Fun Maps," video, April 23, 2020, 1:14:02, https://www.youtube.com/watch?v=xLMkeK3_KTI.

103 Ibid.

ADDITIONAL RESOURCES

Dare to Lead:
Brave Work, Tough Conversations, Whole Hearts
by Brené Brown

Do Hard Things
by Steve Magness

The Emotional Lives of Teenagers: Raising Connected,
Capable, and Compassionate Adolescents
by Lisa Damour

Good for a Girl
by Lauren Fleshman

How to Be Less Stupid about Race:
On Racism, White Supremacy, and the Racial Divide
by Crystal M. Fleming

Long-Term Athlete Development
by Istvan Balyi, Richard Way, and Colin Higgs

Sport for Life's Quality Sport Checklist, which can be found at:
https://sportforlife.ca/portfolio-view/quality-sport-checklist-for
-communities-and-clubs/

ACKNOWLEDGMENTS

Amanda

Writing *Protect the Joy* was a very rewarding experience for me and one that would not have been possible without the steadfast support of others. First, thank you to Ben Simpson, acquisitions director at Amplify Publishing. Ben was the first person at a publishing company that I pitched the idea of this book to. At the time, Ben's first child was a little under one year old and he had coached little league baseball in recent years. His instant enthusiasm for the project was both validating and motivating because he was exactly the type of person I wanted to write the book for—a thoughtful parent who is willing to step up and help kids have a great experience in sport. Thank you, Ben, for your support and for truly making this happen. Thank you as well to senior production editor at Amplify, Myles Schrag. Myles's ability to laugh at our antics and help get this book on the shelf is appreciated beyond words. To round off my gratitude for Amplify Publishing, I want to thank my writing coach, Rebecca Andersen. Rebecca's responsiveness, interest in the topic, and positive comments along the way made what could have been an exhausting process a fun one! It was especially serendipitous that her partner happens to be a physical educator. This only made our creative sessions more enjoyable. I didn't just get a writing coach with Rebecca, I got a dear friend.

To everyone who contributed to the book, thank you! Richard, when I sought out a collaborator for this project, I immediately thought of you. You've been a great colleague over the years. I appreciate how you're always respectful of others' thoughts and ideas and that you're in constant pursuit of what's best for kids. Also, I knew we would have some fun debates in the process, which I have loved. Never once did I regret my decision. Thank you. To friends, colleagues, and even family who added insight, Dr. Beth McCharles, Dr. Gail Moolsintong, Lauren Cornthwaite, Jake Stewart, Sean Stewart, Mia Duchars, and those who asked not to be named as you shared your wisdom and stories in hopes of helping others—thank you.

I want to send a special shout out to Dr. Jessica Kirby for her collaborative spirit and for sending pertinent research articles my way. I met Jessica through my involvement with TrueSport USA and also want to thank TrueSport for their support on this project.

Thank you to my sister-in-law, Amy Stanec, for the incredible book cover and internal design. You're so phenomenal at what you do and I'm very grateful you took this project on. Thanks as well to you and Jenny Grant for nailing the chapter titles. As you know, design and taglines are not my forte.

To my running buddies Alison Riley West, Edna Rodriguez, Scott Solsvig, Amy Stanec, and Ellen Weiss. We solve a lot of the world's problems as we log our miles, eh? Thanks for asking deep questions and for questioning my responses. As with past running buddies from each season of my life, you are so important to me.

To my dear friends that I've met on the sidelines of my kids' sports, Dr. Carolyn Duchars, Erin Krewet, Eliza Stewart, and Carrie Mauch — you're support has been incredible during this book writing process. Thank you for your ongoing encouragement. I'm so lucky to have you in my life.

Throughout my career, I've worked with incredible people and learned from master teachers and coaches alike. Fortunately, despite my many flaws, I take notice and am reflective when I see others shine. Whether I taught you or with you at The Collegiate School, Red Hill Elementary, The Principia School, The University of Virginia, or at St. Francis Xavier University, thank you for helping me to question norms and to think more critically about the experiences kids have in school and in sport. In recent years, I've spent a lot of time with Coach Sarah Grigsby, Coach Nigel Marples, and Coach Shawn Brown. I'm not sure if I've ever met a team more deserving of the special title. This coach appreciates you three more than you know. To every teacher and coach I've been able to serve since founding Move + Live + Learn in 2010, each of you are reflected in this book. Thanks to you, I've learned much more than I've ever dreamed of teaching, and I know how much more I have to learn.

To my mum and dad, thank you for every sacrifice and effort you made so that I could participate in sport. You never complained about taking me or my four siblings to or from practice or competition. You never asked for more than my best, and if I fell short you simply presented it as a chance for me to get it right next time. Thanks to your encouragement and high expectations, I normalized setting goals and this has not only served me well, it's something I'm trying really hard to pass on to my own children. I love you.

Speaking of kids…

Scottie, Kassie, and Ginny. Mama did it! The book is complete. Through sport I learned that I can achieve a lot, even if it seems scary at first. I suppose this is all I hope for you to get out of sport, along with life-lasting bonds I hope you'll form with your teammates. Your best is undoubtedly enough. I love you and hope you'll continue to strive to be the teammate you dream of having.

To my teammate for life…

Jim, you know me better than anyone in the world. So, when I first mentioned this book idea to you over fifteen years ago and you told me to "get after it," it meant the world to me. I can't imagine navigating parenthood with anyone else, and I'm glad I don't have to. I didn't let you read a draft of the book because I care most if you'll like it (and your poker face is brutal). Watching you coach brings me joy as you emulate what this book is selling in such a beautiful way. I love you.

movelivelearn.com
𝕏 @movelivelearn

Richard

I got a call one dreary COVID day from my brilliant friend, who is all fired up for a half-rant, half-inspirational discussion. Then Amanda blurted out, "What do you think of the idea of writing a book to help parents protect the joy of their children playing sports?" How could I say no to Amanda with her fountain of positive energy? We quickly agreed that it's easy to rant, but it's not easy to collect your thoughts, put them on paper, and open yourself to criticism while trying to bring JOY to people. Leaping from the couch in the COVID room, we soon had Amplify Publishing enthusiastic, which gave us the confidence to forge forward. Then once we teamed up with Rebecca Andersen, our writing coach (everyone needs a great coach), the self-belief grew.

I am so fortunate to be part of a talented, positive team. In life's journey from the farming fields to soccer fields to racing down iced mountain roads, I had the pleasure of meeting and working with great people who influenced and inspired me. Shout out to the late Bob Bearpark who trusted my ideas with responsibility and Wendy Pattenden, who trusted me with the freedom to act. I also appreciate that I had the opportunity to work with a group of super smart experts around long-term athlete development, such as Dr. Vicki Harber, Dr. Colin Higgs, Istvan Balyi, Charles Cardinal, Dr. Stephen Norris, and Dr. Mary Bluechardt, to name a few, while of course there are many others who contributed to shape my thoughts in the evolution of Sport for Life. From those early days to now, I am thankful for the current team at Sport for Life who are passionate about creating positive change in the lives of everyone through the power of sport and physical literacy.

Having children who were born in 1997, 1999, and 2001, it's been very fascinating to follow their journeys through multiple sports with friends and family. I hold special gratitude to coaches who were guides toward health, happiness, and success. They know who they are, and there are too many to mention by name.

Anything I have achieved is rooted in my family. With my partner, Vanessa, and three sisters, I am surrounded by love. With that foundation, I so appreciate my kids' (Aidan, Anika, and Cecilia's) humor and joy in collaborating on taking on big challenges. What's next…?

citius.ca
🄾 𝕏 **@Richard_Way**